CAVE CANEM

The goddess Diana and her dog. Rome. Second century AD. Musei Vaticani, Rome. (Photo: Author).

CAVE CANEM
ANIMALS AND ROMAN SOCIETY

IAIN FERRIS

AMBERLEY

Thinking of pets past and present: Waterproof, Perkins, Molesworth, Roadworthy, Kevin, Chester, Socks, Charlie, and Hester.

Mosaic of animals and handlers at an arena, Rome. On display at Colosseum, Rome. First century BC to first century AD. (Photo: Author)

First published 2018

Amberley Publishing
The Hill, Stroud
Gloucestershire, GL5 4EP

www.amberley-books.com

British Library Cataloguing in Publication Data.
A catalogue record for this book is available from the British Library.

ISBN 978 1 4456 5293 1 (hardback)
ISBN 978 1 4456 5294 8 (ebook)

Typesetting and Origination by Amberley Publishing.
Printed in the UK.

Contents

Acknowledgements

In writing this book I have received help from a number of individuals and organisations and I would like to take the opportunity to thank them all here.

For providing a number of images for reproduction in the book I would like to thank Professor R.J.A. Wilson and Dr Genevra Kornbluth. Once again, I must thank the British Museum for the creation of its wonderful web-based image research resource and for its incredibly generous facility for researchers and academics to make use of these images without charge, as I have done with some images in this book. Graham Norrie is thanked for the print of part of the frieze on the Column of Marcus Aurelius.

Thanks to Gianfranco Mastrangeli of the Vatican Museums' *Segreteria dei Dipartimenti e Reparti* who kindly arranged for me to visit the Museo Gregoriano Profano in summer 2014 when it was otherwise closed to the public, a visit during which I examined a number of artworks germane to this study while it was just a notion in my head. Dr Umberto Albarella of the University of Sheffield kindly replied to my queries about an alleged archaeological find of camel bones in Roman deposits in London. Julian Parker once more gave help in locating an image for the book and for technical advice with images.

The staff of the Institute of Classical Studies Library, London, the British Library, London, University of Wales Trinity St David Lampeter library, and Swansea University library were unfailingly helpful in obtaining books and journals for my reference while researching this book.

As always, my colleague and wife Dr Lynne Bevan read and commented on a draft of the book, much to the benefit of the finished work. At Amberley Publishing I would like to thank Eleri Pipien for commissioning this book in the first place and Cathy Stagg for her editorial work and advice in seeing the book into print.

Preface

This is the first recent book to attempt to present a broad analysis of the place and role of animals in ancient Roman society and to interpret their meaning and significance in cultural terms. In order to achieve this, by necessity the range of topics discussed here has had to be very broad, so important were animals in the Roman imagination at that time. Most obviously, there would have been working animals on most Roman farms and animals were often kept as household pets. Meat and fish were highly important ingredients in Roman cookery and supplies had to be located and maintained. Animals were also commonly employed in warfare in the Roman period, far more so than today. The story of the extraordinary slaughter of animals in the Roman arena and by hunting inevitably hangs heavily over this study. Animal sacrifice was considered as central to the practice and rites of Roman religion according to many authorities. Less obvious, but no less important, has been analysis of the widespread appearance of images of animals as attributes of various gods and goddesses, the creation and acceptance of the idea of mythological animals and beasts, and the meaning of the symbolism of animals. Finally, consideration has had to be given to the concept of Nature and the natural world as filtered through the Roman cultural gaze and how this may have impacted on various manifestations of apparent cruelty to animals.

The study encompasses consideration of both ancient contemporary written and visual sources. There is a considerable body of Greek and Roman writing dedicated to the discussion of the natural world and to the philosophical exploration of the human place in that world and its relationship to animals. However, this does not necessarily mean that we understand the relationship of Romans to their contemporary animals because they wrote about it, any more than a future historian could claim that they understood twentieth and twenty-first century views on animals by reading the diametrically opposed writings of right wing libertarian Roger Scruton on hunting and the leaflets and propaganda of the radical Animal Liberation Front. While literary references to animals and philosophical ideas relating to the natural world are highly important as sources, equal weight has been given to looking at archaeological sources, from animal bones dug up during archaeological excavations to artefacts and material culture more broadly. As has been the case with all my previous books there is a great deal of reliance here on visual evidence, that is representations of animals in Roman art and particularly in the form of sculptures, and as images on coins, mosaics, wall paintings, and decorated everyday items. The book is also a story of how art depicting animals became as much a part of Roman culture as real animals played in Roman society. There can be no doubt that image and imagination together helped shape the Romans' understanding of Nature. I believe that archaeological evidence and particularly visual sources both supplement and enhance the picture provided by the Roman writers to a very great degree.

Remarkably, considering the great significance of the subject and the relevance of green and environmental issues today, there has been no accessible general publication on animals in the Roman world available in English since Jocelyn Toynbee's ground-breaking 1973 book *Animals in Roman Life and Art*, written before the overt politicisation of the analysis of human-animal relationships from the later 1970s onwards. There have, however, been numerous articles on various aspects of the subject, particularly studies of animals in the Roman arena, published in academic journals from the 1970s up to the present day. A recent, extremely thorough *Oxford Handbook on Animals in Roman Life and Thought*[1] brought together numerous excellent short papers on virtually every aspect of the subject but seemed to lack a coherent, unified voice and, perhaps surprisingly, any kind of theoretical perspective. This present book should therefore hopefully fill an evident gap in the market. It should be read alongside Toynbee's book and the Oxford Handbook, and is aimed at undergraduate students studying introductory modules in Roman archaeology and history or Roman art and lay readers interested in these subjects. The book will also hopefully have an appeal to visitors to the museums and sites of Rome.

The book consists of an introductory chapter setting out the scope and scale of the study, a chapter on animals as pets or companion animals in the Roman world, a chapter analysing the role of working animals and animals reared and kept by farmers, a chapter investigating food animals and meat and fish in Roman cooking, a chapter on the appalling slaughter of animals in the Roman arena and in hunting, a chapter on the widespread use of images of animals as attributes of various gods and goddesses and mythological animals and beasts in various contexts, a chapter on animals in Roman sacrifice and on various aspects of Roman religion, including augury and festivals, a chapter examining the Roman concept of Nature and the natural world, and a final chapter setting discussion of animals and images of animals in the Roman world in the broader geographical, chronological, political, religious, artistic, and cultural context of the Republic and empire and of Late Antiquity. In the course of this book a number of esoteric topics will also inevitably be covered. For instance, did the Romans keep pets in the same way that we do today? Did the Romans keep domesticated weasels in their homes to combat mice, rats, and snakes? And did the Romans really eat dormice? The book also includes academic notes and a full bibliography to aid those who might want to pursue certain issues further and in more detail.

This study is not in any way a natural history of any particular species of animal, but rather of humans at a certain point in time and the way they behaved towards animals, as far as we can gauge and understand such a set of relationships. Readers of books on so-called Celtic religion will often have come across the thesis that Celtic peoples were somehow more attuned to Nature than their Roman and Romanised counterparts and that their religious beliefs and practices reflected a symbiotic link between Nature and Celtic culture that simply did not exist in the Roman world or was not as well developed. However, this would appear to be somewhat of an academic straw man, and it is difficult to see that this was, in fact, true when it can be demonstrated without doubt that Roman culture and religion were equally in touch with the natural world, as we shall see throughout the course of this book.

Of course there were animals in the Roman countryside, both wild and farmed. But one might deduce from many modern studies of the Roman world that there was a complete split between town and country and that city life was antipathetic if not exactly opposite to Nature and to most extents free of animal life in general. From nits in their hair and intestinal worms, from mosquitos in the marshes in and around Rome, from thrips in their milled grain to mice in their kitchens, from passerine birds in their gardens to scavenging, opportunistic foxes in the back alleys of houses and on the fringes of the cities animals were indeed ever present, providing a kind of murmuring undercurrent and susurration to Roman urban life. Throw consideration of guard dogs and other working animals and pets into the mix and then suddenly the Roman city seems a natural host to animal life.

In an academic study of any aspect of life in the past care should be taken with presenting the facts and interpreting them in their contemporary social and cultural context. Sometimes it may be tempting to view certain past actions or phenomena from a twenty-first century perspective, although some writers overtly shun such an approach, but indeed on many occasions this can in fact prove highly illuminating. The question of animal cruelty and exploitation in Roman times looms very large indeed in this study and casts a giant shadow over the interpretation of cultural mores that condoned sometimes unbelievable viciousness and scant or callous regard for animal lives, while in other ways Roman society was highly enlightened. I must declare that as a trustee of a small, local animal charity where I live, my own views on human and animal relationships today are inevitably biased in certain ways and I have tried to avoid projecting these views back to Roman times when presenting evidence of practices so alien to most western societies today as to make them outlandish and very questionable.

But as historians or archaeologists we *can* and perhaps *should* make judgements on the past, as long as the basic evidence is first presented without bias and the systems of interpretation are opaque. No one but the looniest libertarian today would write a book about how great slavery was in the ancient world, or how Roman infanticide was an admirable practice we could perhaps learn from and be wise to reintroduce to facilitate savings in the British National Health Service, so in this book the killing of animals in the arena for entertainment or, for instance, the tying of flaming torches to foxes' tails as part of the celebration of a religious festival will almost inevitably be presented as cultural practices with negative connotations. But not all was doom and gloom, as this study will show. However, when we learn how much some Romans loved their pets and set up expensive funerary memorials to them the greater body of evidence for abject cruelty in public spectacles does not simply fall away. It becomes tempered with the positivity of individual acts of kindness, and a more complex but at the same time nuanced view of the Roman past in relation to human and animal interaction emerges.

Iain Ferris
Pembrey
August 2015–August 2017

1

Of Mice and Men

When investigating the history of Roman and animal relationships in the ancient world there are three main kinds of evidence that can be drawn upon: contemporary written sources; contemporary visual sources; and archaeological evidence in the form of excavated animal bone assemblages. Contemporary Roman written sources that can be accessed to provide information on Roman and animal inter-relationships at this time are numerous, and indeed many of these were examined and presented by George Jennison when he wrote his classic book *Animals for Show and Pleasure in Ancient Rome*, published in 1937. His book is of further value in that Jennison himself was not only a writer but primarily worked with animals directly in his role as superintendent of the former Belle Vue Zoological Gardens in Manchester, northern England and, as a result, his book is infused with insider knowledge of animal behaviour gleaned through years of direct observation and study.

There are also extensive ancient Roman visual resources available, in the form of mosaic images, wall paintings, animal statuary both large and small, images of animals on coins, and on many different kinds of everyday objects. My own interest lies in Roman art and material culture and I have therefore drawn particularly heavily on such material to flesh out the narrative of this study and indeed in many places to drive that narrative. In this respect Jocelyn Toynbee's book *Animals in Roman Life and Art* still remains the leading source in this field.

A third and equally vital source has been zooarchaeological evidence, that is evidence derived from the scientific analysis of animal bones and other faunal remains from archaeological deposits. This is a highly specialised field of study, in fact a recognised sub-set of the discipline of archaeology since the 1950s and 1960s, though its full integration into Roman archaeological studies came much later than this and thus much later than it should have done. While I have looked at some published excavation site reports I have otherwise largely relied on synthetic analyses of animal bone evidence for the Roman period, and particularly those produced by Anthony King.[1]

The wide geographical spread of the Roman empire around the Mediterranean and into temperate northern Europe meant that a huge variety of species of animals existed within the boundaries of the empire and in contingent regions bordering the empire. Even within present-day Italy, the contrast between the flora and fauna of the high Alpine north and the scorching far south could not be more marked. Thus peoples in different provinces would have experienced the natural world in different ways and would have had differing knowledge of animal species depending on their location. The situation in the provinces would have been further complicated by the overlaying of the experiences of incomers such as soldiers, administrators, merchants and traders, and slaves on those of the native provincials. The picture would have been different again for many of the elite citizens of Rome who might have collected animals as pets, or in private menageries, or exotic birds in aviaries. Most Roman citizens would probably also at some time have seen exotic, unusual, or rare animals in triumphs, on display in the city, or more commonly in the arena during the animal games. Or, of course, they might have seen images of exotic animals in wall paintings, on mosaic pavements, or in the form of other artworks. To what extent provincial amphitheatres hosted games with exotic animals is open to debate.

It is also highly likely that each region of the Roman Empire would have had vernacular traditions in the naming of plants and animals, in much the same way as was true for Medieval to early modern England and Europe, but this is something we will never be able to assess, as all our evidence for names derives from written sources in Latin only. Certainly we will consider the issue of the naming of new animal species and the use of animal metaphor and simile in Roman literature.

The sheer cultural diversity of the empire and the significance of urbanisation at this time means that an anthropological approach to the study of human and animal relationships has its limitations. In some contexts animals were assimilated into the social system and thus might have been considered as an indissoluble part of that system while in other contexts animals might simply have been seen as prey or food, thus being Other in societal terms.

Egyptomania

In many ways this study could be said to be divided into two threads. The first is linked to the Romans' interaction and relationships with native species, that is in their local or regional natural environment. The second is linked to their interaction with and disruption of other, distant natural environments and ecosystems by the capture and enforced movement of what were viewed as exotic species and the depiction of these exotic creatures in Roman art, another form of 'capture' perhaps linked to the imagination. The systems for the procurement of exotic animals for the Roman arena will be considered in detail in a later chapter, while the acquiring and keeping of exotic pets, usually as a symbol of status, will also be considered elsewhere in the book. Discussion here therefore will concentrate on the depiction of the exotic in the form of what are known as Nilotic scenes, images of Egyptian landscapes along the River Nile, that were popular in Egyptian art itself, in early Roman art in particular, and in later Byzantine art (Plate 1).[2]

While consideration is going to be given to Nilotic scenes, Nilotica, on Roman wall paintings and mosaics, it should be borne in mind that the commissioning of such scenes was just a small manifestation of a broader Roman interest in all things Egyptian, indeed what has been called a veritable Egyptomania (Plate 2).[3] This took the form of an almost random collection of influences, appropriations, and adoptions as varied as the building of the Pyramid of Gaius Cestius, a tomb at the end of the Via Ostiensis in Rome, the removal from Egypt of a number of basalt obelisks and their setting up at various locations around Rome under imperial authority, and the appearance of sphinxes on tombs or on table legs. Perhaps surprisingly, the veneration of certain Egyptian deities, especially the goddess Isis, also became common in Rome and other larger towns in Italy, and not just among an expatriate Egyptian community.

The evident popularity of Egyptian imagery and symbolism within Romanised society in Italy can perhaps be gauged by the fact that around 130 Nilotic scenes on mosaics and wall paintings have been recorded at Pompeii, for example, a perhaps surprising number in what was a small provincial town. Nilotic scenes took many forms, often involving the perceived semi-humorous depiction of pygmies, but interest here is obviously quite specifically on those scenes that incorporated depictions of animals. The most spectacular of the surviving Nilotic mosaics in Roman Italy is the huge pavement from the site of ancient Praeneste, modern Palestrina, to the south of Rome.[4] Dating to around the first two decades of the second century AD, it was commissioned for a large basilican hall in the centre of Roman Praeneste, a public building of some kind, though whether a temple to Fortuna, a civic basilica, an *Iseum* or temple to Isis, or a building incorporating a nymphaeum remains uncertain.

The mosaic today can be viewed in the town's museum, *Il Museo Archeologico Nazionale* in *Palazzo Colonna Barberini*, where it is mounted on a wall on the uppermost floor and approached up flights of stairs from the museum's lobby (Plates 3–7). While the wall mounting allows a clear view of the design in its entirety to the modern viewer it perhaps forces consideration of its original context and the ancient act of viewing in that context to become obscured. It can also be forgotten that the mosaic as we see it today consists of only perhaps half of the original mosaic, with the rest restored to create a unified whole. While I do not necessarily accept the description of the restored mosaic as 'a pastiche', as it has been referred to by one academic commentator, discussion of the style of the mosaic must take the fact of heavy restoration into account.[5]

The Palestrina Nile Mosaic takes the form of a panorama or bird's eye view of the course of the river from its mountain source to the Nile delta and the annual flooding of the river, that great natural regenerative event. The peoples of the uplands, of Middle Egypt, and of the delta, appear – as do rustic buildings and grand architectural complexes. Ritual or religious scenes are portrayed. Locals participate in animal hunts, most notably a hippopotamus hunt prominently positioned in the lower half of the pavement. The river and its banks can be seen to be teeming with wildlife. Here we see a virtual celebration of the fecundity of the country as represented by the great river, the environments through which it flows, and, of course, its distinctive and abundant fauna and flora. The labelling of many creatures on the mosaic suggests that this was to act as an aid to some contemporary viewers who might have had no idea as to what these exotic creatures were. Interestingly, the artist has quite carefully distinguished between the characteristic fauna of the Upper Nile in Nubia – the lion, giraffe, boar, rhinoceros, hyena, and elephant – and that of the Lower Nile and delta of Egypt – the hippopotamus, the crocodile, and the ibis. Monkeys, birds, lizards, otters, turtles, bears, dromedaries, peacocks, and onagers are also depicted.

The Nile Mosaic displays a totality that encompasses human life, experience, and endeavour, the coexistence of primitive, unsophisticated life with civilization, as represented by architectural images, and natural phenomena and the environment as represented here by indigenous, yet to the Romans exotic, flora and fauna.

The Nile Mosaic was, in fact, one of two great tessellated pavements adorning the basilica at Praeneste, pendants to one another inside apsidal-ended rooms leading off either end of the great hall. The second mosaic pavement, a fish mosaic, is today still in situ inside the remains of the basilica and though very badly damaged, particularly in the centre, its interpretation alongside the Nile Mosaic helps to shed light on the meaning of the overall decorative scheme inside the building. It sits in a recessed basin cut into natural rock. The Fish Mosaic is likely to have depicted marine life, that is fish, squid, crustacea, and octopuses, across its whole surface, representing the great Mediterranean sea. A human figure stands on the foreshore.

Each of these two mosaics can easily be interpreted on its own. Indeed the Nile Mosaic has been variously described as a religious allegory, a historical painting, a topographical scene, a representation of a province, and a genre piece. However, if intended to be considered together as a conceptual whole then further ideas could have been intended to be expressed here, principally the crossing over the sea by the Romans to conquer the distant land of Egypt or that the Nile feeds the great sea on which Roman power and prosperity depended. I cannot agree with a recent suggestion that the two mosaics presented competing conceptions of time and space.

The classical art historian John Clarke has suggested that there were probably three levels of meaning underlying the depiction of Nilotic scenes in Roman art.[6] Firstly, that they could have acted as 'scenic entertainment', as he terms it, celebrating the exotic nature of this highly significant Roman province. Secondly, just as Roman depictions of barbarian peoples often presented them as being 'other' to the Romans, so the same sense of difference, and thus of power differential, could also have been suggested by Nilotic scenes with people and animals. Thirdly, they could have acted as protective or apotropaic images, seeing away evil spirits and negative forces. I believe that a fourth level of meaning pivots on the identification of Nilotic scenes as part of a geography of Roman-ness. The depiction of exotic animals in such scenes was part of a strategy for a Roman urban audience to come to terms with the modernity of their situation, that is, with being part of a vast new world, as represented by the Roman empire, that they would otherwise find difficult to conceptually comprehend.

Crucially, no other Roman province was celebrated and depicted in this way, or indeed in any other way than as a conquered land, through personification or through images of war and decimation. In the case of Dacia on Trajan's Column and Germany on the Column of Marcus Aurelius we see depicted there foreign lands through their battling and ultimately defeated peoples, sometimes through their villages, huts, and strongholds, and sometimes their farm animals and flocks appear. We get no sense of the actual appearance of these foreign landscapes – their topography, their rivers (unless being bridged or crossed by Roman forces), their flora, and their wild fauna – as we do of Egypt in so many of the Nilotic mosaics and wall paintings known to us. Painted topographical scenes, known as battle paintings, are known to have been carried in the procession at Roman triumphs – though none has come down to us. In contrast, it is worth noting here how the visual idealisation of Roman and Italian landscapes in bucolic scenes was a common trope on wall paintings.

In many of these Nilotic scenes the depiction of crocodiles and hippopotamuses were far from realistic. This does not mean that they were bad art and we should therefore dismiss them. Rather, they depicted the idea of the exotic creature rather than the creature itself. This is remarkably similar to the way in which barbarians were often portrayed in Roman imperial art as generic types, reduced to a form of visual shorthand that would be understood by most viewers, without recourse to depicting ethnic features, clothing, or weapons. It also has some resonance with regard to the depiction of Australian fauna by artists on the Cook expeditions, of so-called First Fleet painters and illustrators, and of an artist like George Stubbs back in England, as we will see elsewhere in this book.[7]

One particular aspect of this study that I can only touch upon here, as I am not an expert in the development of the Latin language, is how Roman encounters with exotic animals inevitably led to the need to name these animals with Latin names, even if they already possessed given names in their home locales, and thus to 'conquer' them through the very act of naming, to bring them into the remit of the Roman world and to become part of its ever-expanding world view. As with alien peoples and lands, so with animals, though it is difficult to imagine which other aspects of the expansion of the Roman world would have required such a marked degree of linguistic invention and novelty to deal with these encounters, though some names appeared through the adoption of given Greek names. Thus these encounters were not just simply physical encounters but rather were also linguistic and highly conceptual ones. In many ways, the partial incorporation of alien elements into the discourses congruent with the Roman cultural mainstream was a demonstration of how the ideology of power and later of empire allowed for more discursive and potentially disruptive or incongruous elements such as these to be 'domesticated'. One strategy adopted to achieve this was to establish a distinction between concentration on acts of transformation performed upon animals or objects themselves and on the animals or objects in themselves. In other words, some elements of deconstruction of the natural character and context of certain animals needed to be presented as congruent to Roman needs

A chronology of the naming of exotic beasts in Latin would be fascinating to construct and interrogate. The act of naming, the choosing of a specific word or words as a name, can take different forms in terms of generating expectations among those hearing and interpreting those names. Animals could not establish their own identities, at least not outside of their natural habitat, and in Roman times the markers of identity were in fact thrust upon them through processes such as being named and written about by encyclopedists such as Pliny. For instance, the Latin name for the giraffe *camelolepardis*, quite literally camel leopard, was in many ways highly pedantic. A giraffe is not really anything like a camel or a leopard: it might be thought to possess certain physical or visual traits in common with each of those highly individual creatures but in no respects is it an actual amalgam of the two, as the name might suggest. This name takes on a motivated relation to the animal, highlighting some of its physical characteristics, using analogies that might allow the listener or reader who has not seen a giraffe to imagine or conceptualise it. Whether the name was intended to demystify the exotic and unusual, to help in the process of negating the shock of its otherness, is uncertain. Would knowing the name have helped someone to mentally assimilate the giraffe when one might finally be viewed in the arena or in an artist's image on a mosaic or in a wall painting? The naming of the Nile crocodile – *crocodilus* in Latin and literally 'pebble worm' in translation – again represented an amalgamation of two descriptive terms to try to conjure up the image of the creature basking on the sunny banks of the Nile.

Once the shock of the new had been diluted or neutralised through familiarity, names of exotic animals, perhaps like the animals themselves, would have become naturalised and would no longer have drawn attention to their invented nature. In Roman culture the various instances and processes of naming taken together were more crucial than the connotations of any one individual animal name. By creating Latin names for exotic creatures, by denoting them as transparent signs, they were Romanised but in most cases without losing their exotic characteristics: they were free from external associations but nonetheless retained certain connotations of novelty and otherness.

The displaying of exotic animals in the arena and their induction into forced and unfair combat, resulting in their inevitable slaughter, would appear to have been a form of intentional shock on the part of the shows' organisers. The social theorist Walter Benjamin, when considering the avant garde nature of the writing of Charles Baudelaire, considered two types of shocked response to such deliberate provocations, the first being purely defensive and thus neutralising the shock, and the second being integrative, that is contextualising the shock into a category of experience mitigated by a conscious parrying of its power to damage.[8] In the case of the second of these responses it is quite possible to see how an individual or group of individuals forming a crowd could possibly become inured to repetitious violence in the arena or indeed to repetitious games where the cycles of violent combat and death were played out anew on an almost continuous loop. Once a discourse of arena violence was established, both in terms of the nature of the shows and the reception of those shows in the attuned minds of the audiences, then only unexpected or unfamiliar things and actions could invade or disrupt this discourse. Context would then be crucial, and in a later chapter some key events involving just such psychic schisms in the arena involving animals will be discussed.

Cataloguing

If naming was the first stage of this Roman linguistic imperialism, then describing or cataloguing animals constituted a second stage, even if such writings can hardly be termed scientific in terms of our present-day definition of the word. It brought Nature under control but also helped to demonstrate its diversity and multiplicity in ways that were stimulating to both the intellect and the imagination. It changed nothing fundamental about animals themselves but it helped codify cultural attitudes to individual species or subspecies of creatures. Latin is rich with words to describe animal anatomy, animal colours, animal bodily functions, and animal sexual behaviour.[9]

There are indeed numerous written sources that can be called upon to testify to various aspects of human-animal relationships in the ancient world. Perhaps the best such sources are the writings of Aristotle, Pliny the Elder, and Aelian.[10] Aristotle's *Historia Animalium, The History of Animals,* his work on biology and the natural world, was written in the fourth century BC but remained fundamental in its field – indeed it could be said to have single-handedly created this field of study – into the Roman period and way beyond, almost up to the sixteenth and seventeenth century rebirth of Natural History as a scientific discipline. Pliny's *Naturalis Historia, Natural History,* of the first century AD obviously owed a huge debt to the work of Aristotle and other earlier writers but if its somewhat anecdotal nature and lack of basic scientific originality slightly compromises the work, its encyclopaedic nature and its insights into Roman cultural attitudes and practices towards animals make it highly significant in its own right, particularly in the context of the present study. Claudius Aelianus, otherwise known simply as Aelian, composed his *De Natura Animalium, On the Nature of Animals,* probably in the early third century AD. It is a work not of biological and scientific observation, but rather an excursive and largely anecdotal series of accounts of animal lives, underwritten by moralising observations of contrasting human behaviour. Notwithstanding this, *De Natura Animalium* still provides much useful information on human-animal inter-relationships beyond its moralising film.

Other useful sources include Oppian's late second century AD Greek poem *Halieutica* which concentrates on the subject of fish and fishing in both a philosophical and comedic manner, Apicius's *De Re Coquinaria,* a cookbook or collection of recipes, of the mid to later first century AD, and Titus Lucretius Carus or Lucretius's *De Rerum Natura – On the Nature of Things*, a now-prescient philosophical examination of the natural world of the first century BC.

Equally, there is a long history of man portraying animals through images going back to prehistoric cave art and while portrayals of animals at any period between then and now were always culturally specific to their original context, they nevertheless have one particular thing in common. That is, that they all represent attempts to narrate the separation of humans from all other animal species, but by their very nature these images also build a bridge between the two. Such images also played a role in providing visual descriptions of certain animals, even if sometimes the portrayals were fanciful or somehow inaccurate.

We should not always just consider the Romans interacting with Nature and retaining agency in all their dealings with animals, for on occasions there was conversely a need to react against certain pests and vermin, as there is in any society. For instance, while the earliest settlement in Rome was centred around enclosed areas on certain of the hills, eventually the need was felt to expand settlement into the lower-lying areas alongside the Tiber and on its floodplain, areas which were marshy and prone to flooding. Not only this, there were also mosquitos breeding in the marshes in and around Rome and it was recognised that these constituted a health hazard as long as there was standing, sometimes stagnant, water in these areas. Thus engineering solutions were needed to drain the marshy areas, to bring in clean drinkable water from outside the city, and to design and build a sewerage system which would help to combat disease and avert public health crises. Thus the humble mosquito could be said to have been the prime motivator behind the draining of the area of the Forum and the Campus Martius and of the marshes directly outside Rome, the building of Rome's aqueducts, and the construction of the *Cloaca Maxima* and its related network of sewers and drains.

There is a remarkable modern echo of this ancient hygienic crusade married with political expediency and an ideological narrative in Mussolini's 1930s' campaign to reclaim the Agro Pontino marshland – the Pontine Marshes – and combat the malign effect of the mosquito there. As Il Duce himself announced in December 1934 on the inauguration of the new town of Littorio there, 'this is the war we prefer', hinting at Italian fascism's need to channel its energies into economic and infrastructural projects as a manifestation of its power and as a cleansing form of surrogate war.

Dolphins and Mice
This study has been arranged thematically, examining Roman relationships with animals in different cultural contexts rather than being systematised by the discussion of each of the most significant species of animal known to the Romans in turn. However, in order to illustrate the potential complexity of such

relationships, discussion will now turn to two case studies, of the dolphin and the mouse, creatures which both occurred commonly in Roman art and which might perhaps be thought to have had little symbolic hinterland.

The first case study that I would like to raise now is that of the dolphin because it illustrates how conceptually rich Roman allusion and metaphor linked to animals sometimes could be and therefore how carefully one has to tread in tracing the path of meaning when interpreting ancient artefacts, artworks, or written sources.[11] Sometimes though one has to accept that in certain contexts there is no hidden meaning to be found: in relation to the present study that sometimes there is no meaning other than there having been a common joy in the depiction of the natural world and its beasts. Roman fishermen and seamen operating in the Mediterranean would have been quite familiar with pods of dolphins and sightings of them accompanying the boats or breaking the surface of the water nearby. Indeed, Pliny relates a number of rather anecdotal stories about their aiding fishermen and their sometimes surprising docility in the presence of humans. The Greeks even believed that dolphins were somehow attuned to the pleasure of music. Most interestingly, stories even circulated not only of dolphins rescuing live humans from the sea but also of them carrying ashore dead bodies, as if ensuring the presence of mortal remains for a funeral.

The sea was as entrenched in the Roman imagination as it was in the Greek mind, and, just as in Greek art and culture the dolphin became a familiar and very common image in Roman art and literature, both of itself and as a signifier and metaphor for a wide range of concepts. Folk tales had it renowned for its speed in the water and its friendliness to man, and it was thought that it was some kind of weather prophet and was able to foretell the time of its own death, when it would then beach itself and die. Folk observations of other dolphins respecting and attending on their dying or dead fellow creatures only served to enhance the mental association of dolphins with underworld forces and currents. This attributed gift of foresight or prophecy gave the creature considerable cultural currency in the Roman imagination.

The fact that dolphins as mammals suckled their young almost inevitably led to their sometimes being equated with human women and vice versa. Such an equation often took the form of dolphins appearing with images of Venus or of water nymphs. A more general link between women and the sea was also fostered. A number of Greek mythological stories, such as those of Rhoeo and Auge, also evidently familiar to the Romans, in which women were cast into the sea by their fathers for being deemed to have brought shame on their families by conceiving a child following a rape, made the sea an indeterminate space where those thought to be outside of society's norms, in these cases by being unmarried mothers, could literally be set adrift. Though both women in this story survived their ordeal, in a way they had faced symbolic death or had hovered between life and death away from the natural human environment of dry land.

The most common medium for the portrayal of the dolphin in Roman art was the bath house mosaic, as indeed it was also the most common medium for the representation of the Mediterranean's teeming fish stocks and its aquatic life in general. Therefore when images of dolphins occurred on bath mosaics it can be interpreted most commonly as the manifestation of what had become an almost cliched Roman trope: the equation of human bathing with non-human aquatic life. And yet, other meanings could also be manifested at the same time. For instance, the dolphin figured quite prominently in a number of Greek colonisation myths, such as those relating to the founding of colonies on Lesbos, at Delphi, and at Tarentum. Enalos, one of the first colonists on Lesbos, was said to have jumped into the sea to kill himself after his great love had been thrown in to satisfy the demands of an oracle, and both were rescued by dolphins. Apollo was said to have first come to Delphi in the form of a dolphin, guiding a Cretan ship carrying priests into the safety of the harbour at Kirrha. They then went on to found a sanctuary there to the god and its famous oracle. Taras, son of the sea god Poseidon and the nymph Satirion, was said to have ridden on the back of a dolphin across the sea from Greece to southern Italy to found the colony of Tarentum. Indeed the dolphin was considered to be a messenger of Neptune/Poseidon. The Romans cannot have been unaware of this perception of the creature as a living beacon guiding people to new lands, something that would fit well with the Romans' own ideology and mythology of empire. Thus in a provincial context a dolphin on a mosaic perhaps could have represented an allusion to Roman maritime power and to conquest, as, for example, in the case of the dolphin mosaic at Fishbourne palace in Sussex, in southern Roman Britain. The dolphin thus could be seen as some kind of bridge to new lands and unknown geographies – an active agent in the creation and expansion of the contemporary human landscape, territorialising the world.

Dolphins on mosaics often were depicted with cupids or putti riding on their backs, and depictions of the story of Arion being carried to safety on a dolphin as related by Herodotus occur on a number of mosaics, most notably at Piazza Armerina in Sicily, on a mosaic at Thina in Tunisia, and in a Pompeian wall painting. Arion, a lyre-playing lyric poet and singer from Methymna on Lesbos, had been travelling around Magna Graecia and had earned a considerable sum from performing there. On his way home on a Corinthian vessel, the ship's crew became aware of his money and decided to rob and kill him or force him to jump into the sea and drown. Pleading for his life, Arion's last request was to be allowed to play and sing one final time, his beautiful voice attracting a pod of dolphins alongside the ship. He then jumped overboard and was surrounded by the dolphins – one of which, or all of them depending on which version of the story one follows, helped him to dry land at Cape Taenarum, at the end of the Mani peninsula in the southern Peloponnese, an area believed to house one of the entrances to the underworld of Hades. Once home he informed on the ship's crew, who had intended to turn up there with their news of his accidental death at sea. King Periander then punished the pirates and Arion gave thanks to the gods, and dolphins, by commissioning and dedicating a statue of himself astride a dolphin for the shrine of Poseidon Taenarum. Once more a link was also being made here between dolphins and travel between the world of the living and that of the dead, in other words, that they mediated between these worlds.

In both Greek and Roman art Poseidon/Neptune, Amphitrite, Thetis, and Nereids are all commonly depicted riding dolphins or with their feet on dolphins' backs. Dolphins were also closely associated with the god Dionysus/Bacchus. Indeed, in the

Homeric Hymn to Dionysus it is related how a band of Tyrrhenian pirates abducted the young god, not knowing who this youth really was, in order to sell him into slavery. Once onboard their vessel, Bacchus started to extract his revenge and slowly sent the pirates mad and attacked them in the form of a lion, till all but one jumped overboard into the sea and were turned into dolphins by him.

If the sea, as opposed to land, represented an environment of which humans were not naturally part, then it is hardly surprising that it was seen by both the Greeks and the Romans in their mythologies as a mediating space between men and the gods and men and the dead. Greek and Roman writers often attributed almost human-like traits to dolphins and it was this supposed link that made them mediating creatures between the living and the dead and thus appropriate to portray in images in funerary art. The intermediary role, facilitating transitions, moving between land and sea, between Rome and foreign territories and lands accessed by the sea, made it easy to equate them with moving between the land of the living and Hades, the land of the dead. Nereids or sea nymphs were thought to convey warrior's souls to the underworld, often accompanied as images by dolphins.

Cupid/Eros mounted on a dolphin became one of many defining images of Augustan art and can most spectacularly and tellingly be seen in a small depiction at the feet of Augustus in what is known as the Prima Porta statue of the emperor, perhaps the defining imperial image of his reign. The statue today has pride of place in the *Musei Vaticani* in Rome. While it was undoubtedly originally stressing the mythological lineage from Aphrodite, down through Aeneas, to the Julio-Claudian family, to Augustus through Julius Caesar, it is also a historically-specific reference to the naval Battle of Actium of 31 BC at which Augustus finally defeated Mark Antony. Thus the image here was not in any way a neutral one: rather, it was highly politically charged.

Images of dolphins also appeared quite commonly on gladiatorial equipment, such as the helmets and greaves from Pompeii and now in the *Museo Archeologico Nazionale* in Naples. In this particular context the dolphins appeared as symbols of both death and hope. They were both *memento mori* and harbingers of unavoidable fate, something that one would have thought gladiators needed little reminding of.

Racing contests at the hippodrome could also be alluded to by the depiction of the speedy dolphin, so quick to cut through the Mediterranean waters. Dolphins were also associated with Neptune/Poseidon who himself was especially associated with horses. Figures of dolphins decorated the *spina* or central dividing wall of the Circus Maximus at Rome, and probably at other racing circuits elsewhere, and, along with eggs, were used to count laps. At the Circus of Maxentius, part of a funerary complex just outside Rome on the Via Appia, bronze dolphins on the *spina* could be turned tail up or tail down to help in the counting of laps raced.

In Christian art the dolphin was almost as common a motif as the fish, and represented the idea of salvation and eventual resurrection. Just as it had often been portrayed in Roman art transporting gods and goddesses, so in Christian art it commonly appeared transporting souls across the ocean. Depicted in tandem with an anchor or a boat, it came to symbolise Christ's redeeming message.

Dolphins were also common in wall paintings, as decorative supports for statues, as figures adorning metalwork, and indeed represented in jewellery items. When they appeared on metal vessels this was often on drinking vessels, equating seawater with wine, some of these vessels possibly having religious or funerary connotations which would once more have placed the dolphin image in an apotropaic or protective role.

The appearance of images of dolphins in Roman funerary contexts (Plate 8) can be suggested to have been partly influenced by Greek and Etruscan antecedents. Frescos from two Etruscan tombs, the Tomb of Hunting and Fishing, and the Tomb of the Lioness in Tarquinia, for example, include representations of dolphins in direct parallel with funerary feasting and drinking scenes, evoking ideas of spiritual transition. Numerous Roman cinerary urns also carried such designs and they became particularly common on sarcophagi, on the front or sides and quite regularly on sarcophagus lids.

One particular image from a Roman funerary context illustrates the complexity of the dolphin motif in such situations. The image is of a waitress or bar-keeper serving a drink, and appeared on the front of a sarcophagus from the Isola Sacra necropolis at Ostia, the port of Rome. To some extent this was subsidiary to the main scene on the sarcophagus panel which is taken up with the depiction of a ship and rowing boat coming into a harbour, presumably at the port of Ostia itself, with a landmark *pharos* or lighthouse guiding their way. Moving to the right across the panel, the decoration segues into a scene inside a tavern, again presumably at the port. Behind the tavern counter, decorated with a dolphin carving, can be seen a well-stocked bar of jars, jugs, and wine amphorae. A woman walks across the tavern to a table where two men are seated. She is carrying a glass or beaker of beer or wine and proffers it to one of the men who holds out his hand ready to take it. The second man has already been served his drink and is in the process of downing it. A small dog reaches up towards the table, flexing his front paws ready to scratch the woodwork.

While the scene depicted here can be taken at face value as representing a contemporary genre scene quite specific to the geographical location, at the same time it includes motifs and symbols quite commonly linked to funerary contexts. These include journeys across water, travelling or voyaging in general, dolphins, dogs, and funerary drinking scenes. It is as if a very local set of themes has been applied to a more universal concept. For whom the sarcophagus was made remains unknown.

Dolphin themed statuary was also common in the house gardens of Pompeii, as it would have been in Rome and elsewhere in Italy. The theme of a dolphin rescuing a cupid from the clutches of an octopus recurs many times here in large and small statuary groups. It is curious that the Romans did not differentiate in certain contexts between sea water and fresh water: sea creatures appear on bath house mosaics, yet the water in the baths was fresh water. Dolphins also regularly appeared as decorative elements of garden and public fountains, fresh water spouting out of their beaked mouths most commonly.

Dolphins appeared regularly on drinking vessels, symbolic there as Bacchic companions or messengers, as they did on other items of Bacchic art, artefacts, and paraphernalia, the god's relationships with dolphins being complex, involving as it did ideas of companionship and celebration, along with darker themes linked to matters of life and death and funerary beliefs and practice. Bacchus's turning of the Tyrrhenian pirates into dolphins was perhaps both a punishment and a symbol of their eventual salvation. A dolphin could symbolise the presence of the god and his power to transform man through frenzy.

Thus it can be seen from the brief review of the types of contexts in which images of dolphins appeared in Roman art that what might at first appear to be nothing more than an anodyne image could in certain contexts be charged with multiple, complex meanings. The notion of the sea and movement across it, as exemplified by the image of the dolphin, underpinned the Roman economy in the form of seaborne trade and driving expansionism and conquest or colonisation. It is of no great surprise therefore that as far as we are aware there was a cultural taboo among the Romans concerning the hunting of dolphins and eating them.

Again, it might be thought that there was very little to say about the mouse in Roman times, the subject of our second case study. However, this would not be true and while Roman authors wrote little about the creature, once more a plethora of images in Roman art signified a number of different attitudes towards this ubiquitous small creature that is generally considered to be a pest when living inside a human's house or eating stored agricultural produce.[12] Mice would have been the major rodent pest in Italy for the early Roman period as the more voracious, tenacious, and troublesome black rat, a native species of Egypt and the Near East, did not establish itself in Italy until possibly as late as the second century BC, as suggested by small numbers of rat bones in deposits of this date at Pompeii.[13] Rats would initially have reached Italy hidden on board merchant sailing vessels and then have established themselves at port sites such as Ostia and Pozzuoli before spreading inland and further afield, and eventually to the provinces. A model of rodent spread involving long distance dispersal at numerous locations followed by neighbourhood diffusion can be surmised throughout the empire. Such isolated populations would have been maintained and periodically enlarged by new arrivals at port sites. In Roman Britain, for example, rat bones from London and York attest to colonies there in the third and fourth centuries

AD, with fifth century examples from the midlands inland site of Wroxeter representing an example of the diffusion of rats from port populations.

Of course, there are many different types of mouse. At Pompeii bones of the garden dormouse, the edible dormouse, the hazel dormouse, the wood mouse, the house mouse, and possibly the Algerian mouse have been recorded as excavated remains.[14] The wood mouse appears twice in the sculptural frieze at the portal of the Building of Eumachia in the forum at Pompeii, as does the garden dormouse, depicted there chewing on an acorn. Most of the known Roman bronze and silver mice are figures of common house mice, though some figures of dormice are also known.

The curious appellation of the god Apollo Smintheus, literally Apollo 'mouse slayer', indicates a firm link between the god and this prepossessing animal. Apollo Smintheus is mentioned in the opening book of the Iliad, inflicting a plague upon the Greeks, is named and depicted on coins, and is attested in inscriptions. There were a number of temples to the deity in ancient Greece and particularly in western Asia Minor where his localised importance there continued well into the Roman period, with a first or second century AD inscription being recorded on a column base at Alexandreia Troas on the Turkish Aegean coast, dedicated by Lucius Curiatius Onesimus, a priest of Hecate. At Chrysa in northern Greece Aelian recorded live mice being kept and fed, and the geographer Strabo tells us that there stood there a cult statue of the god crushing a mouse under his foot. A number of second to third century AD inscribed copper alloy handles with mouse terminals probably from Ephesus in Asia Minor may be linked to the worship of Apollo Smintheus in the region. The inscribed names of Elpidephoros and Hygeinos Kanpylios may be of temple officials.

It had long been thought that stray site finds of small cast bronze mice were somehow linked to Apollo Smintheus, these mice being attached to oil lamps, candleabra, lampstands and other pieces of lighting equipment and furniture, items that possibly were used inside his temples. However, recent research suggests that these might after all simply have been domestic items and that their common occurrence on such types of items may though simply have been allusions to the mouse's well attested propensity for chewing on wicks and candle wax.[15]

Roman metal genre figurines of mice, generally munching on food items of one sort or another, are relatively common in bronze (Plate 9), but silver examples are also known.[16] Mice also appear on bone knife handles, on other sorts of handles, in the form of weights, and on the spouts of metal vessels. Representations are also quite common on ceramic and bronze oil lamps and engraved gemstones. A figurine of a mouse playing a trumpet-like instrument while holding one paw over its ear, and a metal lamp lid in the form of a mouse holding a theatrical or stage mask, were probably both intended to be humorous pieces, respectively parodying an incompetent arena musician perhaps and an outrageously mugging actor. Humour probably was also behind the image on a ceramic lamp in the British Museum collections of a stork holding a balance to weigh a mouse and an elephant, each of whom sit in the opposing balance pans. The joke is doubled by the mouse outweighing the elephant in a subversive inversion of reality. On a Roman Niedermörmter type military helmet of the first century AD, in the Axel Guttmann collection, two mice appear with a segmented food item which has been suggested to be cheese but which is more likely to be bread or cake. The significance of this image is not apparent in this context, though in Roman North Africa, for instance, images of animals in mock combat probably represented allusions to gladiatorial contests.

An image of a mouse also appeared on one of the silver items in the Boscoreale treasure, buried there in AD 79 before the eruption of Vesuvius. The treasure is now in the *Musée du Louvre* in Paris. As two of the items from the treasure also feature images of feasting skeletons, it seems altogether appropriate for a scavenging mouse to be there as well, in that a mouse as an image might be seen as an image of plenty, of agricultural surplus, of abundant food in a household. A mouse feasting on dropped or discarded food on a three-dimensional 'unswept floor' mosaic from Rome symbolised just that and will indeed be discussed further in Chapter Four.

Mouse nests must have been regularly disturbed in the countryside and indoors in Roman houses, and the maternal nature of a nesting female mouse with her brood of pups may then have been observed.

It is therefore a small step from the mouse being a symbol of plenty to it being linked to ideas of fertility and fecundity, and it is in this context that we might interpret a mouse figure, possibly an amulet, from a disturbed burial in Roman York in northern England; wood mouse bones from possible ritual deposits of the second to first century BC under the House of Amarantus at Pompeii; a mouse emerging from out of a womb-like nautilus shell on a red jasper intaglio from Corbridge, again in northern England; and the localised southern Italian phenomenon of the fourth century BC of making and using mouse-shaped baby feeders and depositing them as grave goods. Certain mouse-image-bearing items may therefore have been linked to Venus and, occasionally, to regional manifestations of less obvious deities such as Somnus, as has been suggested for Gaul.

On a second-century AD mosaic pavement in the House of the Venus Mosaic in the city of Volubilis in Roman Mauretania, now in Morocco, appears the image of a cat in a red collar with a bell, named in an accompanying inscription on the mosaic as *Vincentius*, meaning *Conqueror*, pouncing on and killing a mouse named *Luxurius*. It is likely that this depiction of single combat to the death by named protagonists is a humorous take on the kind of gladiator mosaics that were so popular in this part of the empire. Indeed, in the same house a mock chariot race mosaic carries images of racing chariots in a hippodrome pulled by ducks, geese, and peacocks. However, in a Roman dining room the theme of the punishment of luxury, of excess and overindulgence, might have been considered appropriate and a metaphorical depiction of this on a mosaic might indeed be what we are seeing here in tandem with the gladiatorial combat mockery. It must also be considered whether the learned owner of the house and commissioner of the mosaic was familiar with Aesop's fable of Venus and the cat, a depiction of part of this would thence have been altogether appropriate as a theme linked to the major Venus mosaic elsewhere in the house. In this story the goddess turned a cat who was besotted with a handsome young man into a beautiful woman, at the cat's request. After their wedding the goddess decided to test whether the transformed creature had indeed shed her natural cat instincts and bodied forth a mouse into the room where the woman lay with her new husband. Reverting to type, the woman chased after the mouse, probably much to the surprise of her husband, and a disappointed Venus then changed her back into a feline. A less allusive cat and mouse struggle was depicted on a mosaic panel from Orange in Gaul on which a manic or over-excited cat is shown with a dead mouse between its paws.

Thus images of the humble mouse in Roman art can be ascertained to have been symbols of a number of diverse ideas linked to abundance, fertility, fecundity, and plenty, and to well known deities such as Venus and to the more esoteric figure of Apollo Smintheus. If the mouse was seen as a pest in certain situations, it is perhaps surprising that the scavenging mouse on the unswept floor mosaic is portrayed in an almost benign way, there to provide amusement rather than to invite hysteria.

Nature and Culture

This book constitutes a cultural history rather than an archaeological study, though a great emphasis will be placed on the interrogation and interpretation of visual sources alongside written ones. The nature of the vast amount of evidence available, often though in disparate and contradictory forms, means this book is inevitably a record of a series of natural, mediated, or staged encounters between Romans and Romanised peoples and animals.

Attitudes then to different sorts of animals must have varied just as they do today: in all probability such attitudes were more marked, and seemingly quite stark and polarised in the Roman period. Attitudes about livestock animals would have differed from attitudes to pet animals or favoured animals such as a riding horse, as again attitudes would have been different towards wild animals, and finally towards exotic animals, that is animals transported far away from their own natural habitat. What at first sight therefore might appear a straightforward area of study is nothing of the kind, as we will now see. However, it will be demonstrated time after time in this book that there simply was no schism in Roman society between the rational on the one side and the irrational on the other, the former linked to culture and the latter to Nature.

A history of the emotions such as this cannot but foreground the experiences of those Romans who witnessed unbelievable acts of cruelty to animals in the guise of public entertainment. This thought-provoking and particularly telling narrative of cruelty cannot be ignored or underplayed. Despite this study being of a very specific era, one with a common vocabulary and a common conceptual framework, then, as now, there were probably some universals when it came to human and animal relationships, underpinned by basic biology, that is Nature, rather than culture. Looking at animals and their role in Roman society allows us to uncover and think about tracing networks in the past, and the cultural contacts and knowledge exchange that resulted from these contacts, however negative at times.

2

I Know Why the
Caged Bird Sings

There is a considerable amount of evidence for the keeping of animals as pets or companion animals in the Roman world in the form of written sources, funerary monuments and their accompanying inscriptions, and statuary.[1] In some cases the names of these pets have come down to us through these channels, the naming of an animal, bird, or other creature being an important symbolic step towards the breaking down of any culture's self-imposed inter-species barriers. Indeed, the anthropologist Claude Lévi-Strauss coined the term 'metonymical humans' to describe animals who were integral to their societies – for instance, pet dogs and other domestic household pets, hunting dogs, riding horses and so on. As very few of the recorded named Roman pets were given human names – Brutus or Livia, for example – we can interpret this as a distancing mechanism while naming being at the same time a bonding exercise between human and animal.

Some previous writers on this subject have perhaps spent too long questioning the use of the term pet, to distinguish ancient from modern attitudes to companion animals, the latter term they argue being a far more suitable one to use in order to avoid what they see as this evident dilemma.[2] I have opted here to use the term pet for any animal which appears to have been in some way commemorated in death, and thus which can be assumed to have been loved in life, and/or which has been named, thus singling it out for special consideration, or creatures which have been written about by ancient authors or historians in a way which would broadly fit with our present-day definition of the word. Under these terms a pet could also principally have been a working animal, a guard dog or a hunting dog and so on, but have been further loved and treasured in its own right as a companion creature. Evidence for pets in the Roman period is mostly positive, in that those we know about were loved. As today, and indeed at any time in history, it is likely that some Roman pet keepers were bad pet keepers and it is likely that as much cruelty to animals took place in the guise of pet keeping in Roman times as it does today. If such cruelty, neglect and indifference were not common today there would be no need for organisations like the RSPCA and other animal charities, dogs and cats homes, and animal rescue centres to exist.

In certain instances the evidence for the keeping of pets allows us a glimpse of the symbiotic relationship between the cultural and the natural spheres in the ancient world and between convention and impropriety at the time. In this chapter I will also examine and discuss the evidence for sick pets or farm animals being taken to healing shrines to seek a cure, events which were imbued with significant emotional currency and tension. This is a rather neglected field of study and one that will probably repay further research in the future.

Perhaps the most extraordinary contemporary reference to pet keeping in Roman times is in the form of a letter written by Pliny the Younger in AD 104 to his friend Attius Clemens and describing the violent and disturbing events that had occurred at the funeral of Marcus Aquilius Regulus's sixteen-year-old son.[3] Regulus, in his hysterical grief, is said to have sacrificed his son's pet animals and birds by the funeral pyre, slaughtering two Gallic ponies, a number of dogs, and pet nightingales, parrots, and blackbirds. The number of pet animals kept by Regulus's son, or probably more properly looked after by slaves on the son's behalf, attests to his father's wealth and status, or rather, it would appear, to his aspirations towards high social status and his ostentatious indulgence of his son. Perhaps tellingly Regulus's late wife Caepia had left her considerable fortune to their son rather than to Regulus. The father's seeming lack of any scruples in having the pets killed probably reflected not the madness of incalculable grief but rather the cold, calculating machinations of a schemer, out to draw attention to himself in all probability and to gain public sympathy, if Pliny can be taken to be an unbiased source. As Pliny noted: 'that was not grief but a show of grief'.

It has been argued that there is sufficient evidence to suggest that pet keeping was to some extent an integral part of a Roman elite childhood.[4] However, as we will see, pet owners were not exclusively children at this time. Not surprisingly, the most commonly attested pets in the Roman world were birds, dogs and cats, and these will now each be discussed in turn.

Gilded Cages

The popularity of caged birds is clearly demonstrated and highlighted by various ancient Roman authors, especially in Latin love poetry where description and metaphor were interwoven to sully the general and panoptical focus on the particular and individual.[5] Read together as a group, it is surprising how these literary works contrived to convey a significant amount of observed information about the appearance and behaviour of individual bird species through both description and allusion while at the same time often anchoring the use of such creatures as domestic, quotidian poetic subjects within a hinterland of mythological connections and references. The catching of birds often was used as a metaphor for human pursuit and seduction, caged birds for a 'captured' lover, and dying or dead birds for the withering of love or the end of an affair. There is perhaps no more famous pet bird from the ancient world than Lesbia's pet 'sparrow' whose life and death was described by the poet Catullus in two poems.[6] It is generally accepted that the Lesbia of the poems was none other than Catullus's real life lover Clodia (Claudia), the wife of Quintus Caecilius Metellus Celer.

In two of what are known to academics as *the Lesbia Poems*, Catullus paints a picture of a Roman matron playing with her pet bird as a displacement activity from thinking passionately about her lover. Nevertheless, at times in the poems we must accept that the bird was simply a surrogate for this absent lover and that its death in the second poem could also have been a metaphor for the death of love and passion. However, it must be noted that the Latin word for a sparrow – *passer* – could also be used as a euphemism for the male member or penis, hence the ubiquity of winged phalluses in Roman erotic art, and it has indeed been suggested that just such a double meaning makes the *Lesbia Poems* an altogether different and more salacious proposition.[7] It is not the place here to explore this controversy but simply to flag up its existence. It is likely that the 'sparrow' in question was actually a blue rock thrush, a *passer solitarius*, a more decorative and tameable bird than the common sparrow. However, if found as an abandoned fledgling, sparrows can be tamed and domesticated.

The poem spawned a host of imitations and we have elegies to Corinna's dead parrot by her lover Ovid and Statius's mention of his friend Atedius Melior's equally dead parrot, while Martial refers to his patron Lucius Arruntius Stella as writing a poem about the death of his wife's pet dove, all of which suggests that the keeping of single birds, both native and exotic, was a particularly female pursuit, if we can take these poetic expressions at face value.[8] In total, it has been estimated that in Roman poetry there are more than 700 individual references to birds both wild and tame, most to wild species. These fall into four broad categories: mere mention of a bird, in flight or roosting for example; a mythological context in which a bird appears or is alluded to; an epithet, such as white swan; and a purely poetic simile or metaphor involving a bird, its characteristics, or behaviour.[9]

It should come as no surprise that in the fantastical wall paintings from the garden room at the Villa of Livia at Prima Porta, just outside Rome, there appear images of dozens of birds in a verdant garden setting (Plates 10–11).[10] There also appears a bird in a cage, probably a nightingale, which like a surrogate viewer is depicted looking out into the painted gardens with their lush vegetation and trees and a plethora of wild birds. Now restored and recreated as a room inside the *Palazzo Massimo* branch of the *Museo Nazionale Romano* in Rome, these paintings can be interpreted as having been part of a deeply political narrative, marrying the conquest of the seasons and of wild Nature, and ultimately of other lands and other peoples. Not only are we seeing here a contrast being made between Nature and Nature tamed but also an extraordinarily powerful metaphor for power and control.

Of course, as we have seen in the case of Lesbia's sparrow, imagery involving pet birds was often just that, imagery and metaphor rather than solid evidence about pet keeping. Nevertheless, it does tell us something about ancient attitudes and stances with regard to certain types of animals and birds. It would appear that domestic caged birds were very much a specifically Roman cultural phenomenon, a cultural artefact of sorts. Caged birds did not feature particularly in either Greek or Egyptian cultures and therefore some explanation needs to be sought for this. Bird keeping can be thought of as having been part of a much wider phenomenon of display and the acquisition of luxury goods. However, it would not appear that the keeping of caged birds was an exclusively aristocratic interest, but most of our evidence relates to this class. Keeping birds in cages or in aviaries was a fashion; part of an arena of competition, from the time of the late Republic onwards, that encompassed the collecting of Greek statues, architectural munificence and benefaction, the design and laying out of great gardens, and the creation of menageries, aviaries, and fishponds. Marcus Tullius Cicero's brother Quintus added an aviary to one of his villas in 54 BC and in doing so was simply following a fashionable trend.

In the imperial period the emperors and their families continued the trend. According to Pliny, the empress Agrippina, wife of the emperor Claudius, was gifted a nightingale which had cost the extraordinary sum of 600,000 *sesterces*, an exorbitant and ostentatious purchase and gift. He also tells us about Agrippina's talking thrush and other talking birds, a starling and a nightingale, belonging to Britannicus and Nero.[11] In the Augustan period and later, flamingos were brought from Egypt and North Africa. Faustinus, the friend of the poet Martial, is known to have had some of these birds on his farm at Baiae on the Gulf of Naples.[12] As we will see in a later chapter, flamingo flesh and indeed tongues may have been eaten as exotic meat at ostentatious and pretentious Roman feasts. The birds are also recorded as having been sacrificed to Caligula, though any story of this kind promulgated by Suetonius in his book *The Twelve Caesars* needs to be taken with a proverbial pinch of salt.[13] The green Indian parrot was another exotic bird which at first was a rare, occasional exhibit in Rome according to Varro but which apparently became relatively common in the city after the trade between Egypt and India increased during the reign of Augustus, and the birds thus came on to Rome via Egypt.[14] The scandalous emperor Elegabalus was said to have fed both parrots and pheasants to his pet lions and to have eaten, presumably cooked, parrot himself.

A recent systematic study of images of birds on artworks, mainly in garden paintings and interior wall paintings at Pompeii, and of actual bird bones present in excavated deposits, revealed some interesting but confusing information.[15] More than a hundred different bird species were represented as painted or sculptural images in the town, most of them native Campanian birds. Three species of Egyptian ibis appeared in Nilotic scenes, mostly in the Temple of Isis complex and also in a number of private homes, while the flamingo, Egyptian goose, peacock, grey parrot, and three species of parakeet are also represented in small numbers. There was obviously a common and highly developed liking for birds in the town. Caged birds were nowhere depicted, though on one wall painting we can see two bird catchers carrying baskets of live birds for sale, either for sale at a food market or as household pet birds, or even for religious sacrifices. Again, there is virtually no evidence from bone assemblages of the presence in the town of either garden birds, carrion birds, or pet birds at the time of the eruption of Vesuvius in AD 79. Such evidence is most likely to have been destroyed or was ignored by excavators whose priorities were the recovery of artefacts rather than bones. Absence of evidence in this case should not be taken as evidence of the absence of pet birds here.

As well as individual birds or pairs of birds being kept as pets, there is also considerable written evidence for the creation of formal aviaries by the better-off citizens and members of the imperial families. Marcus Terentius Varro, the chronicler of agricultural life in the Roman countryside in his invaluable *De Re Rustica*, himself created an aviary or *ornithon* in the gardens of his villa at Casinum.[16] The design of the gardens here has fascinated scholars from the Renaissance period onwards and numerous attempts have been made to draw up reconstructions of the aviary based on Varro's description. The aviary basically took the form of a high walled enclosure, with the birds being kept in by netting. There was also a duck pond and a fishpond. Varro's collection of birds included 'birds of all sorts, especially songbirds, such as nightingales and blackbirds'. Given his own personal and genuine interest in bird-keeping, it is probably of no surprise that Varro had looked into the history of the practice in Italy and records that the very first collection of birds was established by Marcus Laenius Strabo of Brundisium in the first half of the first century BC.[17]

It would therefore appear that real pet birds were common and accepted in Rome and more widely in Roman Italy while poetic and literary metaphors and allusions to pet birds inhabited the Roman imagination in a way that was highly culturally significant. As we have seen, a cage, a home for a bird, could be used poetically to act as a metaphor for a human home, indeed for the human body or rather some container for its soul. Apotheosis when depicted in Roman art, such as on the base of the Column of Antoninus Pius and Faustina, usually took the form of individuals in flight up to the heavens or being carried up there. A caged bird was a trapped lifeform, which in its uncaged state represented a particular kind of freedom. It could also represent a particular type of luxurious lifestyle. As a recent study has pointed out, caged birds could be linked to ideas around luxury and craftsmanship, metaphoric content, cognition, mental modelling and drama, as well as more banal societal contexts relating to collectability, value, and fashion. A talking bird could be seen by the Romans as a symbol of education and aspiration to knowledge. It could represent human qualities or even be metaphorically human. Single or paired birds could be used to symbolise marriage, fidelity and concord. Doves and peacocks were used in this way, the dove being particularly associated with Venus and thus with the concept of love (Plate 12), and the peacock with Juno, a goddess of marriage. Childhood innocence could also be depicted in this way, as suggested by a relief panel of a girl holding a dove, dated 120–140 AD, from Rome and now in the Getty Villa, Malibu. More darkly, the cock could be used as a symbol of sexual love or even violent lust and as an image in Roman art that had dark links to certain raped women such as Persephone and abused male youths such as Ganymede.

Dog Days

In towns and cities in the Roman period large dogs would have been kept principally as guard dogs (Plate 13), but this does not necessarily mean that they were not also regarded at the same time as pets by their owners. The same dual role may also have been played by hunting dogs and animal herding dogs,[18] all of these types of dogs probably commonly falling into Lévi-Strauss's category of 'metonymical humans'. There would not appear to have been the same social cachet involved in keeping dogs as pets as we have seen happened with regard to the keeping of birds in Rome and Italy. In one of Martial's epigrams is a passage relating perhaps to an aristocratic friend's pet dog,[19] though this is open to other interpretations and perhaps should not be taken at face value:

> Issa's more pert than Lesbia's sparrow,
> Purer than kisses of a turtle-dove,
> More sweet than a hundred maidens rolled into one,
> Rarer than wealthy India's precious stone,
> She is the pet of Publius,
> Issa dear,
> She whines, a human voice you seem to hear.

There are a number of black and white threshold mosaic panels from houses in Pompeii depicting guard dogs/pet dogs, including the most famous example, the *Cave Canem – Beware of the Dog* pavement from the House of the Tragic Poet which gives this book its name (Plate 14). The large shaggy black dog depicted there, with white on its limbs and head, is chained up but is caught barking and snapping at someone at the door. Another chained dog on a mosaic protects the House of Paquius Proculus and a dog with a studded collar, secured by a rope, appears on a portion of pavement now on display in the *Museo Archeologico Nazionale* in Naples. A fourth Pompeian dog mosaic comes from the House of Caecilius Iucundus, though in this case the hound lies curled up sleeping. An attentive guard dog, sat up ready on his haunches, was also painted on a pillar at the entrance to the Taverna of Sotericus. A dog lies sleeping in a busy metalworking shop on a relief from the town (Plate 15). If we project the common use of guard dogs at Pompeii to cover their use in Rome and in cities and towns throughout the Roman empire, then it can be argued that dogs played a crucial and highly significant role in household and urban security in the absence of organised police forces at this time.

Of course, we cannot leave the topic of dogs at Pompeii without making mention of the skeletal remains of dogs excavated at the site over the years and particularly of the very well known plaster cast of a dying dog found during excavations in 1874 at the House of Marcus Vesonius Primus. The poor creature, restrained by a bronze studded collar on a leash, lies on its back, doubled up in evident agony, its legs in the air, as it doubtless writhed on the ground gasping for air in its death throes. This is a pathetic relic of the tragedy which overtook Pompeii and which killed its pets and resident wildlife, as well as its human inhabitants. The American artist Allan McCollum produced a remarkable installation in 1991 called *The Dog From Pompei*, consisting of more than sixty cast fibre-glass dogs taken directly from a mould of the second generation cast at Pompeii. The work was concerned with issues connected to commemoration, voyeurism, death, and other themes, explored through the use of multiples, by repetition, and by exploring the idea of the value or devaluation of the original object or item. Cleverly, and even more poignantly, in the exhibition of the work McCollum laid out the casts not so much that they appeared as multiples, identical casts stressing pathos through repetition, but rather like figures in a stop-go animation, with each cast subtly different in its positioning and alignment from its neighbour, giving the work a feeling of movement rather than isolated stillness. A sub-section of sixteen of McCollum's dogs has also subsequently been displayed in the same way to great effect.

Further skeletal remains of dogs have been recorded at a number of other locations within Pompeii, the most interesting of which would appear to be the bones of a large dog lying on its side, shut inside the House of Menander, a creature that seems to have survived being buried by ash but which sadly then would have died from asphyxiation.[20]

Roman statues of dogs (Plates 16–19), tombstones of pet dogs, inscriptions or epitaphs naming pet dogs, and depictions of dogs on their owners' funerary monuments occur in sufficiently large numbers to suggest they were popular pets at this time, and a number of these will now be considered here. The dog breeds include huge Molossian hounds, dogs like Irish wolf hounds, greyhound or lurcher type dogs, smaller Maltese-like dogs, and tiny lap dogs.

A marble grave relief dedicated to *Helena*, a Greek name very rare in Rome, is in the collection of the Getty Museum, Los Angeles, and dates to AD 150–200.[21] On it is depicted a small but plump Maltese dog framed within a *naiskos* or small shrine. It is uncertain whether the dog was named Helena, and was thus a pet being commemorated, or whether Helena was the dog's proud owner who went undepicted on her own funerary monument for some reason, being symbolically represented by the depiction of her beloved pet dog. The inscription on the stele reads *Helena Alumnae Animae Incomparabili et Bene Merenti*, translated as *To Helena, foster child, soul without comparison and well deserving*. Interpretation of this stone, as always, hinges on the inter-relationship between image and text. The depiction of a dog on its own on the stele suggests a pet memorial, yet the word *alumna* used quite carefully and deliberately in the inscription refers to the Roman system around foster children, sometimes freeborn and sometimes freed slaves, chosen for special treatment and fostering in elite homes.

Totally unequivocal in its being an epitaph for a pet dog is a marble tablet with a lengthy inscription acquired by the British Museum, London, in the eighteenth century and otherwise being without precise provenance (Plate 20). However, there is no question of its authenticity as a genuine ancient piece. The epitaph for *Margarita-Pearl* is written in verse, as if penned by the dog herself. In it can be found a number of clever allusions to well-known lines from the poet Virgil's funerary epitaph and from poems of Ovid in his *Ars Amatoria – The Art of Love* and *Medicamine Faciei Feminae – The Art of Beauty*. It is worth reproducing the text here in full, in translation:

Gaul gave me my birth and the pearl-oysters from the seas full of treasure

my name, an honour fitting to my beauty.

I was trained to run boldly through strange forests

and to hunt out furry wild beasts in the hills
never accustomed to be held by heavy chains
nor endure cruel beatings on my snow-white body.
I used to lie on the soft lap of my master and mistress
and knew to go bed when tired on my spread mattress
and I did not speak more than allowed as a dog, given a silent mouth
No one was scared by my barking
but now I have been overcome by death from an ill-fated birth
and earth has covered me beneath this small piece of marble.
Margarita.

Margarita resoundingly represented the animal that played a dual role in its owner's life, principally a trained hunting dog but one that had become pampered and as much a pet as a hunter, and one that was so valued that money was spent on her commemoration and due grieving was displayed over her untimely, early death.

Another lengthy encomium to a beloved pet dog is provided on the tombstone to *Patricus* from Salernum in Campania (CIL X 639). Mention can also be made of the tombstones of *Aminnaracus* from Rome (the name appears alone beneath an image of the dog CIL VI 29895), of *Heuresis* or *Tracker*, again from Rome (CIL VI 39093), and of the female dog *Aeolis* from Praeneste (AE 1994 348).[22] Below the inscription on the first century AD funerary altar from Aquileia in northern Italy dedicated to Caius Vitullius Priscus sits a large dog with a collar and bell around its neck (Plate 21). The dog is depicted as if suddenly distracted by a noise, turning its head, pricking up its ears, and rising up off its haunches, with its front legs stretched out. Had the dog here simply been intended to represent an image of fidelity, a generalised character trait possessed by the recently deceased Priscus, it would seem unlikely that such care would have been taken over the depiction of this particular dog, its stance and its unusual collar with bell: rather, we are more likely to be seeing a portrait of Priscus's own pet dog or beloved guard dog. A number of stone cinerary urns from Aquileia have lids topped off by a carving of a sleeping dog or lion (Plate 22). In these cases the animals may simply have been apotropaic or protective figures, the dogs possibly linked to a strong local cult of Silvanus.

The famous funerary relief from Rome of the Flavian woman Ulpia Epigone in the guise of the goddess Venus is now in the collections of the *Musei Vaticani* in Rome. Lying on a couch, propped up by her left arm, she is accompanied by a tiny lapdog that peers out from under that arm, perhaps a portrait of a cherished pet, though equally the animal could have been somehow symbolic in this context (Plate 23). Many other such portrayals of small dogs such as this are known (Plate 24).

Images of dogs, unaccompanied by gods or humans, could also be employed on Roman tombstones and sarcophagi as symbols of fidelity, a good example being a tombstone from the *columbarium* of Vigna Codini on the Via Appia in Rome on which appears *Synoris, sweet pet,* perhaps not a pet dog after all but possibly a favourite slave. A very specific link between the image of the dog as a symbol both of fidelity or faithfulness in life and at the same time with links to the underworld, is made on a tombstone from Shirva, Dumbartonshire, Scotland. On this appears a bearded man lying on a couch, clearly a representation of a funerary banquet, with a small dog standing on a cushion behind his legs, but with no food set out on a table that appears in the foreground as is usual in such depictions. A gravestone from Bathford, Somerset in south western England, carries a relief image of a man holding on to the lead of a large dog who is captured in the act of jumping up after a leaping hare, the symbolic meaning of this scene being open to a number of interpretations.

Nine Ancient Lives

It is generally accepted that cats were first domesticated in Egypt and Mesopotamia and that they would have come to Europe through trade or accompanying travellers to Rome from those regions. The well known and well attested religious associations of cats in Egypt continued into the Roman period and it is likely that the same strictures about acknowledging the cat and not harming it were applied by the large ex-patriot Egyptian community in Rome.[23] In Egypt the goddess Bastet was commonly depicted in the form of a cat or sometimes as a woman with a cat's head.

At Pompeii the number of cat bones from excavated deposits is very small indeed, literally a handful, and no cats are among the casts of creatures killed in the town.[24] It has been suggested that in this provincial town before AD 79 there was not yet a fashion for keeping cats as pets, as may have already started in Rome.[25] Certainly, much greater numbers of cat bones are found in later archaeological deposits in Roman Naples. And yet by the mid to late fourth century AD the presence of cat bones from excavated sites throughout the empire, for instance in the *praetorium* or commandant's house at Binchester Roman fort, County Durham in the empire's northern frontier zone, shows how common cats had become by then.

Just as with guard dogs and hunting dogs, so it may have been the case that cats were viewed by the Romans principally as mouse and rat killers, keeping down vermin in houses, shops, and public buildings, and that they came to be regarded as pets as a secondary consideration. One can occasionally find reference to the theory that cats may not have at first been kept in Rome as rodent controllers: indeed, that the Romans commonly kept domesticated weasels for this task. This would appear to be a complete fallacy, based on a misunderstanding of the small number of ancient sources such as Petronius, Pliny, and Cicero who make mention of weasels.[26] At Pompeii a small number of weasel bones have been found in secure archaeological deposits in the Forum and the precinct of the Temple of Apollo, for instance, but not in sufficient numbers to support this bizarre theory.[27]

Pictorial representations of cats in domestic settings are relatively rare. When they do occur they generally reference the cat's natural hunting and stalking instincts rather than its more peaceable and loving qualities. Perhaps the most famous of these images appears on a mosaic pavement from Santa Maria Capua Vetere and now in the *Museo Archeologico Nazionale* in Naples and takes the form of a stalking cat down on all fours at the foot of a birdbath or fountain and hissing at its prey, two parrots and a dove, with one clawed paw extended as if ready to move to strike (Plate 25). Another well known mosaic panel from the House of the Faun in Pompeii carries a depiction of a cat holding a dead game bird, perhaps a quail, in its mouth. Below the scene with the cat are two ducks, other birds and seafood (Plate 26). Two almost identical mosaic *emblemata* panels are known from Rome, the best, from Via Ardeatina, now in the *Palazzo Massimo* collection of the *Museo Nazionale Romano* in Rome (Plate 27), suggesting a common pictorial source for the motif.

On a small marble relief in the *Museo Capitolino* in Rome appears a curious image of a child playing a lyre while a cat reaches up to pull down a brace of dead ducks hanging from a tree branch in a courtyard. This image has sometimes been referred to erroneously as 'a dancing cat', but this observation rather misrepresents the cat's natural instinct to acquire food often at any cost and without scruples or dignity. On a ceramic oil lamp in the British Museum, London, a street entertainer is shown with a monkey and a cat, the cat climbing up a small ladder (Plate 28).

While we know the names of many pet dogs of the Roman period from inscriptions, as far as I am aware not a single cat name is known, apart from Vincentius mentioned earlier, perhaps indicating their respective popularity as pets at the time.

With the Shades

When images of animals appeared on Roman tombstones, stele, sarcophagi, and other types of funerary monuments it was usually for one of three reasons: to act as a symbolic guardian of the deceased, or of his or her burial place; to provide an allusion to either the name, appearance, character, or personality traits of the deceased; or simply as a favourite and well loved pet, as has been discussed above in the case of birds, dogs, and cats. Not surprisingly then, depicting pets on funerary monuments, usually with their owners, was relatively common, and indeed depictions of some more unusual pet animals in such contexts are worth mentioning briefly here.

A mid-first century AD funerary altar of five-year-old Aulus Egrilios Magnus from Ostia carries the depiction of the boy holding the horns of what may be his pet goat or kid, though it is equally possible that he is leading a goat to sacrifice (Plate 29). Also from Ostia, and now in the collection of the Getty Villa, Malibu, comes the late Antonine, AD 161–180, sarcophagus of Titus Aelius Evangelus, evidently a prominent local wool merchant, and his wife Gaudenia Nicene. On the front panel is depicted a funerary banqueting scene with busy peripheral activity. Here we see the bearded Evangelus, reclining on a couch holding a goblet of wine with one hand and a bunch of grapes in the other which he proffers to a woman, presumably his wife. She approaches the end of the couch, holding her own wine cup in one hand and a funerary garland in the other. A small creature, variously identified by different authorities as either a dog or a goat, stands on the floor at her feet, partially obscured by her legs. Behind Gaudenia Nicene sits another bearded man engaged in some sort of textile-related craft activity, with what may be a wool winding frame in front of him and a ball of wool on a table nearby. Behind him is a tree and possibly two further animals, one reaching up into the tree to nibble at its leaves, but this area of the sarcophagus is unfortunately damaged, so identifications of the creatures are unclear. Their stances suggest that they are indeed goats. Other unusual scenes appear on ground lines both in front of the *kline*, daybed, and behind it. In front appear representations of scales. Behind we see a cockerel, a man in a Phrygian cap leading a horse through an arched entranceway, with another cap-wearing man and a woman present. In the foreground, towards the edge of the panel, sits a young man on a chair winding wool, a wool basket visible on the floor under his chair. Images of sheep appear on the sarcophagus sides.

The scene on the front of this sarcophagus appears to represent a not altogether successful melange of a number of different types of symbolic representation: that is, standard funerary symbolism and funerary feast symbolism, biographical symbolism relating to trade or business, pastoral symbolism, and mythological symbolism of some kind. But what do the animals therefore represent: the goat or dog indoors, the feeding goats outside, the sheep, the cockerel, and the horse?

While the presence of the cockerel might most easily be explained by its use as a symbol of awakening and therefore it is altogether appropriate and indeed quite common in a funerary context such as this, it might also symbolise Evangelus's male virility or reference Mercury, god of commerce, and thus an appropriate god to have overseen Evangelus's business affairs when he was alive. But what of the other animals? It has been suggested that the two young men with the horse may be the Dioscuri, being welcomed to Olympus by their sister Helena. The goats may simply be pets.

A number of provincial funerary artworks depict children with pet animals, the most famous of which is a relief from Bordeaux, of Laetus's daughter (the inscription is fragmentary) in the *Musée d'Aquitaine*, which carries an image of a girl holding a small dog or a cat while a cockerel or rooster, perhaps also a pet, struts around in the foreground at the child's feet, pecking at the dangling tail of the pet above.

Emotion, Necessity, and Healing

It is possible that in these images of children holding pets we are seeing the animals being used metaphorically to indicate to the viewer some facet of the child's personality or a particular, positive character trait. However, the possibility also exists that these works could have been votive. The Greek and later Italic tradition of dedicating *ex votos* at healing shrines, often in the form of what are known as medical or anatomical *ex votos*, that is models of body parts in various materials, is also well attested elsewhere in the empire at a later period, especially in Gaul. These gifts to the gods were dedicated either in anticipation of the resident deity intervening to cure the sick dedicatee or in thanks for a cure having been successful. Others may simply be the record of a pilgrimage with an uncertain outcome. At some of these sites images of animals were also dedicated, albeit in very small numbers, and various possible explanations for the presence of these images at the sites can be put forward. They may have represented animals linked to certain deities or have been representations of animals brought to the site to be offered for sacrifice or have been given in lieu of an actual animal sacrifice taking place. In some cases the animal images could have been of family pets. In many cases it is likely that the image could have been of a valuable working animal whose illness was economically detrimental to its owners and whose death would have been in some way disastrous. As we have seen, sometimes working animals could also be considered as beloved pets. In order to examine these various options we will look at material from a major healing shrine in Italy and from later sites in Gaul.

At the Republican healing sanctuary at Ponte di Nona, 9 miles to the east of Rome, among the more than 8,000 dedicated terracotta *ex voto* items, mainly model human body parts, were 138 animal models.[28] Roughly similar percentages of animal models were recorded at the sanctuaries of Veii and Lavinium. At Ponte di Nona many of the animal figures were fragmentary and could not be firmly identified to species. Of the more complete models fifty-three were of bulls, three of horses, three of boars, and a single ram and a bird were also identified. At other Italian sanctuaries models of bulls or cattle were most popular, with horses, boars, and various types of bird also common. Rams, dogs and, in two instances, at Cagliari and Conca, a lion have also been found. The excavators at Ponte di Nona felt that the animal models there must have represented farm livestock valuable to their owners.

From the healing sanctuary of *Fontes Sequanae* at the Sources de la Seine in Burgundy in France, and now in the *Musée Archéologique de Dijon*, comes a remarkable assemblage of wooden, stone, and metal *ex votos* recovered by excavation, many of them in the form of dedicated anatomical *ex votos*, though a good number of statues of pilgrims to the shrine were also found.[29] Most notably from here comes a stone statue of a child wearing an amulet and cradling a small dog in both arms (Plate 30). A further eight, fragmentary stone statues from the site are of pilgrims holding dogs and two holding birds, something that requires explanation in the context of the healing function of the shrine here and at other healing sites in Gaul where other such statues have been found (Plate 31). At the Sources de la Seine stone statue fragments of cockerels, oxen, and possibly also a horse, may have been free-standing or might have been parts of larger statuary compositions, with the birds and animals being animal attributes accompanying an image of a god or goddess. Among the wooden statue figures there were twenty-five small figures of animals, mostly well carved and highly detailed, almost equally of bovines (bulls or cows) and horses.

An assemblage of about 2,000 animal bones excavated from the site, an assemblage dominated by pig and sheep bones, certainly points to feasting here and probably to animal sacrifice.

Other species represented at the site included cattle, goats, horses, dogs, chickens, deer, wild boar, foxes, and hares.

The small cult bronze figure of the presiding goddess Sequana stands in a boat with a swan's head prow, linking her to both Nature and water. From nearby Blessey, just 2 kilometres away from the Sources de la Seine, comes a first century AD bronze of a 'swan boat' with the figure of a man at one end of the boat. There was a long tradition in parts of pre-Roman Europe of decorating items with the swan boat motif, going back to the Bronze Age, and the figures from both the Sources de la Seine and Blessey would appear to have been part of that continuum, while also reflecting the artistic modes of Romanised art.

Again, from the sanctuary at Beire-le-Châtel, Côte-d'Or, where the presiding deity would appear to have been Minerva, many carved stone bovines have been found, along with carved groups of doves, and the head of an owl, a bird linked with Minerva.

The demonstration of the significance of animals to their owners in emotional or economic terms through the dedication of *ex votos* in religious contexts is a universal occurrence, both geographically and temporally, as is the seeking of divine protection for such animals. A visitor to the ethnographic Pitt Rivers Museum in Oxford, England, can view display cases full of amulets and protective charms for animals such as horses, cows, pigs, camels and donkeys, collected variously from places in northern Europe, the Mediterranean region, the Middle East and India and dating from prehistoric times up to the early and mid-twentieth century. If a sick or injured working animal represented an economic disaster for its owner, so did a stolen animal. Inscribed lead curse tablets requesting the gods to punish animal thieves are relatively common finds at temple sites throughout the Roman world. For instance, at the temple to Mercury at West Hill, Uley in south western Britain, Cenacus dedicated a tablet on which he accused Vitalinus and his son Natalinus of stealing his draught animal and implored Mercury to take away their health till the animal was returned. At the same site Honoratus bemoaned his loss of two wheels, four cows, and many small belongings from his home, urging the god to intervene on his behalf.[30]

Dog figurines and statuary have been found at many healing shrines, and at temples and sanctuaries linked with healing deities or deities who were tangentially associated with healing as one of their many roles. These images may have represented animals brought to the sites for healing, they may be images of dogs who 'worked' at the sites in the healing process (dog saliva was thought to have healing properties), or they might have been imagistic attributes of the presiding deities. I am most familiar with the dog figurines and images from sites in Roman Britain, though these are common finds across the empire in such religious contexts. At British sites such as Lydney Park temple, Gloucestershire, Coventina's Well, Northumberland, and Llys Awel, Wales, for example, all the dog images probably related to the attested religious function of their find-spots.

Ten bronze or copper alloy images of different breeds and sizes of dogs have been recovered by excavations at the temple site at Lydney Park, Gloucestershire, along with six images in stone. The most well known of these is the so-called Lydney dog, a small copper alloy figurine of a dog with a long muzzle and a slightly rough coat, probably identifying it as being similar to an Irish wolfhound. One of the other copper alloy items from the site comprises a sheet metal figure of a possible dog with a human face and another is in the form of an inscribed copper alloy plaque bearing a depiction of a small dog and declaring that 'Pectillus hereby gives the vow which he promised to the god Nodens deservedly'.

The Lydney temple and its residing god Nodens were inextricably linked to the process of healing of pilgrims to the site, with perhaps real dogs also being present on the site, in addition to images of dogs, the healing power of their saliva being one of the physical elements of the healing process here, as mentioned above. As well as being linked to Nodens, dogs were also linked in mythology to the healing god Aesculapius, who would also have been deemed to have been present at the temple. Another dog image possibly linked to Aesculapius comes from Bath, Avon in south western England, and takes the form of an altar carved on three sides, a small dog with an upturned, bushy tail standing beneath a tree on the back face of the altar. On the front sits a reclining figure of a woman holding out her arm to a second standing, nude female, in company with a possible feline. On the third carved face is a snake coiled around a tree. The presence of the snake and dog attest to a link with Aesculapius and therefore identify the two figures as Coronis, mother of Aesculapius, and Apollo.

A small bronze figurine of an Aberdeen terrier possibly comes from Coventina's Well, Carrawburgh, Northumberland in northern England. Its presence fits with the make-up of the overall assemblage from the site, which suggests that it too was linked to a healing cult. Again, two bronze statuettes of dogs from a group of religious items found at Llys Awel, near Pen-Y-Corddyn-Mawr hillfort, Abergele, Wales, were probably once more linked to the site's function as a healing shrine.

Other finds of dog images at British temple sites include the now-fragmentary stone statue of a greyhound-type dog from the temple site at Pagans Hill, Somerset in the south west, while a dog, a raven, and a stag, with other creatures, appear with Sucellus and Taranis on one of the sceptre bindings from the Farley Heath temple, Surrey in the south. Enamelled plate brooches in the shape of dogs are also known from Roman Britain, as indeed are such brooches in the shape of horses, stags, hares, felines, birds, fish, and insects. It has been demonstrated that such plate brooches are more often than not associated with religious sites in Roman Britain where they probably represent *ex votos* dedicated by visitors to the sites. A number of bronze skillet or *patera* handles with a dog's head forming the terminal of the handle are also known from Roman Britain, a good example of the type coming from Canterbury, Kent; such items may have been used for pouring libations on an altar rather than for purely domestic purposes.

Images of dogs were not only often associated with specialised healing shrines, with Aesculapius and Nodens, and with other types of temples where the presiding deity may have had a healing role among its other powers, but often with specific deities and mythological figures including Mother Goddesses, the goddess Diana, male hunter deities including Silvanus, Hercules, and eastern figures such as Mithras and Orpheus.

Finally, it is worth considering the image of a lapdog which appears on a relief of three Mother Goddesses from Cirencester,

Gloucestershire in south western England. The goddesses sit together, on a bench of some kind, with three children. The right-hand figure nurses a small dog on her lap, similar to a modern-day Dachshund. A dog, fish and fruits also appear with Mother Goddesses on a relief from Ancaster, Lincolnshire in the English east midlands. In both cases the figures of the dogs appear as attributes of Mother Goddesses who belonged to both this world and the underworld, and whose fertility was crucial to both realms. Thus the dogs were linked both to concepts of healing/birth/fertility and to death and the afterlife, just as they were when featuring as attributes of Aesculapius, the healing god who also most probably had chthonian powers.

Mischievous Irreverence

In the Roman period, as today, certain pets, indeed certain types of pets, would often have been acquired and kept simply as status symbols, to enhance the sense of self of the owner rather than necessarily through any feelings of love or compassion for the pet in the first instance, though such feelings can inevitably evolve and grow over time. It is perhaps to be expected that we can find many manifestations of status-related pet keeping and display of unusual or freakish creatures in Roman aristocratic circles, particularly among some of the imperial families. The story of Caligula and the reported strange infatuation with a horse is probably the best-known amusing story about an emperor and an animal, while Tiberius was said to have kept a pet snake. Equally open to satire and ridicule was the emperor Domitian and his acquisition of a huge fish, a '*monstrum*', which, according to the writer Juvenal in one of his *Satires*, represented uncontrolled imperial power which had grown, like the massive turbot, out of control.[31] The fisherman who caught the turbot and sold it to the emperor had done so because it was a fitting fish for such a powerful man. But Domitian by owning the fish was somehow then also displaying megalomania in invoking his authority over the known world's oceans and all life within it and in the lands around.

Another facet of the owning of a pet is its naming: the breaking down of a considerable barrier between human and animal. While farm animals and some working animals might also have acquired individual or generic pet names in the Roman period, it is generally household pets, stabled horses, racing horses and other animals used in sporting activities such as cock fighting, guard dogs, and hunting dogs and trained raptors or birds of prey that were subject to naming. Particularly famous or infamous animals were also named.[32]

While the most common Roman pets were birds, dogs, and cats it is worth noting here that monkeys and apes were sometimes also kept as pets by the Roman wealthy or by merchants who might have acquired the beasts on their travels.[33] The many similarities of these creatures to humans were not lost on the Romans, it would appear, and this sets them apart from the other kinds of household pets discussed in this chapter. Certainly monkeys of various sorts were well known enough to be the regular butt of Roman humorous writers and indeed occasionally appeared in genre art in the parodical playing of a musical instrument. At Pompeii the bones of a pet monkey, possibly a macaque, have been recoded in archaeological deposits.[34] Genre images of performing Barbary apes appeared in a number of wall paintings there and in the form of statuary. In two instances the animal was depicted in a more serious context, at the Temple of Isis as one of the animals sacred to Isis and a symbol of the Egyptian god Thoth who indeed often appeared in images with a baboon's head or the head of an ibis bird.

Apes were quite often considered as a symbol of bad fortune. An extraordinary depiction of an ape/man hybrid appears on a section of painted wall plaster from Pompeii that is now in the *Museo Archeologico Nazionale* in Naples and which does not have a specific provenance recorded to allow us to consider its proper context at the site. The scene depicted is one of the famous incidents in Virgil's *Aeneid* – Aeneas fleeing Troy carrying his father Anchises and in the company of his son Ascanius – brought to life in dramatic fashion, as it often was in Roman art, though in this instance the drama and pathos of the scene had been totally subverted by Aeneas and Ascanius having apes' heads and tails and being ithyphallic, that is with large erect penises. Either this can be taken as being a humorous illustration in its own right or a politically and ideologically charged piece of humorous invective, mocking part of Rome's founding myth of Trojan royal origins, attacking Virgil's canonical book, or questioning Augustus who claimed direct ancestry from Aeneas and the Roman Julio-Claudian emperors for whom the myth and book were also somehow sacrosanct. It is even possible that this Thoth-like transformation of mythical heroes could have been lampooning the fashionability of Egyptian religions with the upper classes in the town. This though was private humour expressed in a private space and not publicly served up ridicule. The house owner and his or her guests could have enjoyed the sharing of this subversive artwork but its existence would only ever have been known to a handful of people.

In eighteenth century England there emerged something akin to the Roman and present-day regimes of pet keeping, particularly among the aristocracy and gentry. Cosseted pets, including large house dogs, lapdogs, kittens, parrots, monkeys, and, most peculiarly, squirrels, appeared alongside their host families in numerous family portraits of the time. In many instances these animals would probably have been genuine pets, in others they were simply symbolic of human qualities or characteristics. As the historian Keith Thomas has noted, they might have been included in the portraits 'as a symbol of fidelity, domesticity and completeness, though sometimes (as in the case of dogs) as an emblem of mischievous irreverence.'[35]

Thus in this chapter it has been demonstrated how pet keeping among women and children in particular in Rome was relatively common from the late Republic onwards and how the acquisition of pets became one facet in the arena of competition among the Roman aristocracy, particularly the acquisition of more pets than other families or of more unusual and exotic specimens. Related to the keeping of pets by children would appear to have been the popularity of children's toys in the form or shape of animals. Indeed, even babies' rattles in the form of ducks, chickens, dogs, pigs, and bears are known. The keeping of pets by adults is also well attested and it would appear that both real animals, and images of animals in artworks or in poetry and satire, came to represent cultural and philosophical concepts linked to fidelity, faithfulness, and love and loss. Evidence has also been discussed of pet keeping in certain of the provinces of the empire, and there is sufficient evidence to suggest that pet animals and possibly also farm animals were sometimes taken to healing shrines to obtain cures for them when sick, imbuing these poor sick creatures with an emotional resonance which contributed towards the breaking down of the barrier between Nature and culture.

Animal Farm

Rural Rides

In contrast to the complexities of Roman pet keeping and animal collection discussed in the previous chapter, analysing the role of working animals and animals reared and kept by farmers is relatively easy. There is a huge amount of Roman writing on both the countryside, real and imagined, and on agricultural practice, much of which is germane to this present study. In particular Virgil's *Georgics* paints a literary picture of a bucolic rural paradise that includes man and animal together, while Marcus Portius Cato's *De Agri Cultura* and Marcus Terentius Varro's *De Re Rustica* provide us with a nitty-gritty practical guide to farming in general and in passing to animal husbandry, as do Columella in *Res Rustica* and Palladius in *Opus Agriculturae*.[1]

Information on the farming of animals for food and the selling or utilisation of animal by-products from farming not only comes from ancient written sources such as these but also, most usefully, through the integration of zooarchaeological evidence, that is the study of animal bones from archaeological sites, with the ancient sources.[2] Sometimes these two very different types of evidence are complementary and sometimes contradictory, but on the whole an integrated approach to the study of ancient Roman animal husbandry and farming regimes pays academic dividends in the kind of nuanced information that emerges from such a project.

A recent academic study of production and consumption of animals in Roman Italy utilised the osteological data from the study of animal bones recovered from excavations at a sample of ninety-seven sites analysed alongside textual references.[3] Leaving aside the potential dangers of extrapolating generalities from a sample such as this, interesting conclusions have emerged. Perhaps not surprisingly, it was found that cattle, sheep, goats, and pigs dominated the animal economy of all regions in the study and at all periods during Roman times. Cattle were kept most commonly for meat and dairy products and quite significantly for hides, but large numbers were also likely to have been working animals, a very large number indeed employed in traction such as pulling ploughs or carts and wagons. Both sheep and goats were widely kept, sometimes in what must have been huge transhumant flocks and sometimes in small numbers on farms. Wool was an incredibly important commodity in the ancient world, as we will see later in the chapter. Pigs too were common, often in surprisingly large numbers, and it would seem that the consumption of pork in Italy became more popular in the later Roman period.

Farming regimes would have differed widely across the empire, given the vast range of differing climate regimes, soils, geology and topography. Even within Italy there probably would have been quite marked regional differences in breeds of farm animals and once the Roman conquest of Italy had taken place it is likely that moves towards selective breeding of animals using the best stock would have occurred on an *ad hoc* basis to begin with, but eventually on a scale to produce improved breeds over time.

It would seem the Roman economy prized cattle principally for their work contribution in rural life and osteological data suggest that most beef consumed at the table would have come from older animals, probably at the end of their working lives and thus of their economic usefulness. A great deal of the beef eaten would have been sacrificial meat, as we will see elsewhere in the book. Exactly the same situation would appear to have applied to sheep, these animals principally being valued for their wool and to a much lesser extent for their milk to be used in cheese making. Butchered animal bones from the studied sample pointed towards mutton, derived from older animals, and to a lesser extent hogget, being eaten. Goats were also kept for milk. Pigs were kept for meat only.

Unsurprisingly, pork came from pigs fed up at considerable cost and care and at their peak weight in their prime.

Interestingly, there can be seen to have been marked differences in meat consumption between urban and rural areas in Roman Italy, as suggested by the analysis of butchery patterns among the bones from the analysed site sample. The towns would appear to have received much of their meat supply in the form of whole carcasses or in pre-prepared cuts and joints of the better meat off the animals. It is likely that each town was supplied with fresh meat from relatively local farms and it has been suggested that most farms supplying a town would have been within a 12 to 13 mile radius, though in the case of Rome and perhaps of some other large towns meat on the hoof was probably brought from much further afield, the basic economics of food provision being skewed by the unique nature of Rome, the metropolis. Another factor to bear in mind when considering the provision of live meat animals for Rome is that Rome was also a great pagan religious centre until the mid-fourth century AD and as such required huge numbers of cattle, sheep, and pigs to be brought to the city simply for the purposes of sacrifice. The servicing of this need created an extraordinarily large market for animals in their own right, as we will see in a later chapter. Thus at rural sites bones from poorer cuts might be more common or indeed bones from reared farm animals might indeed be largely absent, with such animals having been reared strictly for sale to urban markets, and farm dwellers must have taken advantage of locally-available game to a great extent to provide their meat and protein.

Of course, domestic fowl – mostly chickens, ducks and geese – were very common indeed, being kept for eggs and meat, and some birds provided feathers through their plucking alive, sometimes twice a year. Pliny tells us about the Roman invention of force feeding geese to enlarge their livers: 'Stuffing the bird with food makes the liver grow to a great size, and when it is removed it can be enlarged more with milk and honey.'[4] The common artificial fattening of other birds such as general domestic fowl, doves, and wood pigeons is also attested, and domesticated hares were also often treated this way to prepare them for the table.[5] Small birds such as quail were bred for the table and were particularly favoured in Roman North Africa.

As an aside, mention should be made of the flock of geese kept at the Temple of Juno on the Capitoline Hill in Rome whose panicked cackling alerted the Romans to a night-time attack on the city by the Gauls under their leader Brennus in around 390 BC. In this case augural or sacrificial birds gained a curious kind of historical agency.

Other smaller animals were also commercially reared, often on a small localised scale, including hedgehogs and dormice for the table, which will be discussed in the next chapter. From the fourth century BC onwards hedgehogs were kept as domesticates and were raised for both their meat and most particularly for their quills, which were used as tools in cloth fulling. As noted by Pliny: '....great frauds and profits have been made from the monopoly of this item; in no other department has the senate made more numerous rulings, and there is no emperor to whom a complaint has not been made from the provinces'.[6]

Farming, then and now, was all a matter of scale, and those scratching out a subsistence living co-existed with those owning and farming massive estates. About the subsistence farmers we know very little. About the great landowners we know a great deal, both from written sources and particularly from archaeological evidence.

Perhaps the most famous late Roman mosaic pavement in the *Musée National du Bardo* in Tunis, known as the *Dominus Julius Mosaic,* probably depicts the family of Julius of Carthage and dates from the later fourth century or early fifth century AD (Plate 32). Found on the Byrsa Hill, the mosaic is divided into three interrelated horizontal registers, which depict the owner's large estate in operation over the seasons. At the very centre of the central register, to which the viewer's gaze is first invited, can be seen a depiction of the great estate house itself, with fortified towers, high walls, and a large bath suite with vaulted roof. The master on horseback is shown riding towards the house with a servant on foot in attendance. Striding away from the house is a group of hunters with dogs, off to pursue hares, among whom is probably the *Dominus* again, one of the attendant men carrying a long pole in one hand and with a catch-net over his shoulder. In the upper register appears the mistress of the estate seated on a couch or bench set under a grove of cypress trees. She fans herself and looks out into the distance. On the bench beside her sits a plate of what might be pastries; around her are servants and slaves: agricultural workers variously carry in ducks or geese for the table and fruit for the mistress, while others harvest olives, bring in lambs and shear sheep. Incidental details are quite delightful: a chained dog sits outside his or her kennel and little birds, perhaps quail, grub around on the ground for food outside their hutch.

The master and mistress of the estate appear together in the bottom register of the mosaic. Julius the master is seated in an orchard with his feet resting on a stool and receives a scroll with his name on it from a messenger, who also carries live waterfowl destined for the dining table. Behind him a grapevine can be seen trailing around the trunk of a tree. The mistress has just stood up from her chair and is depicted leaning on a column and holding out her hand to receive a necklace being handed to her by a female servant holding an open jewellery box against her chest. A boy kneels before her with a basket of freshly-caught fish. On both the left and right outer parts of the register appear male servants bringing in more agricultural produce – flowers, it would appear, in the case of the man proffering a basket on the right, and perhaps a basket of nuts in the case of the male who also holds a dead hare in his left hand.

Follow the Money

So far I have discussed the raising, keeping, and sale of farm animals and their meat in terms of basic economics, trade, marketing, and consumption. However, consideration must also be given to the schism in this system in the Roman world created by taxation in kind. During the Republic modest taxation was levied on individuals and their wealth, property, land, slaves, animals, and personal possessions, Italy being freed from taxation in the second century AD and the burden of taxation being transferred to the provinces of the empire. However, this did not lead to an agricultural revolution, and inflation and political instability affected the Roman countryside as much, if not more so, than the towns of Italy and Rome itself. The need to stabilise the inter-relationship between politics and economics consumed the attentions of numerous emperors in the third century AD. But by the start of the fourth century a comprehensive plan was put in place, though this too would eventually and inevitably fail.

Diocletian's Edict on Maximum Prices of AD 301 represents the best documented, longest, and most detailed economic plan that has come down to us from the ancient world and provides startling and fascinating insights into the complexity and diversity of Roman trade and the procurement and sale of goods and services both in Rome and across the empire. The edict was not intended simply as a toothless guidance document but was backed up by clear sanctions involving execution or exile for anyone who charged or paid higher prices than those stated in the edict and for speculative hoarders and what we might call black marketeers. Much of the detail in the Edict is highly relevant to our discussion of Roman farming.

As might have been expected, caps were produced for the prices of basic foodstuffs by weight, such as cereals of various kinds, beans and pulses, and rice, for meats and fish, for oils, for salt, and for wines and beers. For instance, no one was to pay more than ten *denarii* for a pound of beef mincemeat or 16 *denarii* for ten brace of sparrows. No one was to pay more than 100 *denarii* for a pound of washed wool from Asturia in Spain or 12,000 *denarii* for a pound of white silk, presumably bought through intermediary traders with the Far East. For those working with animals, a muleteer, for example, was to be paid no more and no less than 25 *denarii* a day and to charge 4 *denarii* per mile for his beast's load, a shepherd 20 *denarii* a day, and a camel driver 25 *denarii* a day and to charge 8 *denarii* per mile for his camel's 600 lb load. A vet could charge 6 *denarii* per animal for clipping and preparing its hoofs, and 20 *denarii* per animal for the bizarre service of 'bleeding and cleaning the head'. From a British perspective it is interesting to note that a British hooded wool cloak referred to in the Edict as the *birrus Britannicus* could be sold for no more than 6000 *denarii*. Washed wool was a hugely important commodity and prices stated in the Edict varied from medium quality wool at 50 *denarii* a pound, to more prized wools from Asturia in northwest Spain at 100 *denarii* a pound, Laodicea in the province of Phrygia at 150 *denarii* a pound, and Tarentum in Apulia in Italy at 175 *denarii* a pound.

Other interesting entries in the Edict of relevance here include set prices for meat: 12 *denarii* for a pound of pork and 8 *denarii* for the same quantity of beef, and 20 *denarii* for a Menapic or Cerritane leg of pork. A fattened pheasant was 250 *denarii* and a wild one 125 *denarii*, a brace of chickens 60 *denarii*, ten beccafico were to be 40 *denarii*, ten sparrows 16 *denarii*, ten dormice 40 *denarii*, and a pound of venison 12 *denarii*. For fish a distinction was made between sea fish, between 16–24 *denarii* a pound depending on quality, river fish, at between 8–12 *denarii*, again dependent on quality, and oysters at 100 *denarii* per hundred.

Pastoral Politics

The Roman and Italian countryside did not always feature in the Roman imagination as envisioned through laws and proscriptive edicts. In earlier times the pastoral and political had met in idyllic harmony. If Virgil's *Georgics* painted a rosy picture of peaceful, bucolic country life under the benign reign of his patron Augustus, so some of the artworks on the emperor's own great monument the *Ara Pacis Augustae,* or Augustan Altar of Peace, equally contributed towards the politicisation of pastoral imagery and of an animal paradise in a similar way. The *Ara Pacis Augustae* is one of the most significant surviving monuments from ancient Rome.[7]

Restored and reconstructed today it sits within a glistening white, custom-built modernist museum compound near the banks of the River Tiber and close to Augustus's mausoleum, a short distance away from its original location facing the *Via Flaminia*. Completed and dedicated in 9 BC, the monument comprises a rectangular white Luna marble enclosure wall surrounding an altar inside, with doors or openings at both ends. The high enclosure walls are profusely decorated with relief sculpture. The upper parts of the outer faces of the long sides of the enclosure walls are carved with processional scenes involving the imperial family and participating religious officials. A procession of Vestal Virgins also appears in relief on the inner altar itself. Due to damage in places and perhaps over-zealous restoration of some portrait faces, not all the members of the imperial entourage can be identified with certainty and even then there is not always accord among academics as to the acceptance of certain of these identifications. It is generally accepted that Augustus, Marcus Agrippa, Livia, her sons Tiberius and Drusus, Drusus's wife Antonia the Younger, their son Germanicus, Antonia the Elder, her husband Lucius Domitius Ahenobarbus, and their children Gnaius and Domitia Lepida all appear in the frieze on the south side of the precinct wall of the *Ara Pacis*. On the north side can be seen another family group whose members might have included Augustus's daughter Julia and his sister Octavia. The number of women portrayed here was unusual, as was the presence of children in the processional scenes.

The artistic programme of the monument aimed to demonstrate to the Roman viewers the legitimacy of Augustus within the continuum of Roman history and historic myth through the transformation of reality into symbolic political capital.

At this time Livia was not only wife to the first emperor, she was also a mother, but importantly of a child from her first marriage and therefore not a child of the emperor's. While messages about motherhood and dynasty were part of the propaganda programme of the monument, this was conveyed through another female image on the precinct wall, that of Roma or Tellus and by the more abstract vegetal decoration on the friezes that alluded to concepts of the purity of Nature, and of growth and fertility.

The southeast panel, in the upper register to one side of the entrance, is dominated by images of female fecundity and plenty. At its centre sits a nursing mother figure, a personification, usually identified as being either Tellus – the Earth –, Italia, or Roma (Plate 33). Less convincingly she has been argued to be Venus, Pax, or Rhea Silvia, the mother of Romulus and Remus. In many ways it is not actually important which of these figures she is because of the overall message conveyed by her being first and foremost female and a mother. She holds two naked babies. To either side of her are semi-naked females with their mantles blowing out and billowing in such a manner as to suggest that these are personifications of the winds. Behind and below the three women are luxuriant plants and flowers, while below them in the foreground are a seated cow, a sheep, and a large bird caught in flight. This is a scene of peace and harmony, of growth and abundance, of fertile crops, fertile mothers, contented animals, and contented children. This is the Augustan peace in an image. It is a seemingly non-political image that is actually intensely political.

To some extent Roman imperial culture looked for powerful signs to represent its ideologies and in a beloved woman – the demure, reticent, and exemplary Roman matron – found its perfect expression. The image of the idealised woman excused or legitimised male mutability. The woman as transcendental and desirable, as a local spirit of place, was celebrated. The idealised woman, born of a river and of history, suggested Rome's association with Nature, to form an explanatory figure. She was both Society and Nature, without there being any contradiction expressed about the possible incompatibility of the two. She belonged to sidereal time while most people had to deal in the quotidian. She helped allow a space in which politics, transgressive or not, might be practised. In an age of increasing political disorder the female image was often unmistakably an imperative, beautiful and at one with Nature. So very often the style, composition, and subject matter of certain artworks were melded together in order to allow the viewer to look to the future, this being largely achieved by looking to the past and stressing the woman/Nature duality that the figure of *Roma* herself encapsulated.

The Dignity of Labour

It has already been mentioned that cattle were more often than not working animals in the Roman world, pulling ploughs (Plate 34), pulling carts and wagons (Plate 35) and so on. Other types of common working animals at this time would have included horses, donkeys, mules, asses, and it must not be forgotten that in Roman North Africa, Arabia, and parts of the eastern empire camels were highly significant.[8] In this category I will also discuss animals unlucky enough to take part in warfare, that is cavalry horses, war elephants, or animals that just served the military as pack or transport animals.

The act of ploughing was not only significant in the Roman world because of its role in the cultivation of land and the production of crops but also because of its links to the foundation of the city of Rome itself. Many Roman writers described the symbolic ploughing of the bounds of the city by Romulus and how a formal ritual of ploughing came to accompany the rites carried out during the foundation or refoundation of a town (Plates 36–37).[9]

There is considerable evidence to show that donkey mills and horse mills were common throughout the Roman world and indeed in Diocletian's Edict on Maximum Prices while hand mills were priced at 250 *denarii* and high-tech water mills at 2,000 *denarii*, donkey mills were priced at 1,250 *denarii* and horse mills at 1,500 *denarii*. The fact that all of these types appeared in the Edict demonstrates how relatively common they all were. Representations of both horse and donkey mills are also common. For example, a fragment of a sarcophagus in the *Musei Vaticani* in Rome carries images of two horses working a mill (Plate 38), while the sarcophagus of Publius Nonius Zethus, also in the Vatican collections, features a donkey mill (Plate 39). A funerary relief from the Isola Sacra necropolis at Ostia also carries a similar image.

Animals were then highly important in providing labour on farms – oxen or horses pulling the plough as we have seen and both also sometimes pulling farm carts. The horse was more significant as a means of personal transportation. Traders and merchants in different parts of the empire would also have made use of horse or bullock drawn carts and of pack animals such as donkeys, asses, or mules, and camels in North Africa and parts of the eastern empire. Elephants might also sometimes have been used for moving people and goods.

Mules can be seen singly and in pairs pulling two-wheeled carts on a large Hadrianic black and white mosaic floor in the Baths of the *Cisiarii*, the Coachmen, in Ostia (Plate 40). The names of some of these beasts are inscribed there – *Pudes*, meaning Modest, *Podagrosus*, meaning Gouty, *Barosus*, meaning Silly, and the untranslatable *Potiscus*. A figure holding a whip walks in front of one of the coaches. A stableman can also be seen leading two mules, probably for a staged changeover. Representations of two sets of city walls suggest that both Ostia and Rome are referred to here. Marine creatures also appear on the mosaic, as is more usual on a bath-house mosaic. It is thought that the Ostian guild of coachmen provided what we would call today a shuttle service from just outside the baths to the city of Rome, and that such inter-urban services based on a regular layout of relays or staging posts, *stationes,* running both people and goods operated between many cities in Italy and probably indeed all around the empire both as private enterprises and as part of the official postal system, the *cursus publicus.* Indeed coachman Gaius Julius Crescens of a guild of coachmen based in Thessaloniki in Greece and devoted to Heron Aulonites had a grave monument dedicated to him in AD 159/160 by his colleagues, including the head of the society, Artemon the yoke maker, and Tryphon the priest, and is pictured above the inscription driving his rig. The monument is now in the Archaeological Museum in Thessaloniki.

Certain types of Roman dog and certain individual dogs within those types can also be classified as working dogs, though as we have seen in the previous chapter the guard dog could also have been considered or thought of as a household pet in addition to its role in protecting the home, business, or farm. Sometimes hunting hounds might also have straddled the conceptual boundary between working dog and pet. Perhaps we can distinguish between what have been called 'necessary' dogs, that is working to earn its keep, and 'unnecessary' dogs, that is creatures like lapdogs whose function was nothing other than to provide company, companionship, or comfort to a human owner. In the Medieval and early modern period in Europe, working dogs' tasks could include pulling sleds, small carts, and apparently even ploughs on occasion, acting as turn-spits, and most significantly perhaps as sheep dogs, working for farmers and drovers. There is no reason to think that the range of roles played by working dogs in Roman times would have been any less varied.

The role of the camel as a beast of burden in Roman times is of great interest, although camels were used for such a purpose much earlier by other peoples in the Near and Far East, Arabia, and northern Africa where camel trains became a crucial part of the trading economy (Plate 41). Both the dromedary (one humped) and Bactrian (two humped) camel were used for transportation in some parts of the Roman empire; indeed, there is also evidence for hybrids being bred at this time.[10] While today the dromedary is associated with North Africa and central Asia, and the Bactrian with central Asia and the Far East, this was not always so.

Camel remains have been found at a number of Roman sites in Europe: in the east in Serbia, Bulgaria, Russia (at Tanais) and Slovenia, all of these, when identifiable, being Bactrians. In Spain finds have been of dromedaries, as in France (Gaul) and Belgium, and very possibly even in Britain, though some questions remain as to the status of the camel bones reported as having been found at a site in Greenwich Park, London, and if they do in fact date to the Roman period. Camel bone from excavations at San Giacomo degli Sciavoni in Moilse, central Italy, may also have come from an imported pack animal.[11]

As an aside, a single portrayal of a camel pulling a plough is known from the site of Henscir El-Ausaf, Western Gefara in modern day Libya, and dates to the third century AD. This need not necessarily cause surprise. While oxen and horses were most usually used as plough pullers in the European parts of the empire, and indeed donkeys could even be used for light ploughing according to Columella, this need not have been universal in the non-European provinces. Camels were also employed in warfare, and there is some, albeit scant, evidence that camel meat may have been eaten in some parts of the empire.

Curiously, it may be that the Roman system of slavery, which became a necessity of the project of empire and a product of expansion, fundamentally altered human and animal relationships and interaction in many places as tasks that had traditionally and previously been undertaken using animals now were carried out by human slave labour. This change cannot be quantified in any way but a similar shift in the economic basis of animal labour has been noted as occurring elsewhere at different periods, for instance at a much later period in Ottoman Egypt.[12]

Beasts of War
Consideration also needs to be given here to animals employed in warfare.[13] Unlike the treatment of animals in the arena, which we cannot rationalise by comparison to a modern counterpart other than bull fighting, animals are still used today in warfare to some extent – particularly dogs guarding prisoners, patrolling, hunting

enemies, sniffing for explosives, and so on. Ironically, it is likely that Roman veterinary medicine developed initially as a means to maintain and strengthen a pool of healthy animals for war, though once established as a discipline it is likely that veterinary medicine made a broader social impact on animal welfare and on both human and animal hygiene.[14]

The most common war animals in the Roman world were the horse and, to a much lesser extent, the elephant and camel. Dogs would have been used as camp sentries. Attention must also be given to beasts of burden who carried supplies, pulled supply wagons or carts, and who pulled heavy siege engines and assault towers on occasions. On the decorated frieze of Trajan's Column in Rome we can see images of donkeys being used to carry away war booty and, in one most unusual scene, a messenger is shown falling off a donkey in what must have been intended to be a humorous vignette (Plate 42).

The supply of horses to the Roman army must have been a veritable industry in itself, given the great reliance that the military had on this creature, but we know very little about the economics, mechanisms, and logistics of this business (Plate 43). In the early Republican period the cavalry units of the Roman army were small in comparison to the numbers of infantry, and were all recruited from Rome and Italy, though citizen equestrian units in the army did not continue into the imperial era. While the Romans themselves were not especially famed as horse riders, other ethnic groups of people recruited into the Roman army from the provinces as auxiliaries were, and the Roman army wisely took advantage of these traditional skills. The first mounted auxiliary units were Numidians, to be followed by Gauls, Spaniards and Thracians. Allied Sarmatian cavalrymen were also recruited. Horses were, of course, used by officers and indeed emperors to carry them while on campaign – and the mounted figure of a Roman emperor became a common pictorial trope in Roman imperial art. In the Roman army there were units of both light and heavy armoured cavalry, as well as mounted Scythian archers. The heavy cavalry forces were developed following the lessons learned after the experiences of crushing defeat for the Romans at the battles of Trebia in 218 BC and Cannae in 216 BC against the Carthaginians.

In the ancient world war elephants were most famously employed by Pyrrhus of Epirus in his invasion of Italy in 280 BC and by Hannibal and his Carthaginian army against the Romans when he crossed the Alps in 218 BC with thirty-seven war elephants in his force. Unfortunately, most of Hannibal's elephants died in the process, of the extreme cold. Pyrrhus had employed Indian elephants, while Hannibal had the smaller North African forest elephant at his disposal. In the eastern empire the Romans recruited camel-riding auxiliaries. Elephants appear alongside camels in carved scenes decorating the Arch of Galerius in Thessaloniki, northern Greece. Dating to AD 298 the arch commemorates the emperor's victory over the Sasanid Persians and the capture of their city of Ctesiphon and helps demonstrate how adaptable the Roman army could be in different geographical locations.

A small number of references to the use of carrier pigeons to bring messages into or out of besieged camps suggests that their use might have been common.

Rather more esoterically, it has been suggested that a common Roman siege tactic was to use large siege catapults to fire bees' or wasps' nests into towns or forts under attack, so common in fact that it might have led to a significant decline in the bee population in the later empire.[15] I think this suggestion must be taken with a very large pinch of salt, particularly if one thinks of the practical and logistical problems in locating large numbers of insect nests and then in safely transporting them to a battlefield for their use as missiles. However, there may well have been some truth in the historian Herodian's account of Septimius Severus's siege of the desert town of Hatra, now in Iraq, during the Second Parthian War, where the town's inhabitants were instructed by their leader to gather up stinging and poisonous insects in clay pots which were then thrown down to break on the Roman troops as they attempted to scale the town walls.[16]

To help put the Roman use of animals in warfare into some kind of perspective, in the First World War it has been calculated that as many as 16,000,000 animals played some role on both sides.[17] While cavalry charges were a thing of the past, horses were used to pull artillery, often under fire themselves. One of my grandfathers was in the Royal Horse Artillery and had experience of this.

Depending on the theatre of war, horses and mules were also used to transport soldiers, ammunition, food, and medical supplies to the front, and the wounded and dead back behind the lines. Dogs and pigeons were used to carry messages, dogs and even cats were employed to kill rats in the front-line trenches and ship's cats hunted mice and rats onboard, while miners and tunnellers used their traditional canaries underground to help detect poison gases. Military mascots were imbued with great reverence by various regiments and as well as creatures such as goats, more exotic and unusual animals also occasionally took on this role, with lions and bears, monkeys, and foxes being among the more surprising mascots of the war.

Animals were also used in Roman triumphs that led on, of course, from war and victory (Plate 44)[18]. This was often for both practical and ideological reasons, as well as for religious reasons, given that sacrifice followed the triumphal procession in thanks to the gods and preceded victory games in the arena. Religious sacrifice and the games in the arena form the subject of two later chapters, so discussion here will focus on animals in the actual triumphal parade itself. Viewers of a triumph would expect to see the Roman victor, a general in the Republican era and the emperor in later times, soldiers of the victorious Roman army, enemy prisoners, most of whom would subsequently be sent into slavery, and some of the spoils of war, which often included captured animals, the more exotic the better. Thus no ideological distinction was being made here between human, animal, and inanimate spoils: all were representative of the defeated 'other'. That is not to say though that the show of the defeated might not have elicited a sympathetic response from some viewers or have engendered a sense of wonder in others.

The victorious general or emperor would ride in a *quadriga,* or four horse chariot, the horses very commonly being white from the time of Augustus onwards. They had probably been drilled for hours to co-ordinate seamlessly as a team and to track the required pace of the procession. They had also probably been acclimatised to loud and constant noise, to prepare them for the hysterical clamour of the event and its sheer din, as the procession made its way along the triumphal route.

Various accounts relating to a number of triumphs add more incidental detail about animals present at particular events, each detail confirming the fact that the triumph was a highly stage-managed affair, a veritable piece of street theatre. Mention is made of white sacrificial oxen at some triumphs, as many as 120 oxen to be sacrificed at another, leading the procession, their horns gilded and bedecked with garlands, of 107 mules at the triumph of Lucullus in 63 BC carrying packs or panniers of silver coins and eight carrying silver ingots, and so on.

As to captive foreign animals, these would most usually be horses and flocks of sheep and probably cattle for traction. It is likely that during war and occupation by the Romans the economic basis of those peoples living in affected rural areas would have been devastated, if not crippled, by the damage done to crops or by their requisition, and to livestock. More exotic beasts were displayed as well. It would seem that elephants first appeared in a Roman triumph as early as 285 BC, while Metellus's triumph of 250 BC involved a legendarily spectacular display of 120 captured enemy war elephants. Elephants did not appear in triumphs after the time of Caesar, as they ceased to be employed in war by any of Rome's enemies, and when mention is made of elephants in a third century AD triumph they are likely to have been there displayed as diplomatic gifts. But it is worth noting that when elephants appeared in Pompey's triumph of 81–79 BC and Caesar's quadruple triumph of 46 BC the elephants on show on these occasions actually accompanied the *triumphator* and were there as part of the Roman element of the triumph, rather than being representative of the exotic other, as previously. Josephus, the historian of the failed Jewish revolt, tells us that at Vespasian and Titus's triumph in AD 71 to celebrate the crushing of the unrest 'beasts of many species were led along, all decked out with appropriate adornments'.[19] Much later, from another source, we learn of Aurelian's triumph of AD 273 for his victory over Zenobia at which tigers, presumably in cages, elephants, giraffes, elks, and 200 other beasts from Palestine and Libya were present. Even more grandiose would have been a triumph being planned by Gordian III before his sudden death overseas in AD 244 for which huge numbers of animals had already been collected, including ten tigers, sixty lions, thirty leopards, thirty-two elephants, ten giraffes, ten hyenas, a rhinoceros, twenty wild asses, and forty wild horses. It is likely that all such animals displayed in triumphs ended their lives soon after in the arena and then were butchered and their meat distributed or sold. Some of the exotic animals shown at triumphs were in fact diplomatic gifts from client kings, yet their fate was probably the same as that of beasts captured in battle.

Depictions of animals at war in the service of Rome were relatively common in Roman art, and mention has already been made of mounted emperors on various monuments, military baggage trains on Trajan's Column, and war elephants and camel mounts for soldiers on the Arch of Galerius. Rather rarer, very rare in fact, were images of animals suffering in war or being killed.

One of the best known images in the Greek and Roman worlds was that of Alexander the Great battling with the army of the Persian king Darius III, possibly at the Battle of Issus in 333 BC. Probably originally a Hellenistic third century BC painting, the image has come down to us in the form of a Roman mosaic pavement, probably based on drawings derived from the original, now lost, work. The Alexander Mosaic was installed in the House of the Faun in Pompeii and can now be seen on display in the *Museo Archeologico Nazionale* in Naples (Plate 45). At the very centre of the composition is a wounded Persian warhorse, with bloody mouth, injured hoof, and a broken-off spear stuck in its flank. The agony of this animal's suffering is evidently intense. This agony is contrasted with the ecstatic figure of Alexander himself, mounted on his famous horse Bucephalus and dominating the melée of battling Greek and Persian soldiers. In many ways this is the ancient world's own *Guernica*, foregrounding human and animal suffering within an overall historical narrative.

Horses were regularly portrayed on Roman imperial monuments. Often emperors' mounts rear up to trample barbarians underfoot. Animal slaughter was not depicted on such monuments in general, with the notable exception of the Column of Marcus Aurelius in Rome.[20]

The scene on the column known as the *Miracle of the Rains* occurs quite low down on the column shaft (Scene XVI) and is highly complex in terms of the sheer number of figures involved in the action (Plate 46). Roman and German barbarian forces had clearly been ranged in battle order against each other, the Romans to the right and the barbarians to the left, stalemate having been reached between them, as we know from the historical accounts of this battle. We also know that the Roman forces had been cut off from any water supply and that the troops and doubtless their cavalry mounts and baggage animals were almost literally dying of thirst in the burning summer weather. The infantry troops towards the rear of the Roman forces are depicted standing almost stock still, as if awaiting their fate. In the register of figures above them, camp has been struck, as indicated by the presence of a tent, while a piece of field artillery mounted on the back of a flat-bed wagon pulled by horses stands impotently by. There is more movement among the cavalry, while the viewer's eye is suddenly caught by a melée of agitated cattle in the supply train, literally trampling and climbing over each other, in fear or panic perhaps, as behind them a Roman soldier holds up his right arm to the heavens, either in a plea to the gods above to relieve the drought or as if he has felt the first tentative drops of the rain that will soon turn in to a deluge.

The artist though has chosen to depict the moment at which this desperate stand-off was broken by the coming of rains out of the clear blue skies, like manna from heaven; but, most strikingly, he has depicted the rains as emanating from the divine person of an aged male rain god whose brooding presence and sheer size draws the viewer's eye towards him. Massive in size, with huge wings opened out behind him, he stares out at the viewer with an inscrutable but troubling gaze. His long straggly hair and equally straggly beard merge with the wavy rivulets of rainwater that cascade down from on high. His long arms are outstretched to either side and they too are almost hidden by torrents of water sheeting down from heaven to earth. We can see the effects of this welcoming rain on the Roman forces as almost instantaneously the soldiers towards the front of the line burst into animated movement. Two of the soldiers hold their shields up in the air, either to fend off the torrential downpour or more likely to collect water on the shield surface to quench their debilitating and desperate thirst. Other soldiers, energised by the rain, move into battle against the enemy and there, under the figure of the rain god, we see the aftermath of the Romans' swift, unexpected and obviously devastating attack in the form of a pile of slaughtered bodies of both men and animals, seemingly all cavalry horses, the pile still churning with hints of life. A number of barbarian shields are propped up against this obscene heap, their evident failure to provide much protection against the Roman onslaught having been sadly lamentable.

It was not only in the Roman period that artists produced work for patrons who wished to celebrate or commemorate wars, battles and victories, but evidently did not wish in the process to be presented with images of slaughtered animals as collateral damage. A few notable exceptions can usefully and informatively be highlighted here. Eugène Delacroix (1798–1863) painted *Evening After the Battle* some time around 1824–1826. It now is in the Netherlands, in the collection of Museum Mesdag in The Hague. This small, dark but exquisite oil foregrounds two dead cavalry horses, with a less prominent figure of a trooper trapped beneath one of the inert, cold bodies.[21] A more recent attempt to highlight the unnecessary suffering of animals taken to war and to commemorate those that died in service of the British army is David Backhouse's 2004 *Animals in War* memorial in Hyde Park in London.

Valuable Body Parts

In the Roman world animals were sometimes kept for purposes other than for their indentured labour or their meat, and the singular importance of sheep's wool has already been mentioned. Other notable and significant animal by-products in the Roman period included, for instance, hides for manufacturing leather, bird feathers and down, and animal bones and horn for manufacturing and craft purposes. Marrow was removed from long bones; and cattle mandibles were burned to extract fat for lamps, medicinal products, and cosmetics. Antler could be used from hunted deer and a massive luxury market emerged for ivory taken from hunted elephants and rhinos.

The Roman historian Livy tells us that Lucius Cornelius Scipio Asiaticus had 1,231 tusks of elephant ivory carried in the parade of spoils at his triumph of 189 BC. Pliny notes that ivory was rare and came from India and it was the most valuable organic material known in the Roman world, just slightly less valuable than silver.[22] Indeed, an Egyptian papyrus of the mid-second century AD recording the manifest of a shipment of goods and material from Muziris in southern India to Alexandria, gives the value of the raw ivory in the shipment as being almost the same by weight as silver. However, Diocletian's Edict on Maximum Prices of AD 301 records ivory as being priced at 150 fifty *denarii* a pound, a great deal less than the price of an equivalent weight of silver. A low cost for the material at that time might have led to a fall in demand for the material and a redefinition of ivory as a non-luxury material. Yet in the fifth and sixth centuries AD ivory was used in the manufacture of the prestigious consular diptychs, whose size and number suggest that the raw material was not in short supply or culturally devalued (Plate 47).

That ivory working was a recognised specialist craft is shown by the existence of a *collegium* of ivory workers and inlayers, a *collegium* being both a guild and a social organisation. A copy of their constitution, dating from the Hadrianic period, has come down to us.

Probably the most significant find in relation to the archaeology of the craft of ivory carving in the Roman period was made during excavations on the Palatine Hill in Rome when a huge cache of finished objects, partially made pieces, offcuts and debris derived from an ivory and bone worker's workshop, was recovered from two large pits there.[23] Two distinct chronological periods of working were recognised, the first and second centuries AD, and from the mid-third to fifth centuries. The considerable time spans represented attest to a well-established, continuing, specialist dynasty of artisans operating nearby and some form of guaranteed supply of raw materials. That these two materials seem to have been worked together by the same craftsmen is undeniable from the Palatine evidence. A ratio of nine bone to each ivory item in the assemblage of around 1,500 excavated objects attests to the relative popularity and probably also the affordability of each type of material. How the ivory workshops in Rome obtained their stocks of raw material must remain a matter of conjecture. Obviously tusks from elephants slain in the arena were probably bought but how regular and assured a source must this have been? Presumably tusks were also imported from India or most likely through Egypt and Palestine and there is evidence for ivory working in Alexandria.

Less easy to explain is the evidence for ivory working at the Villa des Tuillières at Selongey, Côte-d'Or, Burgundy in France.[24] The presence here of around 2,500 ivory fragments, partly finished items, and objects such as an ivory fan and casket raise questions with regard to both how significant quantities of raw ivory were brought to the site for working up and indeed why they were brought to this particular site.

Centres of ivory working in and around the immediate Mediterranean area did not correspond to elephant hunting areas.[25] For example, a workshop is known in Palestine operating from the first to the fourth century and sites such as Ugarit along the Syrian Palestinian coastal strip had a long standing tradition of ivory working but the hiatus of this pre-dated the Roman period.

Although easily distinguishable from elephant ivory, even by eye, hippopotamus ivory was also utilised in a number of Mediterranean cultures, but no study or quantification of its use by the Romans has yet been undertaken. It is likely, however, that if some hippopotamus ivory was made available from dead arena animals, it would have been bought and used. Another ivory-like material was camel bone, and decorated faux ivory camel bone plaques and other items made from this material were manufactured in Egypt in particular.

In the earlier Greek world ivory was used in certain specific, special contexts to represent human flesh on large scale statues, in a technique known as chryselephantine work. The most famed examples of this were Phidias's Pallas Athene at the Parthenon and Polykleitos's Hera in her temple at Argos. It is surely therefore no coincidence that ivory, a material symbolising trading and political power in the ancient world, was used to make the curule chair, *sella curulis,* for high ranking magistrates at Rome. Ivory was more generally used as furniture inlay, for chairs, tables, and couches; as door inlay; in the manufacture of small jewellery boxes or pyxes, often decorated with scenes of hunting or from the animal games, and larger caskets; for ceremonial sceptres; for sword and dagger handles or pommels; clasp knife handles; personal items such as combs, hairpins, bracelets, and fan handles; for dolls; and for small-scale, intimate, statuary.[26]

Some astonishingly accomplished individual ivory artefacts of the Roman period are worth noting here. The Goodmanham plane, from excavations in East Yorkshire in northern England in 2000, represents a unique but somewhat enigmatic piece: a functioning woodworking tool whose body is made entirely of ivory, a luxury material. It has been suggested that a small ivory carving of a ship and its crew, possibly dating to the time of Constantine and now in the *Musei Vaticani*, was an apprentice piece, an intricate, impressive work produced by an apprentice to demonstrate the skills attained and the level of competence achieved during the apprenticeship. Conversely, it has also been suggested that it might have been a toy.

It would certainly seem that the use of ivory as a luxury material in the Roman world increased in Late Antiquity and it is probably no coincidence that one of the defining items of material culture of this period was the ivory diptych, generally commissioned by the upper echelons of Roman society to celebrate significant events such as marriage alliances and, most importantly, consulships; indeed, the term consular diptych is generally applied to the latter type of item. The intricacy of many of these carved ivory scenes might suggest that ivory carving had, by then, become the specialist province of the jeweller.

The question must be asked if the market for goods in ivory, this evidently luxury material, had any significant impact on elephant populations in their natural habitat when, of course, viewed in tandem with the capture of elephants for the arena games. The Roman conquest of Egypt probably secured the takeover of the long-established Egyptian trade in raw ivory tusks, largely from the lands to the south of Egypt and to a lesser extent from western Asia – lock, stock, and barrel. It is scientifically impossible to distinguish between ivory from African elephants and Asian ones, so the respective scale of supply from each source cannot be quantified. It is worth noting here that at one time there had been a species of elephant living in western Asia, called either the 'Syrian elephant' or more commonly and properly the 'western Asiatic elephant'. Long before the Roman era, this creature had become extinct – probably as a result of both over hunting by the Assyrians in the early Iron Age to obtain its tusks for ivory, and deforestation and thus destruction of their natural habitat brought about by increased agriculture. The Amarna letters provide details of vast quantities of ivory items, suggesting that until the nineteenth century there was no similar level of economic exploitation of this animal resource. Even by the time Pliny was writing his *Historia Naturalis* in the first century AD, he could imply that levels of exploitation were already impacting on the animal population in North Africa and leading to material shortages of ivory.[27] Themistius, writing in the mid to late fourth century AD bewailed the destruction of the North African elephant and the decline of its population there, though it would seem that it took till the seventh century for the creature to disappear completely from this area as the same claim is again made then by Isidore of Seville.[28] The lust for ivory lay at the root of this destruction.

Bone working seems to have taken place at hundreds if not thousands of sites across the Roman world. Wherever animals were killed their bones were commonly utilised in craft manufacture at various scales. The range of items made of bone in the Roman world is extensive, and it is worth listing many of them here to demonstrate the versatility of the material and the ingenuity of the craftsmen who worked it. As with ivory, bone was widely used as furniture and box inlay, for hinges, and even keys. The range of jewellery in bone was wider and included beads for necklaces, ear-rings, finger rings, bracelets and bangles, hairpins, and amulets. Personal items such as combs in bone were common. Bone dolls with hinged limbs were made. Bone toggles or buttons, and bone buckles, adorned clothing and military dress. Bone dice and counters were used in board games. As with ivory, bone handles were common for swords, daggers, clasp knives, ordinary knives, and hand-tools of all kinds and for bow strengtheners, as well as for scabbard chapes. For use in various activities and crafts there were bone spoons, writing styli, spatulas, modelling tools, needles, awls, fish hooks, spindle whorls, distaffs, bobbins, weaving combs, and weaving tablets. There were also many one-offs of various sorts.

From the first century BC onwards, tortoiseshell and turtleshell became fashionable luxury products at Rome, largely used as furniture inlays, sometimes in their natural state and sometimes dyed. Again, this economically significant business must have had a considerable ecological impact, particularly in the Indian Ocean.

Pearls, derived from oysters, were equally as coveted at Rome as ivory and tortoiseshell were, though the range of items into which they were made was, of course, much narrower, being largely confined to women's jewellery.[29] Pearl-decorated shoes are known to have been worn by some elite women, as well as by the emperors Caligula and Nero. Caligula's clothes and Nero's travelling couches were also said to have been adorned with pearls. In the Hellenistic period pearls were largely sourced from the Red Sea, the Persian Gulf and from India. Roman conquests probably extended the areas for acquisition, though it is hard to see that the pearls Caesar expected to win during his expeditions to Britain could have been of an equal quality. A surprisingly large number of Roman pearl merchants, *margaritarii,* are known through funerary and votive inscriptions at Rome itself, at Aquileia, at Tusculum, and at Anzio, all in Italy, while one *margaritarius* is also known from Roman Spain.

For the Romans, as with the ancient Greeks before them, domesticated animals, both alive and dead, represented wealth. To a subsistence farmer a single animal could be as valuable in real terms as vast flocks and herds were to great estate owners. A life less hard could be lived with the help of a draught animal on a small farm, fortunes could be made from the wool of hundreds of sheep commercially farmed. What could be called the monetisation of animals in this way underwrote Roman society in more ways than simply through its contribution to the life and well-being of the countryside. Providing an animal for sacrifice was as much a demonstration of financial generosity as it was of religious piety, as we will see in a later chapter. The commodification of other kinds of animals as a means of acquiring and demonstrating status and power would reach its zenith with the Roman amphitheatre animal spectaculars, which will also be considered below in great detail.

4

Feasting With Panthers

From Farmyard to Table

Leading on from the discussion of farm animals in the previous chapter, attention will now be turned to investigating food animals and meat, fish, and seafood in Roman cooking (Plates 48–49).[1] This would have seemed particularly logical to the Romans who used both dietary and agricultural change as historical indicators. Some consideration will also be given to the matter of food taboos, as dietary choices or restrictions, whether personal or societal, can tell us a great deal about identity formation. Vegetarianism was not common among the Romans or Romanised communities, certainly not by choice, though economic hardship could have led some urban dwellers to eschew meat in their diet on the grounds of cost alone, rather than through a reasoned philosophical or moral choice. Indeed, in certain circles at certain times it would appear to have been viewed with suspicion, if not actually downright hostility. The philosopher Seneca laid out in detail in his *Epistulae Morales* the philosophy behind his ardent vegetarianism, derived from Pythagoras and Sotion, though in actuality this was only very temporary, being practised for only a year after his swearing off the eating of meat on moral grounds. While on health grounds he averred that a mixed diet including meat was somehow not natural for humans, it was the cruelty involved in the killing of food animals and, as he saw it, the resulting streak of cruelty begat in humans because of this, that informed his personal stance. Consideration of the Pythagorean idea of the transmigration of human and animal souls also helped form his beliefs and strengthen his convictions. However, as Seneca related:

> the days of my youth coincided with the early part of the reign of Tiberius Caesar. Some foreign rites were at that time being inaugurated, and abstinence from certain kinds of animal food was set down as a proof of interest in the strange cult. So at the request of my father, who did not fear gossip, but who detested philosophy, I returned to my previous habits; and it was no very hard matter to induce me to dine more comfortably.[2]

The threat of death or persecution can apparently focus the minds of even the most moral among us. Debates about vegetarianism, cruelty to animals, and indeed the sacrifice of animals occurred throughout the Roman period: for instance, in the later third century AD Porphyry of Tyre's *On Abstinence from Killing Animals* set out the views of his teacher Plotinus on the matter.

As an aside, it is interesting to note that recent scientific analysis of the bones of a number of gladiators buried in a gladiator cemetery at Ephesus in present day Turkey suggested that the fighters had mainly followed a vegetarian diet, consisting on the whole of barley and beans, probably in order to bulk up their bodies for protection in combat.[3] Vegetarianism in antiquity therefore should not necessary be equated to a philosophical stance.

As might be expected, the main farm animals kept in the countryside around Rome and more widely in Italy, as we have seen in the previous chapter, were cattle, pigs, sheep, goats and poultry, providing beef, pork, hogget and mutton, lamb, goat meat and chicken, goose, and duck. In other provinces other animals were kept for meat, particularly different types of poultry, including quail. Depending on the location or the season, or indeed on individual taste, meats could either be fresh or cured in some way, by brining, rubbing with salt, air drying, pickling, or by smoking.

In the countryside much small scale trapping and hunting of game animals and birds would have gone on, adding rabbits and hares, deer, game birds, and pigeons to the pot (Plates 50–51). Indeed game meat was probably more important in the rural diet than farmed meat. Snails might have been collected; they were also farmed.

In rivers and lakes, fish and frogs were caught. On the coast both small scale, sometimes even subsistence, and commercial fishing took place. Shellfish were dug up or collected. While fishing has been listed here last of all, it should be noted that fish played a very significant role in the ancient food economy, and it has even been argued that fresh fish, processed fish and fish by-products, taken together, probably ranked fourth in importance to the Roman economy after wine, olives and olive oil, and grain. The fact that the idea of the sea loomed large in the Roman imagination meant its bounty was also appreciated and could be used to bolster identity and enhance status. While fishing might seem to the uninitiated or naïve simply a demonstration of the interplay of chance with time and resources, the skill, knowledge and dedication of the professional fisherman now or in the past should not be underestimated.

The meat from animals sacrificed in religious rites would have been cooked and eaten, sometimes in formal public feasts, so that the animals could at least be said not to have entirely died in vain. Open public banquets followed the *Saturnalia* and the *Compitalia* each year, while more exclusive banquets were the order of the day for the other six Roman annual festivals that included feasting. Huge quantities of cooked meat were apparently distributed at triumphal processions and sit-down meals at tables set for hundreds, indeed occasionally for thousands, were common at such events in both the Republican and imperial eras in Rome, with an estimated 200,000 people having feasted at Julius Caesar's triumphal banquets.

Likewise, meat from more exotic animals slaughtered in the arena was also distributed or sold afterwards for consumption, as certain contemporary commentators revealed. Some may have been reserved for distribution to the soldiers barracked in Rome. A probable instance of just such an event has recently come to light during excavations in Pompeii. A 2014 press release from the University of Cincinnati's Porta Stabia research project in the town announced the finding of a giraffe's leg bones in refuse deposits associated with a tavern.[4] These are thought to be the first giraffe bones found in Roman period deposits in Italy. Christians, though, were forbidden to eat arena meat, sullied as it was with conceptual and ideological baggage that they abhorred.

Tokens for prizes were also randomly distributed at arena games, sometimes showered down on the crowd from above with the release of loaded nets strung across the width of the arena. Some of the prizes were food related. It was recorded, probably in jest, that the emperor Elagabalus awarded prizes including ten boars or ten dormice and for performers a dead dog or a hundred pounds of beef.

In Rome the *annona*, a system of a dole of food for the poor, was introduced as a populist measure in 58 BC and involved the regulated distribution of grain to the needy. While both Julius Caesar and Augustus cut the numbers of those eligible to receive free or subsidised grain they nevertheless reluctantly continued the programme, as did all subsequent emperors. The late third century AD emperor Aurelian replaced grain with loaves of bread and also introduced the distribution of pork meat, olive oil, salt and wine, his actions illustrating the perhaps significant role that the eating of pork played in the accepted Roman diet.

Bee keeping would seem to have been an important activity, and honey as a natural sweetener played a significant role in Roman cooking.[5] It also had its other uses. Of course, bees could also produce wax for candles and other uses, as a by-product. Columella, Varro, Pliny and Virgil wrote at length about the mechanics and practicalities of keeping bees. Unfortunately no Roman hives have ever been found and it is considered that two artworks published as depicting hives are in one case a vegetable basket rather than a hive and that the other is, in fact, a later forgery. It is likely that honey hunting and bee keeping were of rather more significance in some of the provinces, particularly Egypt where a tradition of widespread bee keeping was officially monitored and overseen by royal officials and linked to broader symbolic systems. Indeed, a bee hieroglyph designated the delta region of Lower Egypt and also subsequently regularly appeared alongside the Pharaonic cartouche.

The Roman diet would also have varied greatly according to social class. In elite literature evident disdain for cookshops, *popinae,* was commonly displayed, the poor eating there being derided for their consumption of dishes such as sausages, made from cheap cuts of meat, or offal, tripe and blood puddings. Feasting was the preserve of the better off and especially of the rich. It is unlikely that anyone rich actually would ever have eaten the outlandish dishes of dormice sprinkled with poppyseeds and drizzled with honey and live birds stitched up inside a cooked pig's carcass as served at Trimalchio's feast in Petronius's biting Neronian satire on the foibles and pretensions of this fictional but symbolic millionaire freedman, although we will return to discuss this famous fictional feast later in the chapter. Again, although a fourth or fifth-century AD Roman cookbook by Apicius has come down to us it is unlikely to provide anything other than a guide to food consumed perhaps by only the very wealthiest people of the day or food that was fashionable and faddish at that time.

The basis of the diet probably consumed by most Romans would have been cereals, such as wheat and barley, commonly made into bread and cakes; dried pulses, particularly broad beans, and lentils; fresh vegetables and fruit, especially apples, pears, plums, berries of various kinds, grapes and figs; nuts such as hazlenuts, pinenuts, walnuts, almonds, and imported pistachios; dried seeds such as watermelon; and occasionally meat, game, and fish if the diner was rich enough. Herbs such as oregano, rosemary, fennel, purslane and bay were commonly used to enhance flavour, as were capers and citrus fruits of some kind, perhaps citrons rather than lemons. Food routinely would have been seasoned with salt, sometimes with the more exotic and expensive white and black peppers or other traded spices, or smothered in robust sauces like the famous *garum*, a potent fermented fish sauce. Olive oil would have been used for cooking, and wine or beer would have been drunk with the meal. Vegetables such as tomatoes, peppers and aubergines, which we think of today as being quintessentially Italian, are relatively modern introductions. It is likely that Rome's foreign residents tried to adhere to their own traditional ethnic foodways if the relevant produce to do so was available to them. Romanised diets were adopted in many places across the empire – witness the ubiquity in all provinces of the *mortaria,* or mixing bowl, and of *amphorae* of various sorts, as recovered from archaeological excavations – but this would very much have had to rely on mainly local, rather than imported, produce.

Shopping at the city's many bustling markets would have taken up much of the early part of the day for those whose job or duty it was to cook for their household or master and mistress. A slave attempting to fulfil his or her master's orders for the day might have had to run numerous errands, for instance buying bread from a bakery such as that owned by Marcus Vergilius Eurysaces and meat from a pork butcher like Tiberius Julius Vitalis. These two named Roman tradesmen and businessmen were indeed real people, commemorated on funerary monuments in the city, though not actually contemporaries, as I have suggested here for purely illustrative purposes. The Forum Boarium, the cattle market, and the Forum Suarium, the pig market, would have been both wholesale and retail spaces.

Of course, there would have been considerable variation in the diet of those at Rome, particularly in terms of being able to afford or procure meat and fish, depending on whether the individuals were rich or poor. Differential access to certain foodstuffs was one of many indicators of class stratification. In a great cosmopolitan city such as Rome, different ethnic communities would also probably have consumed different diets depending on their own cultural foodways and any associated dietary prescriptions or restrictions, depending on the availability of certain imported foodstuffs and exotic produce. Around the provinces of the empire local traditions would have remained important, while issues of Romanisation of diet and an associated attached status would have complicated the picture. Again, even in the provinces larger groupings of ethnically distinct immigrants, in many cases in the form of army units, may have eaten a different diet to the locals, or at least prepared and cooked food in a different way, as has been shown to the case of soldiers of North African descent stationed on Hadrian's Wall in northern England.[6]

A ground-breaking and comprehensive quantitative regional inter-site study of animal bones excavated from Roman period sites throughout the empire suggests considerable variation in the role of meat in the diet and of particular meats in different proportions in different areas and often at different times, as indeed might have been expected over such a huge, diverse area.[7] The nitty-gritty detail of the study is not strictly relevant here, but certain key results are worth considering briefly, principally variation within Italy itself, variation across the empire dependant on context, and diachronic change over time.

Variation within Italy itself is detectable, with the central Italian regions of Campania, Latium and Etruria having a much higher representation of pig bones than both the north and the south. The dominance of pork here would appear to be a Roman phenomenon as well as a wealth and status marker, and one which became more widespread from the late Republican period onwards. This probably reflected not only a cultural preference but also a taste for cured pork products as well as fresh meat.

Variation across the empire was highly dependent on context, though it would appear that 'dietary regions....roughly correspond[ed] to provinces but also to climate/topographic zones'.[8] Nevertheless a marked preference for pork and pork products in some regions or micro-regions and even at specific site types, such as military establishments or elite residences, would seem to have reflected a conscious dietary choice related to status and cultural influences from the centre. Otherwise cattle and sheep/goat were favoured to varying degrees. However, Roman dietary influences were less marked in the eastern empire where Hellenised preferences for sheep and goat meat generally remained constant and strong.

Diachronic change over time in diet encompassed the waxing and waning of elite taste and cultural emulation. In the fourth and fifth centuries AD changes in dietary practices can be detected as starting, as reflected in the western Mediterranean moving more towards the taste of the eastern empire, with less pork being eaten and more sheep and goat meat. The pork-rich diet of the elite at Rome decreased in significance, though in Diocletian's Edict on Maximum Prices of AD 301, pork was at the head of the meat section, priced as the most expensive of the common meats. In the northern and north-western provinces cattle farming and beef eating became more significant than previously.

The Flower of Garum

The industrial manufacture of certain cured products is well attested in the archaeological record. For example, the rotting down of fish heads and fish bones and waste and its salting was part of the process of making a number of different pungent fish sauces, of which the best known was *garum* that was stored in large amphorae and transported all around the Roman world.[9] *Garum* was one of four different types of Roman fish sauce, the others being *allex* or *allec* (also, confusingly, *halex, hallex, hallec, alec,* and *alex*), *liquamen* and *muria. Salsamenta,* salted fish, would also appear to have been a popular product, though this was not shipped in amphorae. These sauces were most commonly made from small shoal fish such as sardines, sardinella and anchovies.

The fact that many of these fish sauce amphorae carried a maker's stamp and often also what is known as *tituli picti,* that is painted commercial inscriptions relating to manufacturers or shippers of the product therein, allows a remarkably nuanced picture to be created of manufacturing centres and trading links. The names of a number of *garum* wholesalers are known, of whom the most famous is probably Aulus Umbricius Scaurus. His fine, sprawling house in Pompeii near the Porta Marina, in which he probably lived from the early to mid-first century AD, possibly up to the eruption of AD 79, was testament to the lucrative nature of the trade. Almost a third of the *garum* amphorae, sometimes also called *urcei,* so far excavated from Pompeii were derived from his manufactory premises. Scaurus, obviously not in the least ashamed of his occupation, even commissioned an unusual black and white mosaic for the secondary atrium of his residence, depicting four *garum* amphorae, some of which bore *tituli picti* naming the product 'the flower of *garum* made of mackerel' and 'the flower of *liquamen*' and 'the best *liquamen*' – and three of which named Scaurus, a fine piece of self promotion and intertextuality.[10] A *titulus pictus* at Pompeii also named one Aulus Umbricius Abascantus, whom we can assume to have been a freedman of Scaurus, perhaps his works manager. *Tituli picti* on a number of amphorae naming Scaurus have been found in the wider Campanian region and at Herculaneum, the villas of Boscoreale and Boscotrecase, and even as far afield as southern France at Fos-sur-Mer, Bouches-du-Rhône. A scientific analysis of remains inside one of the amphorae from Scaurus's house revealed that the sauce had been made from bogues, local small fish that abound in the waters around the Bay of Naples in the summer months.

A description of the preparation of *garum* was provided in the tenth century AD Byzantine agricultural text known as the *Geoponica*:

> Fish entrails are put in a pot and salted (little fish, especially sand-smelt, small red mullet, picarel or anchovy, or any small enough, are used whole) and left to cook in the sun, stirring frequently. When the heat has cooked them, the sauce is extracted thus: a deep, close-woven basket is inserted into the centre of the jar containing the fish, and the sauce seeps into the basket: so liquamen is obtained, filtered through the basket. The solid residue makes allex.[11]

The main manufacturing areas for *garum* were on the Spanish coast, particularly in Lusitania, on both the Atlantic and Mediterranean coasts of Gaul, in North Africa, and on the Black Sea in the Crimea. The markets would appear to have been almost empire wide. In Roman Britain, for example, there is reference to *muria* on one of the famous Vindolanda wooden writing tablets. Concentrations of fish sauce amphorae in the northern provinces are found in Gaul, Germany, Britain, Raetia, Noricum and Pannonia.

Even though there is evidence that production of salted fish products peaked in terms of the extent of their distribution outside the Mediterranean region as early as the first century AD, this does not necessarily mean that such products were not subsequently eaten. Indeed, it would appear that more locally produced variants using colder water fish such as herrings and sprats took the place of exports from the Mediterranean, though direct evidence for this is slight, being more or less restricted so far to Britain and Belgium, though epigraphic evidence suggests this also happened in Germany. The four *negotiatores allecarii* and four *negotiatores salarii*, the first four merchants in salted fish products and the latter four salt merchants, named on inscribed dedicatory votive altars at the sanctuary of Nehalennia at Colijnsplaat in the province of Germania Inferior, probably operated in this region, widely famed at the time for its salt.

At the Roman settlement of *Augusta Raurica*, an inland site at present day Augst in Switzerland, excavations have collected about 10,000 sherds of amphorae of different kinds, principally imported wine amphorae, olive oil amphorae and *garum* amphorae. Their analysis and quantification[12] has revealed that in the earliest phases of the settlement, up to AD 90, the number of *garum* amphorae sherds is greater than both wine and oil amphorae sherds. An attempt to requantify these sherd counts to convert them into estimated actual numbers of whole vessels and then to estimate the carrying capacity of the total number of vessels for each commodity gives a slightly different and more nuanced picture of the relative importance of each of these major food and drink commodities at the site in the first century AD. Estimated annual imports of olive oil at that time were the largest by quantity, at around 17,820 litres, followed by 6,271 litres of *garum*, and 4,285 litres of wine. Nevertheless, if such large quantities of *garum* were transported to an inland site such as *Augusta Raurica* then some perspective can be gained of the overall size of the trade to settlements where the dietary regime of much of the population was Romanised in such a way as to require use of this condiment. A *titulus pictus* on one of the Augst Spanish *garum* amphorae mentions the name Fronto and refers to him as a *vilicus*, that is an overseer or manager, presumably at a *garum* manufactory, and indeed many of the amphorae there would seem to have come from Spanish sources. It is not possible to offer an estimate of overall fish sauce consumption on the frontiers as a whole, as the transport of a lot of the products was probably by barrel, to be decanted into individual amphorae close to the main nodes of consumption.

Punishment of Luxury

A book collection of around 500 Roman recipes, *De Re Coquinaria*, has come down to us, put together probably from different sources in the late fourth or early fifth century AD and subsequently and probably incorrectly attributed to *Apicius*, that is Marcus Gavius Apicius, a famous first-century AD Roman gourmet and glutton who was famed for his banquets during the reign of the emperor Tiberius and who even merited a mention in the writings of Pliny, Athenaeus, and Seneca. Pliny called him 'the most gluttonous gorger of all spendthrifts, [who] established the view that the flamingo's tongue has a specially fine flavour'.[13] This recipe book does not provide us with a guide to what the ordinary Roman ate, in the same way that cookbooks today represent fantasy worlds; rather, it probably reflected the tastes and food fads of the better-off Romans, as evidenced by the use of flamingo meat in one recipe, though on the whole the ingredients used were less exotic and relied on heavy spicing, or use of strong condiments. Indeed, about 400 of the recipes involved the use of *garum* fish sauce. The book was ordered according to the grouping of recipes for meat, vegetables, pulses, fowl, fish and seafood. In the meat section there were few recipes for beef; cattle were more for milk or for traction.

The range of cooking methods was obviously pretty much the same as today, with food being either boiled, fried, grilled, roasted or baked.

There would seem to have been no middle ground between the two extremes of Roman culinary practice: a studied simplicity harking back to earlier times as represented by pleasure in the cooking and eating of humble produce such as cabbages or chickpeas, and a gastronomic feasting that revelled in rich, expensive produce and lavish, not to say excessively ostentatious, display and indulgence.

Of course, dinner – *cena* – in the homes of the elite would have been far more formal and elaborate than in those of the lower classes. However, the more occasional private Roman banquet – the *convivium* – was a cultural phenomenon in its own right and was as much about status and ceremony and the maintenance of social relationships as it was about cooking and dining and entertainment. It was at events like these that luxury or expensive foods such as oysters, lobster, pike, turbot, venison, teal, thrush, peacock or wild boar would have been served, as sometimes would ostentatious or outré foods such as stuffed dormice, birds such as the figpecker (beccafico), or lark's tongues, or foods prohibited by the sumptuary laws, as we will see below, as being thought too decadent or even un-Roman. The rarity of a particular food, the difficulty of procuring it, and the resulting high costs were all factors in establishing the exclusivity, and thus success, of an individual's feast. The emperor Vitellius at one event was said to have served up pike livers, pheasant and peacock brains, flamingos' tongues, and lamprey's milk in a giant cauldron.[14] The presentation and serving of some courses constituted spectacles in their own right. This would even have been enough to deter the most hungry present-day academic buzzing round a free buffet table like a fly.

Varro describes an open air dinner in Hortensius's game park in which the diners were entertained by a slave or actor dressed as the god Orpheus who blew his horn to summon forth stags, boars and other creatures, presumably from a hidden or camouflaged game enclosure or holding pen.[15] Such aristocratic or arriviste events would have provided plenty of prime material for Rome's satirists and comedy writers. In the process, in the hands of these writers and commentators events that might have been merely ostentatious and in bad taste became grotesque displays of conspicuous consumption overseen by deluded, deranged or self-loathing boors and sycophants. Yet were these descriptions of lavish, luxurious meals simply literary rhetorical flourishes or was there some basis of truth in them? No account of Roman food, cooking, and dining would be complete without at least a mention of the fictional narrative describing what is generally known to us today as *Trimalchio's Feast*. Trimalchio, a Neronian self-made man with great wealth but little taste, was a character in the *Satyricon*, a biting first-century AD satire and farce by the writer Petronius.

... the preliminary course was served in very elegant style ... among the hors d'oeuvres stood a little ass of Corinthian bronze with a packsaddle holding olives, white olives on one side black on the other. The animal was flanked right and left by silver dishes, on the rim of which Trimalchio's name was engraved and the weight. On arches built up in the form of miniature bridges were dormice seasoned with honey and poppyseed. There sausages too, smoking hot on a silver grill, and underneath (to imitate coals) Syrian plums and pomegranate seeds.

Roasted pig stuffed with sausages followed, as did other bizarre dishes such as hare decorated with birds' wings to create a monstrous Pegasus-like hybrid creature, and twelve dishes arranged in the shape of the signs of the zodiac.[16] Perhaps there were discernible messages in ancient feast menus which testified to the motives of the hosts, and to the intended nature of their self aggrandisement on display on such occasions. Foods from the earth and common produce and domestic animals might have been deemed as food fit for the ordinary man and woman; food from the forests, the air and the sea might have been thought of as less mundanely human and more fit for the gods and those humans whose status and resources allowed them to aspire to greatness. An inscription on a dining room mosaic in the House of the Buffet Supper in Antioch, Syria, declares: 'Here we shall eat and drink like gods'. Away from the coast, in pre-refrigeration days, the opportunity to enjoy fresh seafood would obviously have been limited by both cost and desire. The transportation of live fish and shellfish is quite well attested, as we will see below.

Ostentatious banquets, and even less conspicuously gross meals, would often and inevitably end with a certain amount of food thrown or accidentally dropped onto the dining room floor, to be swept up by slaves either between courses, immediately after the meal, or first thing in the morning. Such waste, if left on the floor long enough, might have provided rich pickings for household pests such as mice or even rats. That such a thing might have commonly been expected was reflected in the popularity of what were known, after Pliny, as *Asarotos oikos* or *unswept room* mosaics, that is mosaic pavements bearing a trompe l'oeil design of discarded food waste, a type of pavement probably originating from a Hellenistic model by Sosos at Pergamon. The best Roman example, in the collections of the *Musei Vaticani* in Rome, is a Hadrianic work, signed by Heraclitus, from a large residence on the Aventine Hill, which around its edges carries images of chewed meat bones, chicken feet, lobster legs, fishbones, shellfish or snails, walnut shells, date stones, and uneaten grapes on the vine, with an image of a small mouse setting out across the floor to hoover up the food in what for him would surely have been a day to remember. In the centre of the mosaic there was a Nilotic scene, with a design of theatrical masks at the threshold. Other examples of this type are known, including a small third century AD panel from El Djem, Tunisia, and now in the *Musée National du Bardo*, Tunis; a large first-century AD mosaic border with images of a fish with head and tail still intact and central fleshy portion eaten, from Aquileia in northern Italy (Plates 52–53), and a fifth-century AD example from the eastern Mediterranean and now on display in Chateau de Boudry, Neuchâtel, Switzerland, which depicts a group of diners making the mess in a house's *triclinium* and a scavenging pet dog.

Such floor mosaics were obviously intended primarily to illicit laughter and amused banter from the diners, but they were not just humorous exercises for the benefit of guests only. Rather, they also said something about the idea of disposable surplus and thus of the wealth and status of the host. They were statements about moral values and the dangers of excess, like the sumptuary laws which we shall shortly discuss.

Having made mention above of dormice as one of the cooked treats at Trimalchio's feast, I will briefly return to the subject of these small creatures in order to assess whether they were ever regularly used as ingredients in Roman cooking or whether this is some sort of myth about strange Roman tastes. Certainly Apicius provided a recipe for stuffed dormouse. At Pompeii edible dormouse bones, as opposed to those of the garden and common dormouse, have been recovered from the Forum and a single garden but not in huge quantities.[17] The agricultural writer Varro makes mention of special ceramic jars used for the fattening up of dormice and a number of these, with internal divisions and airholes, have been found in a number of houses at Pompeii.

The *Lex Aemilia Sumptuaria* or Sumptuary Regulation Law of 115 BC prohibited the cooking and serving of rats, stuffed dormice, mussels and birds from overseas. This was an extraordinary attempt, one of ten such regulatory laws in the late Republic, to regulate against luxurious over-indulgence, the flaunting of wealth, and any consequent political competition, indeed almost to define it as being somehow un-Roman.[18] The fact dormice were also picked out for prohibition in Claudian sumptuary laws suggests that the earlier prohibition did not work to the advantage of Rome's dormice. Bans were also imposed on the eating of artificially fattened fowl, sows' udders and so on. It could be argued that rather than being simply prescriptively against luxury per se, the sumptuary laws were aimed at returning to earlier notions of the separation of everyday eating from feasting and festival menus, a distinction that perhaps had become blurred by increasing prosperity among the elite classes and by the ready availability of what had previously been thought of as strictly luxury products. Ideas of luxury were thought to have been brought to Rome rather than gestated and birthed there. Negative views of luxury were linked to private or exclusive extravagance and self-indulgence but not to public display, magnificence, or munificence. While satirists might have linked luxurious banquets with offensive (to them) effeminacy, a broader moral condemnation was codified in the various sumptuary laws. Yet it has been argued that the passing of the sumptuary laws was almost an act in itself, the putting down of some kind of moral marker by the Senate, and that the enforcement or policing of the laws was virtually non-existent.

Less ostentatious, but no less luxurious, fictional banquets were invented for satirical purposes by other writers such as Juvenal and Horace, the latter in particular skewering the pretensions of some of his snobbish contemporaries by having the banquet hosts announce the life histories of each animal served up to his guests, in a manner which places our own contemporary obsessions with food provenance seem quaint and acceptable. That many aristocrats like Horace's host kept animals and birds in a private *vivarium* or an aviary to be fattened up for cooking and eating at events such as these is highly likely.

A Nation of Shop Keepers

Our evidence for food retailing largely comes through the records provided by inscriptions on the funerary monuments of Roman merchants and shopkeepers, including a number of butchers such as the pork butcher Tiberius Julius Vitalis, for instance. From Rome comes a shop scene depicted on a relief that could either have been a shop sign or which again might have been derived from a funerary monument. The shop relief is now in the *Museo Torlonia* in Rome and depicts two female game butchers, though the classical appearance of the women almost makes them appear like deities rather than mortal working women. The relief is divided into two zones by a pillar: on the left-hand side of the relief hang six carcasses of dead birds and animals, including two suckling pigs, a hare, and two geese; on the right-hand side are the two young women, one standing and pointing to an inscription on the back wall of the shop and the other seated on a low backed chair and plucking a bird hanging from the ceiling over a small table. The inscription is a four line quotation from Virgil's *Aeneid*, whose reference to remembrance of an individual and everlasting memory suggests a funerary purpose for the relief, if indeed it is a genuine Roman piece and not an eighteenth century pastiche piece in the Roman style, as some authorities have suggested. Again, if genuine, the disparity between the appearance of the women and their dirty task might be explained if they were figures preparing a funerary feast rather than employees in a butcher's shop.

A second shop relief, from Trastevere in Rome, probably dates to the first half of the second century AD and is now in the *Staatlichen Skulpturensammlung* in Dresden, Germany, and again is a relief depicting the inside of a butcher's shop. In this case we see the bearded male butcher at work chopping a joint of meat on his block with a large cleaver. A set of scales hang from a frame, with a second cleaver. A range of cut joints of meat and a pig's head hang on hooks from the frame. A basket for offcuts sits on the shop floor to one side of the chopping block. On the far right-hand side of the scene is a woman with an elaborately braided hairstyle sitting in a high-backed chair. She is writing on tablets resting in her lap and may therefore be identified as a bookkeeper, though some authorities have suggested that she may simply be a customer with a shopping list, which seems less likely an interpretation.

At Ostia a fishmonger in the market advertised his shop with a curious welcoming mosaic depicting a dolphin eating a small octopus and the greeting 'INBIDE CALCO TE', 'Envious One, I tread on you' (Plate 54), presumably some kind of apotropaic or protective device. A female poultry seller from Ostia appears on what is known as the Via della Foce relief, a vibrant and busy scene of shop or market trading, found at the entrance to a building on that street in the ancient port town. It was possibly a shop sign of some kind. A woman and a man stand behind a stall or counter, with the woman being placed in the foreground and the man partially hidden behind her, thus emphasising the relative importance of the two traders. To one side of the counter is a rack or gibbet on which are hung some chickens or other poultry birds. In front of the woman are two large shallow baskets containing either bread, or fruit and vegetables, or indeed both. A tall cylindrical wicker container with clearly delineated air holes cut through it would appear to contain live snails, as shown by the fact that the artist has depicted one snail making its escape from the basket, though this rather large snail may simply be a rebus or ideogram. At the far end of the stall sit two monkeys. Trade at the stall or shop seems very brisk, with one male customer being caught in the act of being served by the female vendor who holds a piece of fruit in her hand while two other men stand to one side of him, deep in animated conversation, one of the men holding a chicken in one hand that he has already purchased. Finally, in the bottom left of the panel can be seen the heads and tell-tale raised ears of two live hares or rabbits poking their heads out through the bars of a wooden crate in which they are housed ready for sale.

Since mention has just been made of snails, I will take the opportunity here to briefly digress to discuss the edible snail which both Pliny and Varro, for instance, tell us was collected and eaten by the Romans and indeed farmed on a large scale in some places. Both land and water snails were eaten. Snail cultivation, or heliciculture, involved collecting wild snails and raising them in snail farms, or *cochlearia,* where they could be bred and those almost ready for the table could be both purged and fattened, often by being fed cereals such as 'must and spelt' according to the methods of Quintus Fulvius Lippinus, also known as Fulvius Lippinus, the individual credited with popularising the consumption of snails in Rome and Italy in the mid-first century BC.[19] In the cookbook *De Re Coquinaria* a number of recipes for milk-fed snails are provided, in one case the snails being prised out of their shells, purged on milk and salt, then fried in oil and served with wine sauce, and in another snail meat is again fried but is served with a broth flavoured with pepper and cumin.

The Riches of Our Sea

The fishing industry in the Mediterranean was large scale and well organised and individual boats and fishing fleets would have operated out of most ports and coastal villages all around the Mediterranean littoral, including North Africa. Highly organised fishing and fish processing also took place in the Black Sea region, the Adriatic and, to a lesser extent, as far as we presently know, on the Atlantic coast, though one of the largest capacity known fish processing factories yet known was in Brittany, at Plomarc'h.[20] Little is known of North Sea fishing in Roman times. The largest concentrations of sites where large scale fish processing took place probably corresponded to areas on the key migration routes of shoals of those fish species most prized for processing. Fishermen were not only catching fish for direct consumption but also, as we have seen, for the production of *garum* and other cured or processed fish products. Techniques included line fishing, drift-net and fixed-net fishing. A great deal can be learned about ancient fishing boats, nets, and fishing gear from archaeological finds, written sources, and especially visual sources such as wall paintings, mosaics, and even decorated pottery such as *terra sigillata* or samian ware from Gaul.

Both private and commercial fish farming, aquaculture, were also important and, it would appear, economically significant. Diocletian's Edict on Maximum Prices of AD 301 listed the price of one pound weight of first quality fish at 24 *denarii* and of second quality fish at 16 *denarii*. Fish farming was a topic discussed by the agricultural writers Columella and Varro, suggesting a certain ubiquity, which makes sense considering the fact that good quality sea fish were considered a luxury premium food and product. On some Italian villa estates that bordered on the coast, large artificial salt water ponds were created, with outlets and inlets to the open sea. The sophisticated nature of these tanks suggests they could have been breeding tanks. Their capacity in some cases is such that it is likely surplus fish were sold on commercially as part of the business of the estate. A concentration of coastal fishtanks and ponds along the Tyrrhenian coast probably reflected the needs of the nearby vast urban market of Rome. Similar, though less elaborate, ponds or tanks for holding fish before they were killed and salted have been found along the Tunisian coast in a number of places and in France and Spain. Perhaps such tanks were indeed more common than present evidence suggests.

Oyster farming would appear to have been a particularly Roman invention and there are literary references to the renown and quality of oysters from Brindisi, Anzio, Baiae, on the Gulf of Naples, and Lacus Lucrinus in Campania. Indeed, so famed were the Baiae and Puteoli oyster beds that they were portrayed on a series of glass vessels, probably tourist souvenirs, probably on sale at the sites. Pliny tells us that Quintus Fulvius Lippinus farmed sea snails,[21] as probably did others, following his lead.

While the transportation of live fish and shellfish short distances from the coast can be expected to have been routine, transportation over greater distances would have been more onerous, both in terms of the cost and of the equipment needed to preserve the commodities alive and fresh. Live fish, and seafood such as oysters, could be transported from fishing ports in barrels of brine, by boat up river or on wagons by road. Much of Rome's fish would have arrived this way. Athenaeus describes the use of custom-built watertight containers for shipping and it would be surprising if simpler transport techniques attested in medieval times, such as wrapping live fish in wet moss and regularly watering them en route, did not also have earlier equivalents in the Roman period. Pliny tells us that small quantities of live parrot fish were shipped from the Black Sea to Naples, in an experiment to breed these fish in the seas there. More large scale were the apparently specialised vessels called *vivariae naves* mentioned by Macrobius in the later Roman period and which must have been kitted out with tanks for the mass transportation of live fish. Examination of the second-century AD Roman shipwreck at Grado, found off the coast of Aquileia in north eastern Italy in 1999, has led to the suggestion that with its other cargo, this ship was specially adapted to carry live fish, with a large lead pipe in the hull of the ship being part of a sophisticated hydraulic apparatus for regulating the inflow and outflow of seawater into the ship.[22]

Some idea of the types of fish and seafood eaten by the Romans can be gauged from the excavated fish bones and shells recovered during modern excavations at Pompeii, though few were recovered from the early excavations at the site due to crude excavation techniques being employed that acted against the facilitation of the routine recovery of such material.[23] Likewise, evidence from wall paintings and mosaics at the site and at nearby Herculaneum allows us to at least consider what knowledge of Mediterranean sea creatures there was among its inhabitants. Scientific analysis of human skeletal remains of the Roman period for palaeodietary study can identify individuals who might have had diets rich in seafood but not enough of a database exists for general observations to be made on larger populations in individual cities and provinces.

Perhaps the most famous mosaic *emblema* depicting Mediterranean fish comes from a house in Regione VIII Insula II at Pompeii and is now in the *Museo Archeologico Nazionale* in Naples (Plate 55). This was used as the front cover illustration in the first editions of Alan Davidson's seminal Penguin paperback cookbook *Mediterranean Fish and Seafood*. The fish depicted on the panel all appear to be in shallow water, a few outcrops of rock around the shallows being shown, one with a barnacle attached to it and another providing a perch for a kingfisher. Twenty-one different fish appear in this panel, including a large octopus at the centre fighting with a spiny lobster, an electric ray, two types of spotted dogfish, moray eel, grey mullet, gilthead, bream, bogue, red mullet, sea bass, two types of comber, gurnard, red gurnard, scorpion fish, grouper and common squid. A murex shell also appears among the fish. As an aside, it should be noted that an unusual luxury product – the purple dye known as *murex* – was made from the crushed *Murex trunculus* shellfish.[24] There is evidence for production of the dye at least eight sites in Roman Tunisia.

Fishponds have been found at quite a number of Pompeian houses, including the House of Meleagro and the House of Julia Felix, and at Herculaneum and in its immediate environs. Obviously the kinds of fish that could be kept in such ponds were not sea fish or freshwater fish for consumption; rather, they would have been decorative species – pets in other words.

Commodification

As we have seen in this chapter we cannot only think of Roman society as one in which so-called nose to tail eating would have been the norm, but also one in which the same waste-not-want-not attitude would have been applied to animal by-products as well, as was discussed in detail in the previous chapter. In terms of the use of animal by-products, skins and hides were extremely important, but it was wool that was the most highly significant such economic by-product – so much so that wool or woollen products from a number of areas of the empire were individually mentioned in the Edict on Maximum Prices issued by Diocletian in AD 301. Elephant ivory was a luxury item and evidently widely traded and greatly coveted, with a concomitant dire environmental impact in North Africa and probably in parts of India as well. Animal bone was used throughout the empire for the manufacture of numerous kinds of everyday items from hairpins to knife handles.

A hunt for luxury food products, inevitably meat of some kind, fish or seafood, again led to a strict commodification of certain creatures, as we will see happened with exotic beasts destined for the arena, and led to minor ruptures in the fabric of the natural order, some temporary and some longer lasting or more profound. According to Plutarch[25] one such rupture might be thought to have occurred when a summer absence of song thrushes in the city of Rome could be put down to the fact that most were then being fattened up in the *vivaria* of the important Republican general and politician Lucius Licinius Lucullus, whose ostentatious banquets were famed in Rome in the mid-first century BC and whose individual selfishness was but one act of societal and cultural jeopardy that threatened the contemporary ecosystem on a small, localised but cumulatively dangerous way every day.

The Atrocity Exhibition

Blood in the Arena

This chapter is primarily concerned with the extraordinary slaughter of animals in the Roman arena. Hunting and the use of horses in chariot racing will also be considered. While some of the exotic animals traded at huge expense to bring them to Rome were bought to be exhibited rather than killed and others were intended for incarceration and display in private zoos or collections, the vast majority of these captured and transported creatures were destined for death in the amphitheatre. Such spectacles continued in various forms without surcease for hundreds of years.

Animal spectacles appear to have begun in Rome in the third century BC, and perhaps their origins lay in the triumphal displays of captured African elephants staged by Marius Curius Dentatus in 275 BC and Lucius Caecilius Metellus in 250.[1] Many early arena shows were simply displays of exotic animals for the general public, allowing them access to the sight of creatures that otherwise at the time might have only been seen by their elite contemporaries and those Roman aristocrats who had used their wealth and connections to stock their own *vivaria* or animal enclosures in Rome and its environs (Plate 56). Exotic animals like elephants were sometimes trained to dance, walk on a tightrope, or pick up items, according to Pliny and others.[2] Animal shows involving violence and combat, known to the Romans as *venationes*, or hunts, possibly began in 186 BC when lions and leopards featured in a show sponsored by Marcus Fulvus Nobilior. Whether the animals fought each other on this occasion or fought against human performers is unknown. Certainly, it would appear that bloody *venatio* shows developed out of the culture of gladiatorial spectacles. The last recorded *venationes* in Rome took place as late as AD 523. While acknowledging the cruelty and human suffering associated with the gladiatorial shows, discussion here will be restricted to the animal games and the arena executions involving animals.

The sponsorship of public gladiatorial and animal shows became a way for the rich and powerful of Rome to display their wealth and enhance their status, influence and power. Sponsorship itself became a locus of political competition in the late Republic and was to become a facet of Roman imperial largesse. In his *Res Gestae*, a quantified justification of his reign and achievements, the first emperor Augustus proudly claimed that at twenty-six *venationes* held during his reign a total of 3,500 African animals had been slain, setting a high bar for those emperors that followed. When the Roman poet Juvenal complained about the political apathy of his fellow citizens of the late first and early second century AD and their failure to react against the unreasonable or eccentric behaviour of autocratic emperors, he coined a famous phrase that would resonate down the years. These citizens craved and were satisfied with *panem et circenses*, that is bread and circuses, he wrote.[3] Many emperors too found that the provision of mass entertainment and the occasional public distribution of free grain easily diverted critical attention away from the more negative aspects of their reigns. The provision of such spectacles was a necessary strategy for making imperial power visible in Rome.

Arena shows in Republican times and in the early empire took place at a number of venues in Rome, until in AD 70 the emperor Vespasian set about the construction of a vast new venue for imperial games, the Colosseum. It was in the Colosseum in Rome that regular shameful bloody spectacles in the guise of entertainment were played out to baying crowds of anywhere between 50,000–80,000 people from AD 80 onwards. The entertainment took the form of public executions, gladiatorial games, *venationes* or wild beast hunts (Plates 57–58 and illustration on Page 4), and mock naval battles. The usual programme consisted of wild animal hunts in the morning, executions at midday, and gladiatorial combat in the afternoon. Inaugurated in AD 80 in the reign of the emperor Titus, the Colosseum continued in use for gladiatorial shows until *c.* AD 435 and for animal hunts up to the AD 520s. Indeed, as has already been mentioned, the last recorded animal hunts at the Colosseum were held in AD 523, given by Flavius Anicius Maximus in celebration of his consulship; the criticism of these games by Theoderic the Great was not on the basis of the cruelty of the event or its anachronistic nature in the sixth century but rather because of excessive costs. However, the nature of these later animal shows was often different from earlier arena games, possibly because of the expense and difficulty of obtaining African animals from the fourth century AD onwards, particularly after AD 439 when the Vandals seized the Roman North African provinces. More herbivores appear to have been used in the later shows and there was more of an emphasis on the skill of human hunters eluding wild beasts during the show rather than necessarily killing them as a priority.

At the Colosseum's inaugural games, lasting 100 days, 9,000 animals were killed – a stand-out performance being recorded from the *bestiaries,* or beast-fighter, Carpophores who slew a bear, a lion and a leopard in a single battle. On another occasion he is said to have killed twenty animals, including a rhinoceros which he despatched with a spear, leading to his acclamation by the crowd as the new Hercules. Another good illustration of the almost stupefying scale of slaughter in the arena is provided by the records relating to celebratory games put on for the Roman people by the emperor Trajan over several months with monies accrued from his bloody conquest of Dacia in AD 107: 10,000 gladiators fought and 11,000 large animals were killed in the *venationes*. Animals as diverse as African elephants and lions, crocodiles, Indian tigers and Dalmatian bears would have evoked wonder in the spectators' eyes, even without the spectacle of their needless butchering for further entertainment. There is even the mention of the killing of a seal at one particular show in Rome. An analysis of the kinds of animals depicted on the numerous animal *venatio* scenes in domestic wall paintings at houses in Pompeii has produced evidence for arena combat involving the following species: brown bear, wolf, dog, possibly fox, lion, leopard, African elephant, horse, possibly the wild ass or onager, wild boar, fallow deer, red deer, ox, Dorcas gazelle, oryx, and even, almost improbably, sheep.[4] A whole industry, probably employing thousands of people, would have been in existence simply geared towards the hunting, trapping and capture of wild and exotic beasts in their natural environments, their shipping overseas to Rome by both land and sea, and their tending and feeding while in transit and at the Colosseum prior to their killing in the name of culture.

It seems likely that most if not all of the 230 or so amphitheatres across the Roman world, from the one at Leptis Magna on the North African littoral to the one at Chester in northern Roman Britain, would have been used for animal games of some sort. Whether exotica such as lions and rhinos would have been seen in Roman Britain is uncertain – there is no evidence to support their presence here at any time. Animal games in Roman Britain might have consisted of dog fights or bear baiting instead.

It is not the place here to provide a chronological history of the Roman animal games and to try to quantify the number of animals slaughtered. Rather, a few particular events can be highlighted to throw further light on the nature of these events. Perhaps the most extraordinary story associated with the animal games in Rome concerns the involvement of the emperor Commodus, the son of Marcus Aurelius, whose tempestuous and erratic reign between AD 180 and 192 marked one of the low points in Roman imperial history. Commodus became obsessed with the games and somewhat over-identified with the figure of the gladiator and the hyper-masculinity of the arena, even taking to appearing there himself, most notably during the fourteen days of games he sponsored in AD 192.[5] He also particularly venerated the hero god Hercules and in one of his most remarkable and chilling portraits had a marble bust created in which he appeared in the guise of the hero, holding a large club and clad in a lion skin. The historian Dio Cassius provides a startling account of one particular appearance by Commodus at the Colosseum in Rome. It is a lengthy and detailed account, which is most certainly worth reading in full in order to understand the perception of the emperor's state of mind among many of the spectators present in the Colosseum that day.

However, just a little will be quoted here to provide a flavour of the occasion.

> On the first day [Commodus] killed a hundred bears all by himself, shooting down at them from the railing of the balustrade....In the midst of the struggle he became weary, and taking from a woman some chilled sweet wine in a cup shaped like a club, he drank it at one gulp. At this both the populace and we [senators] all immediately shouted out the words so familiar at drinking bouts, 'Long life to you!' ... On the other days he descended to the arena from his place above and cut down all the domestic animals that approached him and some also that were led up to him or were brought before him in nets. He also killed a tiger, a hippopotamus, and an elephant. Having performed these exploits he would retire, but later, after luncheon, would fight as a gladiator ...[6]

Dio then goes on to describe the bloody arrangements for the gladiatorial fights and disdainfully describes how Commodus would manipulate contests through sheer cruelty and how he would intervene to abort any instances of mercy being shown to the defeated. While crowds kept turning up for the full fourteen days of these games, Dio suggests that some chose to stay away from the very beginning, spurning the demeaning behaviour of the emperor as they saw it, while others still attended but came to experience some form of moral fatigue at the empty rituals of slaughter and unfettered power. Fear of the emperor was real, as Dio continues:

> And here is another thing that he did to us senators which gave us every reason to look for our death. Having killed an ostrich and cut off its head, he came up to where we were sitting, holding the head in his left hand and in his right hand raising aloft his bloody sword; and though he spoke not a word, yet he wagged his head with a grin, indicating that he would treat us in the same way.[7]

Herodian in his *History of the Empire* also gave an account of Commodus decapitating Mauretanian ostriches with specially adapted arrows with crescent-shaped heads.[8]

If the role of the *venator*, like the gladiator, was to please the crowd by gauging and anticipating the mood of the spectators on any particular day and to plan and temper his actions accordingly, then it would appear from this account that Commodus was considered to have ignored this precedent. The lack of any degree of mercy in his performance and behaviour before this crowd would appear to have been his way of setting some lesson to the Roman people and stating his absolute authority and strict grasp on power. Rather than this being taken as a show of strength, Dio's account suggests rather that this was interpreted as a conspicuous display of abuse of power and therefore of inherent weakness on the emperor's part. We are seeing here highly ambiguous attitudes towards animal life and the natural world being displayed by the crowd and Commodus displaying his own personal power by taming wild Nature through the killing of these animals.

Another lamentable episode was chronicled by no fewer than five separate Roman historians and writers – Cicero, writing at the time, and Plutarch, Pliny, Seneca and Dio, all writing later, Dio in fact around 250 years later. The appalling nature of this event might have been thought to mark some kind of turning point in the organising of the arena games in Rome, but this was not to be. The event took place at the five-day games presented by Pompey the Great in 55 BC to mark the inauguration of the magnificent Theatre of Pompey. While hundreds of animals were apparently killed during these particularly lavish games it was the fate of a group of eighteen to twenty elephants, reported numbers vary from one account to another, which captured the imagination of the writers and of the Roman audience in the arena.[9]

The elephants were pitched against a team of men armed with javelins and shields who managed to dispatch one or two of the elephants during an intense combat that saw the elephants fighting back for all that they were worth. The surviving elephants, some probably horrendously wounded, charged as a group to try to break out of the arena in a state of panic, both scaring the spectators and impressing them with what came next. In a letter Cicero noted that 'the last day was that of the elephants, and on that day the mob and crowd were greatly impressed, but manifested no pleasure. Indeed the result was a certain compassion and a kind of feeling that that huge beast has a fellowship with the human race'.[10] Pliny wrote that 'when they [the elephants]had lost all hope of escape they tried to gain the compassion of the crowd by indescribable gestures of entreaty, deploring their fate with a sort of wailing, so much to the distress of the public that they forgot the general and his munificence carefully devised for their honour, and bursting into tears rose in a body and invoked curses on the head of Pompey'.[11] Seneca did not go into as much detail about this specific event as the other four commentators, but rather alluded to the spectacle and Pompey's part in it in less than flattering turns. He tells us that eighteen elephants were pitted against criminals 'in a mimic battle'. He reserved his condemnatory bile for Pompey in organising this mockery of an entertainment.

> O what blindness does great prosperity cast upon our minds. When he was casting so many troops of wretched human beings to wild beasts born under a different sky, when he was proclaiming war between creatures so ill matched, when he was shedding so much blood before the eyes of the Roman people, who itself was soon to be forced to shed more. He then believed that he was beyond the power of Nature.[12]

Cassius Dio noted that the elephants:

> were pitied by the people when, after being wounded and ceasing to fight, they walked about with their trunks raised towards heaven, lamenting so bitterly as to give rise to the report that they did so not by mere chance, but were crying out against the oaths in which they had trusted when they crossed over from Africa, and were calling upon heaven to avenge them. For it is said that they would not set foot upon the ships before they received a pledge under oath from their drivers that they should suffer no harm.[13]

Like Pliny, Dio claimed that the crowd called upon Pompey to spare the wretched elephants, which he would not do. Unlike the other four commentators, Plutarch did not go into detail about the final day's slaughter or about the crowd's reaction. He makes mention of 500 lions being slain but stressed that a more significant spectacle lay in the elephant fight which he declares to have been 'a most terrifying spectacle'.[14]

A careful analysis and close reading of these five accounts repays the effort by providing a number of remarkable insights into the psychology of the arena games, its patrons and, most importantly, the Roman audience. The fact that we have so many accounts of this particular event is unusual and, given that four of these narratives detail very specific occurrences on that day in a corresponding manner, we can accept these accounts as being largely true. Seneca made a fine comparison between a politician's manipulation of human lives and animal lives for their own selfish ends and appeared to equate war, death in the arena and civil war in his remit of outrage. Such a sophisticated analysis of the stark realities of the arena animal games went straight to the heart of Roman political ideology and the vacuum there filled by nothing but the manipulation and exercise of power. Just as in the other example of political miscalculation on the part of Commodus, discussed above, it would seem that Pompey's failure to react to the mood of the crowd placed him in a momentarily hazardous position, which many believed he did not come back from in terms of regaining automatic public affection.

One wonders if Pompey's blasé attitude to the suffering of the elephants had its roots in an earlier event in which the general attempted to enjoy his first triumphal procession, staged in 81–79 BC to celebrate his victory in Africa, riding in a chariot pulled by four elephants, as if he was Bacchus in his Indian triumph or Alexander the Great. The vehicle with these large beasts pulling it was too wide to fit through the *porta triumphalis* and Pompey had to abandon the idea after two failed attempts to manoeuvre the chariot through and reverted to the usual horse-drawn triumphal chariot. This must have been not only frustrating but humiliating for Pompey, especially as this was recorded for posterity by both Cicero and Plutarch, and one cannot help but ask if twenty or so years later, his refusal to spare the elephants at his games of 55 BC was not in some way a psychological revenge upon the species, the fulfilment of a deep-seated need for some kind of blood revenge? Was the fact that so many writers seized upon this event simply a reflection of anti-Pompey feelings among these authors, or did this event mark a genuine moral crisis of some kind in the Roman psyche?

I am not sure that I in any way agree with the recently mooted idea that of all the different species of exotic animals that appeared in the Roman arena it was the elephant alone that was an especial target of hatred from the audience by dint of its one time service in the armies of some of Rome's greatest enemies, first Pyrrhus and then the Carthaginians in the two Punic Wars.[15] Certainly most Romans would have been aware of Pyrrhus's use of elephants when he invaded southern Italy in 280 BC, and of his defeat at the hands of Manius Curius Dentatus who subsequently exhibited some captured elephants at Rome in 275 BC. In 250 BC Lucius Caecilius Metellus shipped 140 elephants to Rome, captured from the Carthaginians in Sicily, to be goaded and probably killed. In both these instances the elephants were undoubtedly war booty, along with human captives and captured weapons. Later, following his death and deification, Augustus's statue was paraded around the Circus Maximus in a chariot pulled by elephants, an echo of which event could be found in a similar event there for the image of *diva* Livia following her death in AD 42. The stories of the crowd's reaction to Pompey's indifference to the suffering of the elephants at his games suggest no residual hatred of this particular species among members of the defiant and shocked audience.

Another sympathetic account of the death of an animal in the arena is provided by the first century AD writer Statius, although the sympathy expressed here is of a very different kind to that received by Pompey's elephants. His lament was for a famed, veteran fighting lion who had survived a number of contests and evidently had grown to be some kind of crowd favourite. 'You are fallen, skilled ravager of tall beasts ... conquered by a fleeing beast ... the sorrowful populace and senators groaned at your death, as if you had fallen as a famous gladiator on the dismal sand.[16]

In the second century BC the Senate actually banned the importation of African animals to Rome between the years 186 and 170 BC. However, this was not on the grounds of curtailing such cruel and degrading entertainments, as might have been expected, but rather as a precautionary measure against political grandstanding by games' sponsors, dressed up as being linked to public safety issues and concerns. Public dismay and outrage led to the quashing of this measure through the lobbying of a Tribune of the plebs.

When objections were raised to various aspects of Roman spectacle and sport, they generally came from three particular groups: the literary elite and the Stoics; Jews; and Christians. Some of the literary elite, like Pliny and Tacitus, may have raised objections because of their intellectual snobbery and elitism; however, when a figure such as Cicero declared that 'if you've seen one *venatio*, you've seen them all'[17] we must remember his delaying tactics and dissembling over providing a contact at Rome with leopards for his games, as detailed below, and wonder if his dismissals were not actually moral objections after all. Many objections though were made on the grounds of abhorring mindless popularism and escapism rather than animal cruelty per se. Jewish objections as articulated by Josephus did involve the condemnation of certain aspects of Roman games – '... bare faced impiety to throw men to wild beasts ...',[18] but taken together, his objections were more to do with the Roman-ness of these events, their un-Jewishness in other words. Christian criticisms focused on idolatry, the corruption of the soul and cultural difference, thus reinforcing Christian identity by the very act of opposition to such vicarious sinful pleasure. Most peculiarly, some Christian objection was linked to the issue of cannibalism, in that it was argued that men who partook of the meat of slaughtered arena beasts, which had themselves tasted human flesh or blood, were cannibals.

A great deal of media excitement has recently been generated by the dissemination of the published results of the extended and admirable academic study into the mechanical devices in use at the Colosseum, literally behind the scenes and under the main floor of the arena, in the area known as the *hypogeum*.[19] Detailed structural survey over a number of years since 1996, has revealed the former position of up to sixty large capstans for raising caged animals, gladiators, props or scenery through trapdoors in the wooden floor directly into the arena. Cables, ramps, hoists and counterweights were also used to move animals, people and equipment. Media attention has focused on a peculiar and unnuanced reverence for the wonders of this Roman engineering in itself; little consideration has been given to the psychological motivations behind the mechanisation and streamlining of the killing process for animals. This link between the application of architectural and engineering ingenuity and mass killing should have a terrible resonance that reporting of this work failed to appreciate, even in the quality newspapers that ran this story. Such mechanical aids were apparently present at many amphitheatres across the empire, and indeed in Roman North Africa even the smallest amphitheatre had specially constructed equipment for delivering animals into the arena, but the nature and purpose of this equipment will not be considered in any detail here, as it is not altogether strictly relevant to the main narrative of this book. It is uncertain whether animal games would have taken place at every single amphitheatre built, but at sites where complex machinery is recorded it can be assumed that such games did indeed take place regularly.

In mitigation, albeit a very poor mitigation because of its infrequency, it must be remembered that not every animal brought to the arena was necessarily there to be killed. Sometimes the exhibiting of a rare or exotic creature to the populace was an end in itself. This may have been the case with the giraffe that Julius Caesar brought to Rome from Alexandria in 46 BC, the first recorded exhibition of this creature in the city and indeed on the Italian mainland. This giraffe, this *camelopardalis*, half camel and half leopard as it appeared to the Romans, and others like it, entranced its viewers not only with its outlandish appearance but also with its gentle character. Pliny found it almost like a sheep in that respect, while Heliodorus noted that giraffes could be led round on a leash. There is no specific mention in the accounts of Caesar's triumphant victory games in the arena of the animal being then killed; indeed, Dio simply states that it was 'exhibited to all'.[20] It is uncertain whether the Romans were at all aware of the Egyptian view of the giraffe's natural ability to see vast distances both because of its height and its exceptionally acute eyesight as imbuing the creature with a gift of foresight or prescience and thereby linking it to associated prophetic powers.

The fate of all giraffes appearing subsequently in the arena in Rome was probably a grim one. As we have already seen, in the late second century AD Commodus killed not only a rhinoceros in the Colosseum but also a giraffe, five hippopotamuses and two elephants over two tragic days. In AD 248 Philip the Arab marked the millennium of Rome's founding with an arena show that included a group of ten giraffes, the largest group of the animals ever assembled in Rome for an arena show. While giraffes probably were relatively common sights in the arenas of Roman North Africa, they may also have occasionally have been taken to provincial arenas further afield; it is difficult to otherwise account for the presence of giraffe bones recently found at Pompeii, as related in Chapter Four.[21] These bones must have been derived from a slaughtered arena animal.

Less formalised animal fights might also have been common. It is generally accepted that cock fighting, quail fighting and even partridge fighting were popular in ancient Greece, and might have remained so among Greek populations in the Roman empire, being heavily symbolic activities linked to martial display and hyper-masculine identity. However, it is not altogether certain from a general dearth of written allusions to the pastime that such 'sports' found a ready audience in Rome and Italy; indeed, some academics have argued that they were largely unknown there.[22] Yet scenes of cock fighting appeared on a number of decorated Roman funerary altars and sarcophagi, though such scenes, of course, could have had a purely metaphorical meaning in such contexts (Plate 59). A relief from Smyrna carries a depiction of four fighting cocks, one dead on the ground and another strutting around with a victory palm held in its beak. Cock fighting is also depicted in a wall painting from the House of the Labyrinth in Pompeii and on a mosaic elsewhere in the town (Plate 60). Bird bones recovered from excavations at the military fortress at Velsen in Holland and from, for example, a number of urban sites in Roman Britain, along with metal artificial fighting spurs, suggests that cock fighting might have been a popular military and provincial pastime. We can probably consider cock fighting to have been a masculine interest and one that to some extent was a displacement activity in lieu of violent behaviour on the part of the sport's adherents towards their contemporaries. I find it hard to accept one academic's suggestion that cockfighting in Roman times was an activity linked to introducing children to violence involving animals, in order to inure them to witnessing arena violence in later life.[23]

Brief consideration needs to be given to the psychological effects of committing cruelty to animals and exposure to such behaviour. This is not a new philosophical field – indeed, Thomas Aquinas had considered such issues in the thirteenth century. It is today well known that many violent criminals, particularly murderers and serial killers, became desensitized to violence and its consequences by a process of escalation of violence and its staging, the progression thesis, often starting during childhood or adolescence with cruelty to animals and the maiming or killing of animals. Children who commit such acts or attempt to commit them can be identified as potentially posing some significant risk to fellow humans in the future if intervention and rehabilitation does not take place. When violence towards animals, or rather certain types of animals, is state sponsored, as in the Roman period, it raises serious issues about the psychological damage inflicted through the pursuit of linked ideological ends.

So, in summary, it would appear that many of the beasts supplied for games up to the era of the late Republic may well have been gifts or tribute from client kings or from diplomatic contacts or have been war booty, the animals perhaps first being paraded as booty or as novelties in a triumphal procession, and then being disposed of in the arena. However, once we enter the imperial era there was a marked formalisation of the games and they took on a political and ideological value that had not necessarily existed in the same form in the Republican period or which had been otherwise latent.

Adopting Attitudes

The Romans' attitudes towards exotic beasts varied tremendously and not everyone saw their slaughter in the arena as a worthy spectacle, as we have seen in the case of both commentators and crowds witnessing Pompey's lack of empathy for the elephants at his games. Again, attitudes were not fixed in time and it is therefore worth considering the case study of the elephant at Rome more fully, starting with the account of the elephant as given in Pliny's *Natural History*.[24] Of course, all the details of Pliny's account may not necessarily be true or correct: however, it does allow us to at least consider the possibility of changes in attitude over time, as a creature such as this moves from the realm of the extraordinary and exotic, to the slaughtered and the unmourned. Pliny was correct in noting that elephants come from both Africa and India, but he did not assign any difference to these two distinct species. For each region he describes a different method of capturing the animal alive: in India by using an already tame elephant to attract a wild one and then by beating the wild elephant until it too submits; in Africa Pliny described the use of pitfall traps to isolate and secure a wild elephant. If the elephant was simply being hunted for its tusks then he suggests that throwing spears at its feet – the weakest part of the beast he tells us – will eventually help bring down the elephant.

He tells us that the first elephant was brought to Rome for a triumph in 479 BC, but that elephants had first been seen in Lucania in Italy seven years earlier when they were used as war elephants by King Pyrrhus of Epirus. In 251 BC about 140 elephants were subsequently brought to Rome by sea in celebration of the victory of Metellus over the Carthaginians in Sicily. Pliny quotes a number of accounts that give different versions of the fate of these creatures; they may all have been killed during games in the arena or, at the very least, they were mistreated there and died as a result.

Considerable discussion of the fate of the elephants at Pompey's games of 55BC has already been presented above. Pliny's account of the incident is brief but telling:

> When, however, the elephants in the exhibition given by Pompey had lost all hopes of escaping, they implored the compassion of the multitude by attitudes which surpass all description, and with a kind of lamentation bewailed their unhappy fate. So greatly were the people affected by the scene, that, forgetting the general altogether, and the munificence which had been at such pains to do them honour, the whole assembly rose up in tears, and showered curses on Pompey, of which he soon afterwards became the victim.[25]

Elsewhere in the *Natural History* Pliny writes about the behaviour and natural attributes of the elephant in an anecdotal style. He is quite clear that man's 'need' of the creature is to procure its tusks for the manufacture of luxury objects from its highly valuable ivory, a process that he does not view with the same sympathy he appeared to be extending towards the arena elephants.

It must be remembered that the appearance of an exotic animal in the arena was actually the last part of an extended process that would have begun overseas with the hunting and location of the animal, its trapping, its care in transit, its shipping overseas to Rome, and its feeding and training in captivity to prepare it for the games. This is an extraordinary chain of events, mediated simply by the value placed on the animal by the sponsor of the games. Who organised the hunting and trapping and who carried it out? Who cared for the trapped beasts before transportation? Who shipped them to Rome and so on? This was not a series of unrelated activities: animals were not acquired on a piecemeal basis. To keep up the constant flow of animals required by the arena in Rome, and those elsewhere in the empire, there had to be a hard-headed and efficient commercial organisation overseeing this trade, and so it would seem to have been the case. It is thought that housed in the *Piazzale delle Corporazioni,* Square of the Corporations, at Ostia were at least three North African based companies specialising in the shipping of exotic animals from overseas to Rome and indeed the elephant depicted on the black and white mosaic at the office of traders from Sabratha in Libya was probably some kind of company emblem, flagging up their business of trading in wild animals or ivory, or indeed both commodities (Plate 61). An early third-century AD inscription from Noricum, Austria, tells us about the involvement of the prominent local family the Albii in the animal trade.

Caspian tigers were brought from their former habitat south of the Caspian Sea in Turkey, through Iran, into central Asia; possibly Indian tigers and elephants were also bought from intermediary traders with India; from Africa, particularly Egypt and North Africa, would have come lions, leopards, elephants, hippopotamuses, giraffes, and ostriches; and from Europe bears and wild boars. Thousands of animals must have been in transit at any one time. The famous first-century sculptor Pasiteles is described by Pliny in his *Historia Naturalis* as having been mauled and almost killed by an escaped leopard while at the docks on the Tiber in Rome as he was engrossed in drawing a lion in a cage there, presumably a common way for Roman artists to familiarise themselves with exotic creatures.[26]

The mechanics of the animal trade ultimately though relied on the apparatus of the Roman state, with whose political and ideological interests the games were inextricably linked, and was not simply a commercial operation. It has already been mentioned how certain types of exotic animal could be provided for games by the intervention and co-operation of provincial governors and officials on behalf of those at Rome whose political friendship they may have wished to gain. Indeed, the well documented case of Cicero, then governor of Cilicia, between 51 and 50 BC, and the aspiring political player Marcus Caelius Rufus explains the mechanics of this reciprocal arrangement, or rather how it should have worked had Cicero had any interest in complying with his client's repeated requests for help in obtaining leopards for his sponsored games.[27] I will return to this particular example later in the book. There is now considerable evidence for the direct involvement of the Roman army in hunting down animals for shipping. In that respect, it is worth noting, for example, that there was a well attested position of *ursarius,* or bear hunter, in the Roman army, such men being mentioned in inscriptions at a number of military sites. Inscriptions also record *venatores immunes,* exempted hunters, and *vestigiatores,* trackers. An inscription from Cologne records the capture of fifty bears over one particular six-month period.

Large *vivaria,* or animal holding enclosures and pens, are attested as having been present in Rome, near the Porta Praenestina for example. Inscriptions from the city refer to roles here for an *adiutor ad feras,* wild beast keeper, and a *praepositus herbariarum,* herbivore keeper, the latter role played at one time by Aurelius Sabinus. Some distance outside Rome, at Laurentum, there would appear to have been extensive holding and breeding facilities for animals intended for the arena. Inscriptions make mention of specialised animal keepers here such as a *procurator Laurento ad elephantos* (elephant keeper), a role at one time played by Tiberius Claudius Spec(u)lator, and *praepositus camellorum* (camel keeper), a title once held by Titus Flavius Stephanus. These might have been official establishments or they might have been private commercial concerns. In some instances, wild and exotic animals may have been bred or brought to maturity in captivity in or near Rome for the arena. A fine mosaic pavement of around AD 500 from Antioch in Turkey, called The Worcester Hunt as it is now in the Worcester Art Museum, Worcester, Massachusetts, United States, includes an image of a mounted huntsman stealing away some tiger cubs from their mother. It may well be that bringing young beasts to Rome and raising them there was often a safer proposition than capturing mature animals.

In considering the roles that animals were forced to play in the arena, in the hippodrome and on the hunting field, it has been shown that virtually no expense was ever spared in procuring animals and in laying on a dramatic and unusual show or chase. In the emperor Diocletian's Edict on Maximum Prices of AD 301 maximum prices were provided for different grades of lions, leopards, bears, ostriches, boars, deer, and wild asses – the most prized, good quality lion being priced at no more than the astonishingly high sum of 600,000 *sesterces*. Scenes on some of the fourth-century mosaics from the palatial villa at Piazza Armerina in Sicily provide evidence of the organisation of animal procurement, while in Roman North Africa there is considerable evidence for the existence of sodalities of professional animal hunters catering to this lucrative business.

At Villa del Casale, Piazza Armerina, it is the long Great Hunt mosaic that is of particular interest in this context, extending the full width of the building in a corridor in front of an apsidal hall (Plates 62–64). On the mosaic are various scenes of the hunting and capture of wild animals including leopards, antelopes, lions, tigers, rhinos and hippopotamuses in different landscape locations. A senior Roman official, or *dux,* oversees the hunts. Carts are on hand to carry away the captured beasts in cages. Dockside scenes of animals such as ostriches and gazelles being loaded onto ships bring home the sheer complexity of the logistics of the operation, while we also see depicted the offloading operation at the port of Rome, with ostriches being led off the ship and an elephant standing by to disembark. In each of the apsidal ends of the corridor are mosaics of personifications, in one case of Africa or

Mauretania accompanied by a bear and leopard, and in the other of India holding a tusk and accompanied by a tiger, elephant, and phoenix. Contrasting with the Great Hunt mosaic is the Small Hunt pavement elsewhere in the villa, which carries depictions of aristocrats hunting boar, deer, and small game in the local countryside (Plate 65), making a dutiful and appropriate sacrifice to Diana, and enjoying an alfresco meal. Perhaps the villa owner was somehow involved in the animal trade but had used the two pavements to contrast his business of animal shipping with his personal pleasure in leisure hunting.

Turning now to the North African evidence, on the mid-third century AD Magerius Mosaic from a substantial private villa at Smirat, Tunisia, and now in the *Musée Archéologique de Sousse*, appears a depiction of a *venatio*, in the form of a scene of extremely fierce and bloody combat between four leopards and four armed fighters with spears (Plate 66).[28] The fighters' names appear in inscriptions beside their images – they are Spittara (curiously depicted wearing stilts of some kind, as if a novelty act), Bullarius, Hilarinus, and Mamertinus while each of the leopards is also named – as Victor, presumably having appeared in the arena previously to gain such a name, Romanus, Luxurius, and Crispinus – and girded with a laurel crown. The grisly scene shows the leopards either being speared or bleeding out before their deaths. Figures of two deities also appear, one male and possibly to be identified as Liber Pater (and by some authorities as Bacchus, as discussed below) and the other female and generally accepted to be Diana the hunter goddess whose presence here is altogether appropriate. The two deities could have been at the spectacular in spirit, overseeing the events, or it is indeed even possible that actors playing these roles and adopting the personas of Diana and Liber Pater could have been present in the arena on the day of the show, adding to the theatricality of the *venatio*.

Although partially damaged towards the top edge, the head and upper part of a male figure survives, labelled Magerius, an image of the villa owner himself. Towards the centre of the mosaic stands an official or herald holding a tray on which sit four bags of money, one for each of the four combatants represented, there to make some kind of announcement about the games. The steward's announcement forms part of an unusually long inscription sited near him, for all viewers of the pavement to read and take in. The inscription is a complex piece of writing, expecting the reader to understand it comprises not only the words of the steward but also words shouted out by members of the audience at the show and some linking descriptive narrative. While Magerius himself is labelled, we need to also account for the other two appearances of the word Mageri on the pavement. They appear not to be name labels for any individual actually portrayed on the mosaic but rather the most acceptable explanation appears to be that they represent the cheers of the unseen crowd who cry out the name of Magerius who has provided such entertainment for them.

Most notably the herald announces the name of the animal providers and fighters, the *Telegenii*, and refers to the *munus* taking place. The *Telegenii* were a professional guild of itinerant *venatores*, who probably took part in arena shows across most of Roman North Africa. They have left an unusually large epigraphic footprint across the region and were recorded in formal inscriptions, some on mosaics, and even in the form of stamped mottos on pottery vessels, not only here at Smirat but also at Sousse, Timgad, El Djem, Carthage, and across the Sahel.[29] The Latin word *munus* had a number of meanings but in this context almost certainly means spectacle or contest, that is the bloody *venatio* depicted. The herald first announces to the crowd that the *Telegenii* require 500 *denarii* for each of the leopards provided for the spectacle. The crowd then appears to be crying out, presumably to Magerius: 'By your example, may future benefactors understand the spectacle. May its echo reach benefactors of the past! From whom have we had such a spectacle? When did we ever see such a spectacle? On the model of the quaestors you will give a spectacle, at your own expense you will give a spectacle; it will be your day!' The inscription then tersely declares '*Magerius donat*' – 'Magerius pays'.

In the final coda of this extraordinary inscription, the herald, or possibly the crowd as well, lauds Magerius who has financially sponsored the games: 'This is what it is to be rich! That's what it is to be powerful! Yes, that's really it! It's getting dark now, may the *Telegenii* be sent back from your *munus* with their bags full of money!' There can be no better illustration of the politicised nature of the Roman trade in exotic animals than this. It must also be noted that though the herald has set out the charge being made for their provision of these fearsome fighting beasts, each of the money bags on the herald's trays bears a symbol that suggests that each contains twice that amount in coin and we must suppose that Magerius is here further emphasising his power, wealth, and munificence by ostentatiously overpaying the *Telegenii* for their part in staging these magnificent and successful games and thus for enhancing Magerius's status.

Other recorded North African hunting spectacle sodalities include the *Leontii*, the *Pentasii*, the *Tauriscii*, the *Sinematii*, the *Perexii*, the *Tharaxii*, the *Ederii*, and the *Decasii*, though it would appear based on the wealth of evidence that has come down to us about their activities that the *Telegenii* were the most significant of these groups. Each sodality had its own protective deity, symbols and attributes. The *Telegenii* looked to a conflated Bacchus and Liber Pater as their patron god, though it is difficult to understand the presence of Bacchus at the awful slaughter of leopards on the Magerius Mosaic, given his general affection for and affinity with felines. This is why I feel that it is more likely that we are expected to identify the overseeing deity in this particular circumstance as simply Liber Pater. Their symbols included the staff topped by a crescent, heads of millet, and ivy, all of which appear as decorative but symbolic elements in the border of the Magerius Mosaic.

Five sodality leaders appear drinking together on a third-century mosaic from a building near the amphitheatre at El Djem in Tunisia, and now in the *Musée National du Bardo* in Tunis. They appear to be in an arena box or an animal training ring. Drinks are set out on a table and two servants are in attendance. Each appears with the symbol of their individual guild, the man with the staff with a crescent moon represents the *Telegenii*, as we have seen. The men are indulging in drinkers' banter, snippets of their conversation recorded in inscriptions on the pavement. 'We three are getting along fine' declares the *Telegenii* chief. Others say 'Let us amuse ourselves', 'Enough said', and 'We have come to drink'. Another snippet about disrobing is unreadable through damage. One of the servants seems to be gesturing to them to keep the noise down by holding a finger to his lips, perhaps to prevent their drunken, raised voices from disturbing the five huge bulls who are lying together asleep inside the arena. An inscription above the servant's head implores them 'to let sleeping bulls lie'. We might suppose that these beasts were being readied for an imminent appearance fighting in the arena.

It has even been suggested that the *Telegenii* had such an established trading and shipping network to support the animal trade that they also inevitably became involved in the shipping of other lucrative commodities such as olive oil, though the direct evidence for this is somewhat slight.[30] It is likely though that the North African animal trade was severely disrupted, or even possibly more or less curtailed, by the Vandals seizing of the Roman North African provinces in AD 439 and their almost one hundred years' holding of power here.

Fatal Charades

Another manifestation of the use of animals in the Roman arena was the part they were occasionally forced to play in executions, which were staged as mythological enactments.[31] These highly theatrical and contrived set-ups, which became a judicial phenomenon from the early empire onwards, were curiously grotesque in their concept and conceit of placing real people and real animals in fictitious narratives of considerable jeopardy, something that must have confused as many members of the audience as they delighted. The enactments married punishment of criminals with ideas of retribution and humiliation. For spectators there was a sense of seeing justice done, and to some the executions would have also served as a deterrent, albeit one laced with entertainment. A few examples will be considered here.

According to an epigram probably composed by Martial to mark the inaugural games put on by Titus in AD 80, spectacular games that we have already discussed above, in the arena a person dressed as Orpheus, in a stage setting that included high cliffs and thick forest, charmed animals with beautiful music before he was torn apart by a rampaging bear.[32] The costumed figure was doubtless a condemned criminal, dressed up and probably somehow trussed up to prevent his movement or escape. The music would have been played by a musician hidden out of sight of the spectators. Those animals seemingly in thrall to the god were probably a gathering of the most sedate kinds of farm animals or other artificially sedated creatures. The bear would most likely have been goaded and mistreated before its release into the arena to guarantee its frenzied state, and perhaps primed to attack the helpless criminal dressed as Orpheus by laid scents or trails. This extraordinary subversion of the tale of Orpheus, in which his attempts to control Nature itself and to bend it to his will were turned upside down by his death at the paws of a bear, might have been thought to have been setting a dangerous precedent. Two other theatrical staged executions noted by Martial also involved a bear, a Lucanian bear to be precise in one case, tearing apart a criminal dressed as Daedalus. 'How you would wish you had your wings now!', Martial gloatingly declared.[33] In the other charade a Scottish bear killed a man dressed as the bandit leader Laureolus.

As if these three events were not terrible enough, Martial further praised a third grotesque mythological charade based on the story of Pasiphae, the daughter of the sun god Helios and his wife Perse.[34] As the wife of King Minos of Crete, Pasiphae not only bore his children but also gave birth to the terrifying Minotaur, as a result of being raped by a white bull sent to her by the sea god Poseidon/ Neptune. In the arena the poor woman presented as Pasiphae was then forcibly ravaged by a bull. 'You must believe that Pasiphae did couple with the bull of Dicte [a mountain on Crete]: we have seen it, the age-old myth has been vindicated. Don't let the ancient tradition be astonished at itself, Caesar: whatever legend rehearses, the amphitheatre provides for you', crowed Martial. We must assume that the poor woman either died in the assault or was put to the sword shortly afterwards to bring an end to her misery. It is difficult to believe that such a distressing event could have been presented as a public display and entertainment.

How often such fatal charades took place and whether their staging was always quite so elaborate and considered is not known, or indeed what kinds of criminals or prisoners were selected to take part and for what reasons. They must have been quite rare events, and those involving animals rarer still. The important early Christian figure St Clement of Rome, writing in the late first century AD, not that long after Titus's games, suggested that some female Christians were martyred in the arena in the guise of Danaids and Dirces. While this is simply a brief allusion in a longer text and therefore he did not provide any further details on specific martyrdoms, we can certainly assume that the Dirce charade would certainly have involved animals, if it did in fact take place, while we must remain forever in the dark about the Danaids charade. Dirce, the wife of Lycus of Thebes, was the tyrannical mistress of Antiope, who had been placed into slavery with her by her husband, who was also Antiope's uncle. Antiope had a complicated back story. She was married to Epopeus of Sicyon, while pregnant with twins to Zeus who had raped her. Her father died of shame, her uncle Lycus killed her husband, abducted her, and when she gave birth to her twins (later named Amphion and Zethus by a shepherd who rescued them) he left them in a cave to die. Antiope eventually escaped from captivity but was recaptured by Dirce who planned to punish her by tying her between the horns of a wild bull. However, at the last minute Antiope was rescued by her sons who subjected Dirce to the same fate that she had planned for their mother, being torn and trampled to death by the bull. Given the specifics of this story it can be assumed that any criminal or Christian made to dress in character as Dirce would have met a similar grim death in the arena.

In each of the instances cited here of what are commonly known to academics today as fatal charades, none of the animals that had taken part had been killed during the particular execution in which they had been chosen and forced to play a part. It is highly likely though that the bears used had been horribly goaded into a frenzied state to attack whoever they were let loose on in the arena. The Dirce bull was also probably physically mistreated, once the woman had been tied to its horns in order to enrage it and facilitate its homicidal fury. Following the denouement of each particular charade the animals would either have been killed or recaptured and recaged for future fighting.

Pictorial representations of the process of *damnatio ad bestias* are quite rare in Roman art, perhaps quite understandably, though a huge amount can be learned about this, and about the arena games and gladiatorial contests in general, from examination of the so-called Zliten Gladiator Mosaic and the Silin mosaic, both from

Roman North Africa. Dating to the second century AD, the Zliten mosaic pavement decorates the *triclinium,* or dining room, of the Villa Dar Buc Ammera, near Zliten, Leptis Magna, in present day Libya. It is now on display in the Assaraya Alhamra Museum in Tripoli (Plate 67). The large mosaic consists of sixteen square fields decorated with geometric designs and fish, with the arena and gladiatorial scenes being restricted to the border areas around all four sides of the pavement.[35] Two scenes of execution will be considered here and two others of combat with animals.

Both executions are of dark-skinned men and it has been suggested that these were local rebels, though given the date of the pavement it seems more likely that they were in fact condemned criminals. The first execution scene consists of a standing man, held by the hair from behind by a whip-whielding jailor, facing down a lion which is captured at the moment of springing at him, its front paws off the ground, its back paws pushing into the ground to give it traction. The prisoner holds out his arms in a futile gesture of warding off the lion's attack. In the second execution, an almost naked man tied to a stake is wheeled into the arena standing upright on a small trolley. One attendant behind him pushes the trolley and a second stands by with a whip in case the leopard leaping up at the condemned man's chest gets out of control and turns on the jailors. On the Zliten mosaic is also depicted a scene of enforced combat between a bear and a raging bull who are chained together to bring on their aggression, and an image of a man fighting two ostriches.

A mid to later second century mosaic from a villa at Silin in Libya shows victims in a distinctive costume of hooded tunic and trousers being attacked by a massive white bull, which has tossed two of the victims up into the air and awaits a third who is being ushered towards the bull by a handler. A second official with a staff looks on. This is again possibly an execution staged as a mythological re-enactment.

Although animal spectacles continued to be staged in Rome into the fifth and even sixth centuries AD, it would seem that these were far less grand and involved far fewer exotic animals than had taken part in earlier imperial games such as those staged by Augustus, Titus or Trajan. The emphasis in later games, certainly at

Rome if not in North Africa where wild beasts were probably still quite easily and cheaply procured, seems to have been the eluding of fierce animals by athletic human opponents rather than always the animals' slaying.

Racing Colours

In stark contrast to the above stands the huge interest attested among Romans in the equally popular but less vicarious chariot racing that took place in the Circus Maximus, just up the hill from the Colosseum, and in the many other racing hippodromes elsewhere in Italy and further beyond in some of the provinces.[36] More than sixty circuses are known, with five or more being recorded in each of Italy, Greece, Spain, Tunisia and Asia Minor (Turkey). In Rome the sport was highly organised and quite formally factionalised, with racing teams carrying the colours of their stables – the Greens, Blues, Reds, and Whites – and many spectators identifying specifically and ardently with *their* team (Plate 68). The stables established clubhouses for their individual factions in Rome itself and elsewhere in the empire, thereby encouraging partisanship among the racegoers. Faction colour seemed to have been of prime importance.

Appuleius Diocles, a famous second-century AD charioteer, is recorded in an inscription as having joined the Whites at eighteen years of age, raced for them for six years, before being recruited by the Greens, where he stayed for three years. He then moved to the Reds where he raced for fifteen years, retiring at forty-two, having won 1,462 races out of 4,257, winning nearly 36,000,000 *sesterces* in the process. He is one of only four *miliarii,* winners of more than a thousand races, known to us. The others were Publius Aelius Gutta Calpurnianus, Flavius Scorpus and Pompeius Musclosus. While we know from historical sources and inscriptions the names of many of the great racing charioteers such as the four *miliarii,* sources often also name the most famous horses of their era as well, demonstrating an evident and almost equal interest in the horses as in the drivers. The writer Martial compares his own minor fame to that of the great horse *Andraemo*. The quadriga team of Flavius Scorpus – the horses *Ingenuus, Admetus, Passerinus* and *Atmetus* – are named on a funerary altar. While the majority of racing horses were stallions, mares are also attested, such as the famous African horse *Speudusa,* 'Speedy', commemorated with her own tombstone.[37] The horses most commonly raced in harnessed teams of four, though six- or even seven-horse teams are also attested, as are, much less commonly, two-horse teams.

Horse racing also took place at hippodromes and more impromptu races also probably took place in less formal venues, as did camel racing in North Africa, and indeed races between camels and horses also occasionally occurred. Horse racing, though a popular sport, would not appear to have been quite as popular as chariot racing. The recent discovery of an inscribed tablet in Greek at the Lukuyanus Monument in the Beyşehir district of Konya province, central Anatolia, Turkey, is of great interest. The monument is decorated with a relief of a horse, appropriate to the burial here of the jockey Lukuyanus who, the inscription tells us, in translation, 'died before getting married. He is our hero.' The lengthy inscription also provides some fascinating insights into the rules of horse racing in the area, there being a presumed hippodrome nearby. Apparently, in order to give other jockeys, trainers and owners a chance, it was decreed that winning horses and others from the same stables could not compete again, presumably just at the same race meeting, to give others an opportunity for victory and racing glory.

So fervent were many of the chariot racing team supporters that they often commissioned or prepared inscribed curse tablets, most made of lead, invoking the gods or evil spirits to bring disaster down upon the rival teams' named drivers and horses. Some of these tablets might also have been commissioned by chariot drivers themselves, to try to nobble their opponents by magic means if they felt threatened by the more finely honed skills of their rivals. Many of these curse tablets have been found buried at racetracks throughout the Roman world. One such third-century AD curse tablet found at the track in Beirut bears a crude *graffito* drawing of a bound charioteer with holes where nails or spikes would have been driven into his body and head, being assaulted by what appears to be a bird of prey. Listed on the tablet are the names of thirty-five horses also included in the requested spell. The spirits were here asked to 'attack, bind, overturn, cut up, chop into pieces the horses and the charioteers of the Blue colours – Numphikos, Thalophoros...' and so on.[38]

Another tablet, from a first-third century AD grave of a race track official at Carthage is equally frothing:

> bind every limb and sinew of Victoricus – the charioteer of the Blue Team – and of his horses which he is about to race... Bind their legs, their onrush, their bounding, and their running; blind their eyes so that they cannot see and twist their soul and heart so that they cannot breathe. Just as this rooster has been bound by its feet, hands, and head, so bind the legs and hands and head and heart of Victoricus the charioteer of the Blue Team, so that they may not reach victory tomorrow in the circus. Now, now, quickly, quickly.[39]

When an attempt was last made to quantify numbers of known named chariot racing horses from the Roman world, in an academic paper published in 1948, perhaps surprisingly roughly 480 different names were recorded during the exercise.[40] These included names that denoted the beast's colour or markings, its speed and agility, its physical character, or its psychological characteristics. Some were given names alluding to victory, while others got more playful names such as 'Much Beloved' or 'Divine'. Some were named after gods or heroes, some were given place-name epithets, and so on.

Races at the hippodrome were not simply about entertainment but, as with gladiatorial shows in the arena, they represented the manifestation of an ideology that linked spectacle with power and authority. Aristocratic and imperial largesse was here being used to enhance and maintain status. During the imperial era at one stage racing at the *Circus Maximus* took place on sixty-four days of the year, with twenty-four races on each day. There are though many examples of genuine interest in chariot racing displayed by individual emperors, sometimes indeed verging on obsessive fandom. For instance, Caligula was ridiculed in the story of his life as presented in Suetonius's ribald book known to us as *The Twelve Caesars* because of his obsession with the racing horse *Incitatus*, Bounce.[41.] The emperor personally paid for the housing of *Incitatus* in a superbly and ostentatiously adorned marble stable, attended by slaves. He wore jewelled collars and horse coats in the imperial purple. Suetonius also suggests that the bond between emperor and beast was so absurdly strong that Caligula even considered appointing the horse to the consulship, more a dig at the powerlessness of such magistrates at the time than a serious consideration. The later emperor Lucius Verus was said to particularly favour a horse called *Volucer,* Flyer, who he spoiled with tasty titbits and lavish coats. The emperor was even believed to have carried round with him a small gold statuette of the horse which, when it died, was buried in a tomb on the Vatican Hill. Commodus is recorded by the historian Cassius Dio as being most fond of the Green faction horse *Pertinax,* Will to Victory.

Just as the arena entertainments involving animals needed a vast financial and logistical back up to underpin the entertainment, starting far away from Rome by the tracking and capture of wild beasts in their home environment, so too did chariot and horse racing. The buying and selling of horses, their breeding, stabling, training, their transportation and so on was a veritable industry involving vets, farriers, saddlers, blacksmiths, stable staff, trainers, grooms, riders, and chariot drivers. All of this would have been reflected in the number of people involved in the sport at all levels, and the number of dedicated properties and buildings linked to the sport. In this context it is interesting to look at the infrastructure associated with horse racing today in Britain, which might in some ways be comparable. At Newmarket in Suffolk, Charles II built royal stables in 1671 and the town has been associated with the sport of horse racing ever since, uniquely so in Britain. More than a third of the town's population of 15,000 is involved in the racing industry in some capacity, directly or indirectly. Here there are two racecourses, seventy training yards, numerous designated rides – 'gallops' – and paths, eighty stud farms, and approximately 3,000 horses in training.

The popularity of chariot racing was reflected in the number of times images of the races, of the hippodrome, of chariot teams and charioteers also appeared in Roman non-funerary art, both elite art and popular or genre art, on wall paintings and mosaics, metal, pottery, and glass vessels, engraved gemstones and so on (Plates 69–71). As we will see in a later chapter, chariot racing was sometimes featured on funerary monuments (Plate 72) and on many types of funerary objects, such as lamps or the glass bowl placed in a burial at Cologne, Germany.

This is not altogether surprising, given that some Romans attached a cosmological significance to the shape of the circus itself and to the circular motion of the chariot teams as they raced around the circuit.[42] This was both a cosmic allegory and an event symbolically imbued with a ritual significance in a funerary context. In Roman art races of four chariots set within a circular field such as provided by a glass bowl could be thought of as signifying the four seasons following one on another, of time passing. As circus imagery became more common charioteers were more overtly presented as seasons on mosaic pavements, for instance. It must also be remembered that in the later Roman period private circuses came to be associated with imperial funerary complexes, such as the associated circus and mausoleum of Maxentius and those of the empress Helena.

Hunting
Hunting in the ancient world would have taken place on a number of scales. It undoubtedly would have been a widespread, small scale, everyday occurrence, in the form of country dwellers tracking, trapping, netting and stalking wild animals, including birds, for food, or shooting them with bows and arrows or spearing them. Genre illustrations of bird catchers with poles trying to ensnare birds in trees are common in Roman art. The practice of using 'lime twigs', that is switches coated in a sticky substance generically known as bird-lime, to catch quails and small migrating songbirds still goes on, mostly illegally, in parts of North Africa and southern Europe today. The individual hunter might have been alone, or with a trained dog. Hunting in the Roman world was also carried out on a much larger, more formal, scale in the form of organised events including multiple hunters on horseback, beaters and probably packs of dogs. While winning game for the table was the driving force behind the everyday hunt, the more formal large hunt should be seen as having been a social and cultural phenomenon, one often linked to status and display in the ancient world, particularly in the period of Late Antiquity.[43]

Hunting has been described by one of the characters in R.S. Surtees's nineteenth-century book *Handley Cross* as being 'the sport of kings, the image of war without its guilt, and only five-and-twenty percent of its danger', and indeed some elements of this statement could equally have applied to hunting in Roman times, particularly in the later Roman period or Late Antiquity when many imperial and aristocratic activities became ceremonialised to a great extent. Hunting in England from the Medieval period onwards also became associated with the careful management of the hunting landscape and the exclusivity of the use of this land within legal strictures. Roman agricultural writers tell us of the widespread existence of the *leporia*, a kind of small-scale enclosed game reserve initially just for hares, as the name implied, but later commonly used to house deer and other game animals as well. While there would not seem to have been anything similar to large Medieval game parks in the Roman period, certain specific tracts of land certainly became favoured hunting grounds at the time, as an example from northern England will demonstrate.

Scargill Moor in the parish of Barningham, County Durham (previously within the boundary of North Yorkshire) is a remote tract of unfarmed land, difficult to access even today. The moor lies 2 miles to the south of the Roman fort at Bowes and provided the setting for two Roman period rustic shrines set up to the god Vinotonus Silvanus, probably by officers stationed at nearby Bowes fort. I visited the moor in the late 1970s to help investigate reports of erosion at the best-preserved of the shrines and can attest to the extraordinary atmospheric quality of the site and its very isolated location. The dedicatees of altars at the shrines included Julius Secundus, the centurion of the First Cohort of Thracians, and Lucius Caesius Frontinus from Parma in Italy and Titus Orbius Priscinus, both prefects of the same unit.

The name of the deity Vinotonus occurs on a number of the inscribed altars from Scargill Moor[44] and is otherwise unknown elsewhere in Roman Britain and more broadly in the empire. He must, therefore, be considered to have been a local god who, as some of the inscriptions indicated, could be formally equated with the Roman god Silvanus, a protector of forests and fields, and of boundaries. Along with Pan and Faunus, he was one of the rustic gods of the Roman countryside. Silvanus's most common attributes when he was portrayed in Roman art were a *falx*, a sort of pruning knife, a tree branch, a dog, and, occasionally, fruit of some kind. He sometimes was depicted wearing a wolf pelt.

Hunting as a Roman imperial pursuit does not appear to have been one of the defining aspects of imperial behaviour and activity that it subsequently became until the reign of Domitian (AD 81–96), and most certainly there can be said to have been no Republican tradition of formal aristocratic or senatorial hunting either.[45] A consideration of why hunting became enshrined within imperial ideology certainly suggests that its acceptance as a formal, regular pursuit for an emperor corresponded with the redefinition of the concept of manly *virtus*, that is the quality of virtuous conduct but also of bravery and strength. Hand in hand with this review of codified imperial male behaviour went a revival of Philhellenism, a love for and interest in all things ancient Greek, particularly its art and literature, among the aristocratic class at Rome. Thus Macedonian royal hunting iconography, the portrayal of the mythological hunting exploits of the hero god Hercules in both art and literature, and other Greek and Hellenistic sources of hunting imagery together helped focus and fuel the development of an artistic template for Roman imperial figures at leisure and for sport in the countryside. The trend for Greek-inspired hunting imagery might in fact have had its roots in non-imperial circles, and it has been suggested that representations of hunting in a number of wall paintings from houses in Pompeii, including the House of the Ancient Hunt itself, might have reflected just such a manifestation.

Some of the most iconic Roman imperial hunting images date from the reign of the emperor Hadrian. The Hadrianic sculptures reused and reset in the much later Arch of Constantine in Rome comprise eight circular panels or *tondi*, known collectively today as the Hunting *tondi*, given the nature of their subject matter (Plate 73).[46] These eight serial images comprise a programme whose narrative helps define Hadrian's person in terms of the emperor's personal qualities. There has been a considerable amount of academic debate about the type of monument from which these *tondi* originally derived, and it has variously been suggested that they came from an imperial monument celebrating the emperor's travels or his love of hunting, or, less convincingly, that they came from a temple or tomb dedicated to Hadrian's favourite, the beautiful Bithynian youth Antinous. They are of particular interest in terms of their reuse on the arch in that they depict scenes which were not somehow linked to war, to imperial triumph and to conquest, as were the reused Trajanic frieze sections and statues of Dacian prisoners and some of the Aurelian panels. Nor were they linked to imperial ideology as expressed through the concepts of duty and responsibility, and the rites associated with the fulfilment of those things, as so well illustrated on some of the reused panel reliefs of Marcus Aurelius. However, it could be argued that they were expressions of *virtus* personified in the person of the emperor, or indeed that it was simply that the establishing of a link of some kind between Hadrian and Constantine was pre-eminent in their choice for reuse. The fact that the scenes are set in a number of disparate locales perhaps indicates that they were illustrative of Hadrian's travels around the empire and thus representative of the idea of the unity and diversity of the Roman empire, both in terms of its peoples and of the natural environment of each province. An even simpler explanation would be that they were chosen as much for their shape as for any other consideration.

The eight *tondi* of Luna marble comprise scenes of the departure for the hunt, the hunt itself, and sacrifice after the hunt. The game hunted comprises the bear, boar and the lion. The sacrifices depicted are clearly to Silvanus, Diana, Apollo and Hercules. Hadrian's young companion Antinous appears in at least one of the scenes, most certainly to be identified as taking part in the boar hunt. The portraits of Hadrian in these scenes have been recarved; in the sacrifice to Apollo on the north side, and to Hercules on the south side, the new portrait face may be that of Constantius I, Constantine's father, or less likely of Licinius, Constantine's fellow Tetrarch, while on the other *tondi* where the emperor's head still survives it can be seen that Hadrian has been recarved to become Constantine. These *tondi* are positioned four on each long side of the arch, two in a pair above each of the small side passageways. Their arrangement probably did not mirror their original disposition on the Hadrianic monument from which they came.

The *tondo* depicting the boar hunt is of particular interest in that the two main mounted figures in the middle ground in pursuit of the huge boar, their horses depicted charging at a gallop after the magnificent charging boar that dominates the foreground of the scene, almost mirror the pose of the mounted Trajan on the panels set into the sides of the main central passageway of the arch. The hunted boar replaces the prostrate barbarian foes as quarry or victim. The boar hunt was a common and typical heroic theme in both the Greek and Roman worlds, particularly as reflected in the stories of Meleager and the Calydonian Boar and, of course, Hercules and the capture of the mighty Erymanthian Boar, a feat that was considered more significant than the slaying of the Nemean Lion in terms of its fourth position in the telling of the Twelve Labours. The boar symbolically represented the wild wood, the untamed, the space of Artemis. Its killing or capture might indeed have been thought to represent the opening up of the wilderness to civilization, and thus the boar hunt also came to be quite commonly associated in Greece, and to a lesser extent in Italy, with the building of towns and cities, at least in terms perhaps of their foundation myths.

While hunting was an aristocratic, restricted pursuit at the time of Hadrian it became even more marked as a signifier of power and status in the third and fourth centuries and much further beyond, a defining pastime and signifying sport. Hunting became a defining elite male leisure activity in the later Roman empire, even in the most remote of the provinces. In the late Roman period such an activity as hunting would have been the preserve of not only the aristocratic male landowner but also of senior bureaucrats and military officers. It was to become a defining activity linked to a suite of pursuits celebrating hyper masculinity in Late Antiquity. In classical art and mythology the hunt was itself symbolic of the life-course, with death waiting for all of us inevitably at the end of life's chase; this may account for the popularity of the hunt motif in Roman art in general and its ubiquity in many different media, even down to smaller items of material culture such as pottery and knife handles. The hunt also became quite regularly used as an allegorical image for life itself and was often linked to ideas reflecting salvation (Plate 74), something which Christianity would employ in its palette of symbolic expression. However, it is unlikely that the Senate's architect for the decorative scheme on the Arch of Constantine selected these *tondi* for their allusive content. They may simply have been selected on aesthetic grounds and for their links with the good emperor Hadrian.

While writing about the Hadrianic hunting *tondi* in my previous book on the Arch of Constantine I was very much drawn towards thoughts about the Troyes casket, in pride of place in the Treasury of Troyes Cathedral in north-central France. Brought from Constantinople in 1204, this ivory casket is a richly-decorated piece of Byzantine court art that probably dates from the tenth or possibly eleventh century AD. The lid of the casket is decorated with a scene of two emperors in military garb mounted on richly-appointed horses positioned on either side of a walled city. The emperors may be about to enter the city, some of the citizens inside being pictured greeting them with acclaim. A Tyche, the personification of the city, offers a victor's crown to the emperor on the right. On both the front and back faces are hunting scenes; on the front a lion hunt is portrayed, with the two mounted emperors confronting the beast, one armed with a bow, the other with a sword; on the back a boar is being hunted by a single individual with a lance, again in imperial military dress, and accompanied by a pack of dogs. Hunting is here, as so often in ancient art, an affirmation of the emperor's hold over the natural world, its terrain and creatures, acting as a broader metaphor for the control of the Byzantine empire. On the two ends are depicted Chinese imperial phoenixes, suggesting either the reach and influence of the Byzantine court or indicating that the casket might well have been an imperial or diplomatic gift to the Chinese court. There is no doubt that this precious item represents a material manifestation of Byzantine political power, of how imperial ideology was made manifest in artistic production. The juxtaposition here in terms of images of urban and rural imperial roles and pursuits, and between practical and almost existential concerns, between the concerns of the Byzantine empire and of the world beyond, between individual and collective responsibilities, echoes, many centuries later, many of the themes touched upon in the programme of artworks on the Arch of Constantine both in the images on the Hadrianic Hunting *tondi* and in their new setting.

Rhythms of Cruelty

In this chapter extended consideration has been given to an examination of how the use of animals in Roman amphitheatre spectacles, and particularly their killing, led to a commodification of exotic creatures from the farthest reaches of the Roman empire and beyond, on a scale never previously seen and seldom seen since, in a similar manner to the operation of human slavery in Roman times (Plate 75). That a veritable industry grew up to operate this trade and facilitate the political discourse around the sponsorship of such bloody shows testifies to their centrality to Roman imperial and elite society. Discussion of organised hunting, as an almost ritualised elite or imperial pursuit not linked to the pursuit of game as food, has also indicated that animal blood-letting through hunting likewise was another major force in the maintenance of elite identity. It has almost been a relief to also discuss here the vastly popular sport of chariot racing where the be-all and end-all of the event was not the death or suffering of creatures without agency or protection.

Gruesome animal combat scenes and bloody hunting scenes were common subjects in Roman wall paintings and on mosaics, most of them in private houses. This is not altogether surprising within the broader context of the fashion for images of gladiatorial combat and of suffering figures such as Marsyas. The aesthetics of pain in Roman art covers a broad spectrum of suffering and of sufferers.[47] The appeal of animal suffering, and images of animal suffering, was a Roman cultural artefact that it is difficult for us to come to terms with today.

To some extent, to be a real man in the Roman imperial era after Domitian's reign, emperors, aristocrats, senior soldiers and bureaucrats were required to display their keenness for and prowess at hunting and killing animals in the countryside. This blatant hyper-masculinity was of course manifested in many other ways but hunting required not just the kind of passive attendance or financial sponsorship that linked imperial authority to the arena games but rather the active participation of the emperor and represented another forum for the performance of the state rites.

The sheer pointlessness of much of this needless animal cruelty and its links with imperial and aristocratic machismo is well summed up by the tale of one particular spontaneous hunt described by Pliny the Elder in his *Naturalis Historia*,[48] presumably with information garnered from a contemporary informant. The hunter in this case was the emperor Claudius who was visiting his vast new harbour building works at Ostia when a whale happened to become stranded in the shallows inside the harbour, having been feeding there for a number of days previously. Rather than attempting to refloat the whale the emperor had the harbour mouth netted and together with a number of shiploads of soldiers set to hunting the whale, showering the creature with spears and provoking it to sink one of the ships, as an appreciative audience looked on. Pliny does not tell us the final fate of the trapped creature: we can only assume that it was killed.

6

Venus in Furs

Animal Attributes
In this chapter discussion will focus on the widespread use of
images of animals as attributes of various gods and the rationale
behind such specific identifications. In Roman art many of the
gods and goddesses of the Roman pantheon were often depicted
in association with a particular animal, an animal that had played
some part in their lives as codified in myth or which served some
purpose specifically associated with that deity. For instance, we
can commonly see depictions of Jupiter and an eagle, of Minerva
and an owl, Mercury with a ram, a cockerel and sometimes also
with a tortoise, Bacchus with felines of various sorts, Aesculapius
with a snake, Sabazios with snakes and lizards, Faunus with a
woodpecker, Diana with her hounds, and so on. Sometimes, when
certain animals were depicted on their own, we can often assume
that their image was making an allusion to the absent deity. It is
easy to understand that animal attributes might have been intended
to humanise the gods, to make their presence in the human world
more understandable, by linking them to some facet of Nature and
thus of the real world. The reasoning behind the creation of some
of these animal attributes will now be explored, though it is not
intended to provide an exhaustive list of all Roman deities and their
attribute animals, but simply a representative selection. I will start
by discussing the Capitoline Triad, Rome's three most powerful
deities – Jupiter, Juno and Minerva – and will then consider other

major gods and goddesses such as Apollo, Mercury, Venus and Bacchus, some eastern deities, and some provincial deities.

The association of the eagle and thunderbolt with Jupiter, god of the sky and the father of the gods, is relatively easy to understand, as is the appropriation of the eagle as a symbol of Roman imperial authority and power and as a symbol of the Roman army. The high-flying nature of the eagle and its hyper-vigilance in flight doubtless made its association with the all-seeing gods in the heavens a logical one to ancient minds. Its life both in the skies and on the ground linked both heaven and earth. Its potency and its violent power led it to being labelled as the king or ruler of the birds, first among the Greeks and subsequently among the Romans, making this regal association a ubiquitous one.

Many images of the eagle in Roman imperial and military art are of the bird carrying Jupiter's thunderbolt in its beak, acting as the armour-bearer of the god, the winged deliverer of his thunderbolt. Another related image is that of the eagle holding or clutching a snake or serpent, symbolising the defeat of an opponent. The *aquila,* or eagle standard, became the official standard of the Roman legions following the wide-ranging military reforms of Gaius Marius set in place in 107 BC – before that time the eagle had been just one of many animals or creatures represented on standards, including the wolf, the horse, the boar, and the mythical Minotaur. The eagle had a hugely significant prophetic connection in that it was said to portend the will of Jupiter himself, or so it was thought among the Romans, its presence on a battlefield suggesting victory for whichever side its flight or behaviour seemed to favour.

Both the writers Cassius Dio and Herodian described the use of an eagle as an actor in the drama at the imperial funeral of the emperors Pertinax and Septimius Severus respectively. The funerary pyre on such occasions was tall and multi-storeyed, like a pharos or lighthouse, we are told. While Dio simply noted that the bird once released flew from the pyre into the sky,[1] we learn from Herodian that 'from the highest and topmost storey an eagle is released, as if from a battlement, and soars up into the sky with the flame [from the funeral pyre], taking the soul of the emperor from earth to heaven, so the Romans believe.'[2] Some academics have questioned whether such events actually took place, or whether the soaring eagle as representative of the ascending soul of the emperor was simply a literary fantasy, a metaphorical and philosophical construction with no basis in any kind of reality. Some deceased female members of the imperial family were depicted on so-called *consecratio* coins, named after the legend they bore, with an image of a peacock representing their apotheosis, either by an image of the bird on its own or by a peacock depicted in the process of carrying the deceased to the heavens. In his description of Pertinax's funeral Dio also alluded to the use of an eagle at Augustus's funeral almost two hundred years earlier.[3] Some academics remain sceptical of this report too. Indeed, apart from Dio and Herodian, no other Roman writer refers to such a ritual – but few other descriptions of imperial funerals have in fact come down to us. As the bird was not released until the pyre was lit and burning, would not the eagle have died from smoke inhalation or asphyxiation or have been scorched in the licking flames, they ask? And how was it released from a secure cage on top of the pyre? I am not sure that Roman skill and sleight of hand at staging theatrical performances, arena games with animals and fighters seemingly appearing from nowhere, and highly rehearsed state rituals could not be applied to a carefully staged public funeral as well. In support of the rite can be cited evidence from a number of coin issues carrying an image of what appears to be a cage on top of what is most certainly an image of a funerary pyre.

In Judaism and later in Christianity the eagle was to be employed as a symbol of rebirth and rejuvenation. Both Christ and St John the Evangelist can be seen portrayed with eagles in some examples of early Christian art, making them like new Jupiters or indeed new emperors through the appropriation of this pagan symbol. The bird had become an image invoking spiritual power as opposed to the physical power with which it had almost exclusively been associated in Roman imperial times.

Juno was often associated with the peacock, cuckoo and the cow. Each association had a different origin. Peacocks first appeared in Hellenistic portrayals of the goddess, pulling her chariot, and here they must be considered to have been Persian birds, first brought to Greece during the time of Alexander the Great. One of Aesop's fables concerns a peacock soliciting the goddess to give it a beautiful voice like the nightingale, only to be told that it should accept its blessings in having a size and beauty denied the other birds at creation. The cuckoo gained its association with Juno through the fact that her brother Jupiter wheedled his way into her affections when she was coming to sexual maturity in the form of a cuckoo and once he had won her heart, he turned back into his normal state. The association with cows was more prosaic, and simply related to ideas of fertility and motherhood in an agricultural society, with blessings from the goddess being seen as propitious for the breeding cows of the herd and for suckling cows.

The owl represented the companion of Minerva and acted as a signifier of her presence. The story behind the beginning of this symbiotic association is unknown. The owl in the ancient world was considered a symbol of knowledge, of wisdom, and of learning (Plate 76). Its ability to see in the dark also led to its acting as a darker symbol of foresight or prophecy. However, other less obvious uses were made of Minerva's symbolic owl in Roman times. In Pompeii the processing of cloth was an important and economically highly significant local industry and the town's powerful and influential guild of fullers, the *fullones,* used the image of the owl as their symbol, thereby alluding to Minerva as the goddess of craft and weaving and as their patron.[4] Two *graffiti* from there also illustrate this link. The first, from outside the workshop of the fuller Marcus Fabius Ululitremulus, reads: '*Fullones ululamque cano/non arma virumq(ue)*', which translates as 'Of fullers and the owl I sing/not of arms and the man'. This is a knowledgeable pun on the first line of Virgil's epic poem the *Aeneid* and bears relation to a depiction of Aeneas, the book's hero and a mythological early Roman. The second, accompanied by a crude, poor drawing of an owl being held aloft in someone's hands, reads: '*Cresce(n)s fullonibus et ululae suae sal(utem).// ulula est*', translated as 'Crescens to the fuller and his owl greetings.//It's an owl', the latter referring to the poor drawing as way of an explanation to aid the perhaps puzzled viewer. A painted pillar from the *fullonica* of Lucius Veranius Hypsaeus displays on each face scenes from the processing of cloth in the workshop. On one side is depicted the inspection and brushing of cloth and a man holding a cage-like structure, which has been interpreted as a bleaching frame. On top of the frame sits an owl, again alluding to the fullers' guild and to Minerva.

Owls also appeared in a number of wall paintings and on mosaics in the town in contexts where their presence probably displayed no overt symbolism, though in a town such as Pompeii where Minerva was so seriously venerated as an economic patron, we can never altogether be sure of this. A distinction can be made between two different types of owls depicted in various contexts at Pompeii: a tawny owl appears on a fresco on the outer wall of a storeroom at the House of Lucius Ceius Secundus and on a mosaic from the House of the Faun; little owls were the species depicted in all other contexts.[5]

Apollo, son of Jupiter, was associated principally with both the dolphin and the crow. According to mythology, to escape the island of Delos he turned himself into a dolphin and brought about a great storm that allowed him to board a ship in distress and lead it to safety. As a dolphin he was also said to have guided Cretan priests to Delphi to found a temple there. Thus, in his dolphin guise, he became associated in Greek and Roman minds with colonisation and the seeking out of new lands. As for the crow, he was said to have turned himself into this bird when trying to flee from the monster Typhon. On another occasion the story goes that Apollo, incensed at the marriage of his lover Coronis to Ischys, burned the white crow messenger which brought him the news, thus turning all crows black. Thereafter crows were generally accepted as harbingers of death, doom or disaster, and they then assumed the power of announcing important deaths by their presence as an omen. The god was also variously associated with, amongst other creatures, wolves, deer, swans, serpents, and mice, as well as the musical cicada.

Mercury was commonly depicted in Roman art with a veritable pet shop of attribute animals, in the form of the ram or goat, the cockerel, and sometimes also a tortoise. As well as being the messenger of the gods and a deity associated with commerce and travel, among other things, he was also invoked as a protector of flocks and herds, hence the regular presence of the attribute ram, a symbol of animal fertility and male virility. The cockerel represented the dawn of each new day, to be greeted by its call, and hence with his role as a messenger. The tortoise was a rather more obtuse attribute, as it alluded to Mercury's invention of the lyre, made from an empty tortoise's shell. The crane was also associated with the god, and Ovid may have been drawing upon an older tradition when he suggested that the god invented the entire Greek alphabet while observing the daytime flight of cranes in different formations, in the same way that in a Greek myth the hero Palamedes invented several Greek letters while similarly watching these fascinating birds migrating.

Venus, the goddess of love, beauty, fertility and, by extension, marriage, was particularly but not exclusively a deity sympathetic to women. The nature of her birth in the sea, as recounted in mythology, meant that she was often portrayed in Roman art with seashells and with, or riding on the back of, dolphins. White birds, doves, geese and swans also often accompanied her image. Turtle doves were birds that were attributed with the character traits of gentleness, loyalty and monogamy, all redolent of Venus's own character.

Neptune was obviously associated with all marine creatures, especially dolphins, and in Roman art with a host of mythological hybrid sea creatures such as hippocamps. His image was particularly popular on bath house mosaics. Less obvious perhaps was the god's link with horses, animals that he was said to have created and in whose guise he sometimes appeared, and this accounts for the fact that marine imagery often could be found in the context of Roman horse racing and chariot racing, as we saw in the previous chapter.

The god Bacchus, deity of viticulture and ecstatic celebration, became associated with felines during his childhood, according to classical mythology, playing with lions as a child. In Roman art he often appeared in images with lions, particularly with tigers, with panthers (and leopards – of the same family), and sometimes with smaller cats such as lynxes (Plates 77–78). They served to accompany or protect him and sometimes to transport him. He was often shown in a chariot pulled by felines and, less commonly, was depicted riding on the back of a big cat. Thirdly, they represented a type of creature into which he could metamorph or change. Detailed analysis of a corpus of Bacchic images has shown that these felines, where gender can be assigned to them, were predominantly female, and this may have been significant in terms perhaps of making the big cats companions to the god comparable to the female Maenads, stressing the importance of the feminine in the Bacchic sphere and the female aura surrounding the male god.[6] His shoulders were often draped by a deerskin, another animal-linked attribute.

The so-called Indian Triumph of Bacchus was a popular subject in Roman art, particularly on decorated burial sarcophagi of the Antonine and Severan periods (Plate 79). It chimed with contemporary ideas of Roman conquest and triumph, and thus had an ideological and political content, alongside the more obvious mythico-religious themes relating to journey and salvation. In such scenes the god can usually be seen riding in a chariot pulled by panthers or other felines and sometimes riding on the back of an elephant in the triumphal procession. On one sarcophagus, in the Walters Gallery in Baltimore in the United States, an African giraffe also improbably appears in the procession. The god's control of animals and Nature and his generative powers were well illustrated in such vibrant and complex compositions as these.

As an aside, it is worth noting that the elderly satyr Silenus, one-time tutor of Bacchus, was commonly portrayed in Roman art in a drunken stupor being carried home on the back of a donkey (Plate 80).

The goddess Ceres was the most significant and powerful of the many Roman agricultural deities, overseeing crops and herds and being seen as linked to issues of fertility more generally, and she had a particular appeal to Roman women and mothers. Ceres was often associated with pigs and piglets. Pigs could be considered as enemies of the crops in that let loose in a field they will more often than not uproot plants there and trample others. Ceres's role as protector of crops and fields meant that a piglet or pregnant sow therefore was viewed as an appropriate sacrifice to the goddess for this very reason. However, it is interesting to examine the image of Ceres that appeared on a Republican *denarius* coin of 90 BC. Here the goddess was depicted walking to the right and holding two blazing torches, one in each hand, and ahead of her walks a piglet or small pig. This curious scene would appear to represent the goddess in Hades searching for her daughter Proserpina who had been abducted and taken there to be raped and imprisoned.

At the celebration of her *Cerealia* each year the release of foxes with burning brands tied to their tails gruesomely symbolised her protection of the agricultural realm from pests and vermin.

The crippled smith god Vulcan's disability meant that he was sometimes portrayed riding on the back of a donkey. His supposed association with the quail was somewhat more tenuous and rather cruel in the process, linking the god's disability and problems with walking because of his disfigured legs with the curious, limping dance that the quail does in the spring during its mating ritual.

A number of Greco-Roman and eastern deities were associated with snakes, as well as there being a number of Hellenic snake or serpent cults, which had, in some cases, only a localised significance but in others a more broad appeal. Most of these associations stressed the link between snakes and fertility and procreation, something that in a phallocentric culture like that of Rome found a ready audience. The impregnation of Olympia by Jupiter in the disguise of a snake led to the worship of the figure of Jupiter Meilichios and of other serpent-affiliated figures such as Amphiaraos and the extraordinary Glycon as described by the satirist Lucian.[7] The latter was even considered a powerful deity by that seemingly most rational of men, the emperor Marcus Aurelius.

In Roman art Aesculapius, the Roman god of medicine and healing, was most usually depicted holding a staff with a snake or serpent curled around it. He was, of course, as has been mentioned in an earlier chapter, often also associated with dogs, as indeed were other healing deities. It made sense that dogs as symbolic markers could have had both a dark side, being associated with chthonic power and the underworld, and what might be called a light side, that is connected to the process of healing. The healing quality of human and animal saliva was well known and thus having a wound licked by a dog, as probably happened quite commonly at healing shrines, was therefore not quite as strange a remedy as it might appear to some today. The keeping of dogs as pets is recognised today as being good for their owners' mental health. No matter how low a dog owner feels, he or she knows that they have an over-riding responsibility for exercising, feeding and caring for their dog; such a selfless realisation can help stave off many of the worst effects of depression and stress. Today, many hospitals both organise and allow or encourage dogs to be brought as visitors on some wards to be petted and stroked to help raise the spirits of the patients, and charities promoting such schemes are quite common.

Snakes and lizards, so often associated in Greek and Roman thought with the underworld and with ideas of eternal rebirth, were common symbols associated with the powerful image of the hand of Sabazios, an often mounted Thracian or Phrygian deity who became popular in the Roman west from the third century AD onwards. Snake handling may well have been carried out as part of the cult rites. Snakes were likewise associated with the Egyptian cult of Isis that gained a fashionable foothold in Rome and other towns in Italy such as Pompeii. Snakes and lizards were also often depicted alongside dogs as companions of the eastern god Mithras in the great scenes of his bull slaying, gorging on the blood spurting out from the disabled creature's wounds. The Mithraic cult and myth relied on the astonishing and bravura narrative of the bull slaying scene or tauroctony for its power (Plate 81). This image of both creation, salvation, and rebirth appeared in more or less the same form in Mithraea in Rome, Italy, and the provinces both in the far west, for example at Housesteads on Hadrian's Wall in Northumberland in northern England, and in the far east of the empire, for instance at Dura-Europos in Syria. Its universality suggested a common cause and cultic purpose.

That snakes and serpents were more often than not thought of in the Greek and Roman worlds as creatures of darkness and harbingers or signifiers of misfortune or death, is borne out in Greco-Roman mythology. One of the most famous statues in the ancient world was the statuary group depicting the Trojan priest Laocoon and his two sons doing battle with giant sea serpents which were depicted in the process of squeezing the life out of their almost helpless victims. Found on the Esquiline Hill in Rome in the early sixteenth century and now in the collections of the *Musei Vaticani* in Rome, this is probably the self same statue described by Pliny the Elder as being owned by the emperor Titus,[8] or at least a brilliant contemporary copy of the original (Plate 82). Laocoon's fate had been sealed by his denunciation of the Trojan Horse as a Greek ruse, a position which had angered the gods, resulting in divine punishment in the form of the deadly serpents being rained down on him at the behest of Poseidon (Neptune) or of Athena (Minerva) or Apollo.

Rustic Deities

Pan, the son of Hermes (Mercury), was a Greek and Roman god of Nature, wild places, shepherds and flocks, himself half human and half goat. He was often therefore shown in the company of a goat or a herd of goats, which he summoned with a tune on his pipes. Pan, being a rustic deity, was also linked with ideas of human and crop fertility. His own virility and his animalistic sexual appetites reflected his split personality, his place between Nature and culture. Perhaps the most shocking portrayal of Pan in Roman art is the small marble statuary group from the garden of the Villa of the Papyri at Herculaneum in which he is shown having sex with a female goat (Plate 83).[9] Not quite bestiality as such, for Pan was a half animal god in any case, the transgressive nature of this work was surely part of its original power. While deemed to be pornographic following its discovery in the mid-eighteenth century, it spent many years closeted in the *Gabinetto Segreto* at the *Museo Archeologico Nazionale* in Naples, with other erotic works from Pompeii and Herculaneum designated as being morally dangerous to the uneducated general public. Yet its original setting in a villa garden was anything but secretive. While viewers of this statue would have been a select few family members and friends, visitors, and guests, clients and so on, it is now impossible to in any way understand how the work might have been regarded and received by these contemporary viewers in its original setting and context.

The subsequent reception of this divisive and polarising work is interesting. To the Marquis de Sade, who wrote of it in *Juliette,* it was of interest for its dark, subversive allure and its viewing allowed his characters to throw off their moral shackles and subsequently indulge in acts of bestiality of their own. To the excavators and contemporary museum curators it was a dangerous and potentially corrupting work. Some scholars have interpreted the work as part of a continuum of overt, harmless eroticism in classical and Roman art; others still see it as more harmful and insidious.

Faunus was a pre-Roman Italic god of the countryside, of wilderness and of natural places, of primeval woodlands and wastelands, much like Pan. He came to be associated with agriculture and husbandry, and with fertility, and may have been invoked at the annual *Lupercalia* festival in Rome. His father was said to be Picus, the mythological founder of Laurentum near Rome, and the first king of Latium. Legend had it that he very much relied on augury, employing a woodpecker in the process. For this reason, the spurned witch Circe turned Picus into a woodpecker and thus he lived out his life in that form. The woodpecker thus became the attribute and related symbol of his only son Faunus.

The male rustic deity Silvanus, a god of the fields, woods, of boundaries, of the home, and of hunting, was most often depicted holding a *falx,* or pruning knife, and in the company of his dog, though very occasionally he appeared in images with a bear. While he most often appeared as a bearded, older man he sometimes was depicted as a beardless youth. There is in fact one example of the god being syncretised with Antinous, the youthful, vacuous favourite of the emperor Hadrian, on a fine decorated marble panel, perhaps carved by Antoninianus of Aphrodisias, from Lanuvium, where there was a *collegium* and temple dedicated to Antinous and Diana, though the panel may have come from a private shrine (Plate 84). Though at first sight a mismatch, this need not necessarily have been the case, as the syncretism here of Silvanus and Antinous made perfect sense when we consider the particular interest that Hadrian had in hunting, as we have seen in the previous chapter, and how often he hunted in the company of his young companion or lover. The myth of Silvanus's love for the boy Kyparissos, as related slightly differently by Ovid and Virgil, centres around the accidental death of a deer belonging to Apollo, perhaps a metaphor for forbidden love in this case and the consequences of the act, again a tale that might have resonated with the besotted Hadrian.

The most interesting of the Silvanus bear images comes from the legionary fortress at Xanten in Germany and adorns an inscribed votive plinth set up by Cessorinus Ammausius who, the inscription tells us, was an *ursarius*, that is a bear hunter, in the XXXth legion. The stone is now unfortunately damaged, but it can be seen that standing next to the now-headless Silvanus is a bear tucking into some fruit. Bear and animal hunters have been discussed above at length in Chapter Five.

Diana the hunter goddess was seldom portrayed in Roman art without her trusty hounds (illustration on Page 2). According to legend Diana was found bathing naked one day by the hunter Actaeon who had stumbled across her by accident, though he then proceeded to spy upon her. When Diana discovered that her privacy had been invaded in this most blatant of ways she turned Actaeon into a stag. He was then torn to pieces by his own hunting dogs. There are a number of portrayals of this metamorphosis and tragic death at the hands of a vengeful goddess in Roman art, one of the most compelling being on a Romano-British mosaic pavement in Roman Corinium, Cirencester in Gloucestershire, with Actaeon sprouting antlers out of his head as his dogs attack him.

Like Silvanus, Diana (Greek Artemis) in Greek myth was also associated with the bear but in quite a different way.[10] She sent a bear to nurse the infant Atalanta who had been abandoned and exposed in a forest by her father, and in two other mythological stories turned people into bears. The bear in the case of Atalanta was, like the goddess herself, nurturing and protective, particularly of children. It would seem that these two perceived aspects of the bear's natural character led to images of the creature being thought to be imbued with the same qualities and thus to be used in funerary contexts in an apotropaic or protective role. The marrying of the person of Artemis with that of a bear was also reflected in rites and rituals at temple or sanctuary sites in Greece dedicated to the goddess. Figurines of bears have been found at a number of such sites there, dedicated as votive offerings to Artemis, as well as actual bear claws. It is known that bear cubs were sacrificed by burning at Patras. The link between Artemis and the bear continued into the Roman period, as the goddess to the Romans became Diana.

The god Mercury Artaios and the goddess Artio were two other, provincial, local deities also linked to the bear. The Rhône-Alpes region where Artaios was popular and the Rhine-Moselle region where Artio was worshipped are both areas that included the kind of wooded mountain landscape where bears would have been relatively common in the Roman period, particularly close to those human settlements towards the forest margins where bears would quite likely have occasionally gone to forage. Indeed, one of the most remarkable pieces of small scale religious art from the Roman provinces is dedicated to Artio and comes from Muri in Switzerland, and is now in the *Bernisches Historisches* Museum in Bern. This bronze group of figures on an inscribed base, known as the Dea Artio figure group, consists of a huge bear, its mouth gaping open, approaching the seated figure of Artio. She has a basket of fruit on a raised pedestal of some kind at her side. The goddess sits bolt upright, looking straight at the bear, but appears to lean back in her seat, as if in trepidation at the approach of the massive creature, one of her feet virtually in contact with one of the front paws of the bear, who arches its back and pushes its head towards the goddess, though its attention equally could be on the food she has ready. Behind the bear is a starkly rendered tree, representing its natural habitat of the forest. The goddess here seems relatively confident in the presence of the bear, yet also slightly wary, as betrayed by her body language and pose. She seems to both have control of the beast, and thus of wild, ferocious Nature, and at the same time some kind of wary respect for its untamed nature. She is at one with Nature and, as indicated by the bounteous display of fruit, also linked to ideas of plenty and of fertility. This work would seem to operate on two levels in terms of meaning, one linked to the idea of the divine and the control of Nature, as already suggested, and the other linked to the human relationship with wild Nature in the more liminal parts of the region. On the more mundane front the fruit may be here as a lure to bring the bear closer, perhaps to allow her to feed it and nourish it. The inscription on the statue base reads '*Deae Artioni Licinia Sabinilla*', giving us both the name of the deity and of the dedicatee of the votive group.

The Roman chthonic deity Hecate, a goddess linked to boundaries, entrance-ways and the underworld, was often associated with packs of dogs as her attribute animals. She often appeared in Greek and Roman art in triplicate, as great power was thought to be invested in such triplism. Quite regularly one or more of these triple figures of the goddess had an animal head, sometimes of a cow, sometimes of a dog, or of a boar, serpent or horse.

Just as the fertility of wild Nature, of farm animals and of crops was thought to have been of primary concern to the goddess Ceres and to the host of lesser Roman rustic deities, so the importance of the horse in particular was seen to be highly significant in certain regions of the empire. Even though a major deity such as Neptune might have been linked to the protection and welfare of horses in Rome and Italy, in parts of the western empire the female mounted goddess Epona was more popular, while in the east the male Phrygian rider god was of particular significance. The gender of each of these provincial deities was not necessarily exclusionary. Epona was a Celtic goddess, particularly worshipped in Gaul, and she was often the focus of dedications by soldiers, especially cavalrymen.[11] She was a fertility figure, a mother goddess associated with horses, and common in funerary contexts. She was most commonly portrayed riding side saddle on a horse, in rare cases astride a horse, or in the company of horses or foals. The Thracian rider god was a male, martial figure whose origins in the east of the empire belied his eventual much wider appeal and the great influence that images of the god had on Roman military art and perhaps subsequently on Roman imperial art. If Epona had some kind of cross-gender appeal, the male rider god would seem to have been a much more polarising figure, appealing to hyper-masculine men.

Labours Won

The hero god Hercules had as one of his attributes not a live animal but rather an animal pelt, the skin of the Nemean Lion, which he slew during one of his labours. The pelt helped make images of him easily identifiable to viewers. Its loss at one stage to Omphale was a metaphorical form of emasculation (Plate 85). Whatever fearsome animal qualities he had assimilated by the slaying of the lion and the wearing of its pelt was now dissipated by its wearing by Omphale in order to humiliate and tame him.

Hercules, because of his strength and almost superhuman powers, was much revered by the soldiers of the Roman army and men in general who identified with his insouciant blend of hyper-masculinity and vulnerability. Because of this, a temple to Hercules was built in the Forum Boarium in Rome, within the compound of which was sited the so-called greatest altar, the *Ara Maxima*. A most curious sentence in Pliny's *Historia Naturalis* informs his readers that dogs and flies were forbidden to enter the *Ara Maxima*, one of the few explicit exclusions of particular creatures from a god's presence.[12] This makes them almost a form of anti-attribute and perhaps a moment can be taken to try to consider the meaning of this rather enigmatic ruling. From a purely practical point of view, attempting to keep dogs and flies away from a temple where regular sacrifice took place and where meat from the sacrificial animals was cooked and eaten makes great sense, being linked to spiritual purification and sacrificial hygiene. While dogs could be physically kept out of the sacred precinct, flies could only have been kept at bay by the burning of certain herbs to repel them. But there is no other such specific prohibition relating to any other temple site in Rome at any time in the Roman period. It must therefore be concluded that the dreaded dogs and flies banned from this particular site were banned for a reason linked very specifically to Hercules himself. Of course, his twelfth labour had been to venture into the underworld to capture and bring back Cerberus, the fearsome and ferocious black three-headed hound that guarded Hades, a mission which he accomplished through a violent struggle, bringing the dog to Eurystheus who had set him the task in the first place and then returning the dog to the underworld, otherwise unharmed. It would have been no surprise if the god had not had a permanent aversion to dogs after these traumatic events, and if the chthonic associations of dogs in general made them particularly and especially antipathetic to the hero god's cult. As to the flies, explanations for their permanent exclusion are harder to fathom. We know that Hercules rid Oeta in central Greece of locusts and Erythraeans of vine flies or ips, thus gaining a reputation as an averter of insects and a protector of cattle, animals who are often pestered by insects. Alternatively, it has been suggested that rather than dogs and flies Pliny had meant to refer to dogflies, a particularly irritating insect that attacks cattle.

Founding Fathers

A she-wolf and a woodpecker feature significantly in the great Roman foundation myth concerning the twin brothers Romulus and Remus, as indeed does the process of augury by the examination of the flight of birds, something that will be considered in detail in the next chapter.

The story of Romulus and Remus began in the city of Alba Longa in the Alban Hills in the central Italian district of Latium, about 12 miles to the south-east of the site of Rome. The city was ruled by King Numitor who had two sons and a daughter called Rhea Silvia. Numitor had an ambitious and duplicitous younger brother called Amulius who sought to plot against him and indeed eventually deposed him from the throne of Alba Longa and slew his sons whom he saw as a potential danger to him. Rhea Silvia was allowed to live but was forced by her uncle to become a Vestal Virgin, thus to renounce her sexuality and dedicate her life to the service of the goddess Vesta as a virgin. Thus it was intended that through this she would remain forever barren and produce no heirs to threaten Amulius's power.

But this attempt to wipe out Numitor's line was inevitably thwarted by the actions of the gods; Mars sought out Rhea Silvia and sired two sons with her, the twin boys Romulus and Remus. As a result Amulius imprisoned Rhea Silvia and the twin babies were placed in a basket that was then thrown into the River Tiber, which was in flood at the time, and in which the infants were expected to drown. However, fortuitously, the basket floated to safety and the twins were found on the banks by a she-wolf, who suckled and nurtured them (Plate 86), and a woodpecker who brought them food. Both the wolf and the woodpecker were creatures sacred to Mars. Eventually the infants were discovered by the shepherd Faustulus, who took them home and, with his wife Acca Larentia, raised them to maturity.

As youths the brothers were headstrong and courageous but slightly out of control. Remus was arrested and brought before the exiled former king Numitor whose path he had crossed. Romulus rescued him and revealed their true identities to Numitor, that they were in fact his grandsons. Together the three led an army to Alba Longa and deposed the usurper Amulius, restoring Numitor to his rightful throne.

Subsequently the twins went off to found a city of their own on the site of Rome, a schism between the two brothers allegedly being brought about by disagreements over the precise siting of the settlement. Recourse to the ritual of augury to establish the will of the gods by examining the flight of birds in the area apparently favoured Romulus. He therefore founded his own fortified enclosure on the Palatine Hill, while Remus set up another enclosure in competition, possibly on the Aventine Hill. Remus was killed soon after this either by Romulus or by one of his underlings, possibly while trying to breach the defences of the Palatine enclosure. Romulus now became sole founder and ruler of the new city of Rome, named after him.

In this story the significance of the Tiber river and of wild creatures in the area cannot be overestimated. Were it not for those creatures, and of course the god Mars, we are led to understand that the two infants would have died. Mars played such a significant role in the founding of Rome, at least in the mythological founding narrative, that it is of no surprise that he was such a venerated deity within the army, leaving aside his warlike tendencies, highly regarded by emperors, and that he gave his name to the *Campus Martius* or Field of Mars where military training took place before the area became formally consumed within the growing city. Mars was also seen as the protector of cattle, the most significant and economically and religiously important creatures in Roman society, and with the vulture, eater of carrion on the battlefield.

What for many years was considered to be one of the most famous and iconic Roman works of art, referred to by ancient writers – the so-called Capitoline Wolf, which holds pride of place in the *Musei Capitolini* in Rome – keeps the myth of Romulus and Remus fresh in the minds of museum visitors today (Plate 87).[13] This magnificent large, cast bronze is of a she-wolf suckling the two lost infants. Yet this work is not necessarily all that it seems, and some visitors to the museum may not understand why the work is captioned as either being a pre-Roman Etruscan bronze statue of a wolf with the figures of Romulus and Remus added in the Renaissance period or a medieval bronze wolf with Renaissance additions. Scholarly opinion on the dating of this highly significant statue could not be more divided. This statue and the image it represents is an excellent example of how multi-layered in meaning classical reception can be. Mussolini was apparently particularly fond of the statue and had a number of copies made to be given as diplomatic gifts to several cities in the United States in the 1930s. The image is also reproduced in the form of the club badge on the football shirts of A.S. Roma. Interestingly the statue inspired the 2011 art installation 'Look at Me (New Capitoline Wolf)' by Polish artist Pawel Wocial whose take on the iconic work and its meaning helped open up new avenues of interpretation of the original work, in that its deconstruction as an iconic marker of a mythological archetype and its appearance in a different context brought into question its loss of power and context. If the original Capitoline wolf had become a symbol of submissiveness, of maternal care and responsibility, rather than of Roman martial power, then its clothing by Wocial, its adornment with jewellery, and its appearance in cosmetic make-up made it more a symbol of present day vanity and vacuity.

In the Latin sexual vocabulary there were many slang terms or euphemistic words that derived from the names of animals and perceived characteristics of certain animals. The equation of certain aspects of human sexuality with the animal world illustrated the acceptance of a certain fluidity in terms of delineating human and animal differences.[14] Less easy to understand, therefore, was the pejorative and slang use of the Latin word *lupa* – she wolf – to mean a low prostitute and *lupanar* – wolves' den – to mean a low class brothel. Used this way the word was figurative and suggested some kind of connection between the natural predatory nature of the wolf and of prostitutes, a kind of shared rapacity across species. In the same way *milua*, the feminine of *miluus*, a bird of prey or kite, was also used to denote another kind of prostitute. The festival of the *lupercalia* again derived and took its name from *lupus*, as we will see in the next chapter.

Finally, of interest here are the religious cult group known as the *Hirpi Sorani* – literally the wolves of Soranus – and their links to other wolf cults in pre-Roman and Roman central Italy.[15] The *Hirpi Sorani* had their origins in Faliscan culture, *hirpus* being the Faliscan word for wolf, but continued in existence into the Roman period when Soranus, largely an underworld deity, became equated with Roman religion in the form of Apollo Soranus. Their rites, initially practised annually at the site of Mount Soracte in the lower Tiber Valley, involved sacrifice, the handling of entrails, ,and fire-walking or fire-leaping as a purification ritual. The priests and attendees would not seem to have worn animal masks or skins, and the link with wolves may in fact have related to a cult foundation myth involving wolves plundering sacrificial meat and being chased away to caves on the mountain, caves that might have been thought to be gateways to the underworld through which the wolves entered and exited the world. The priests were wolves in name only, acting thus to purify their people, through direct action and metaphor.

The depiction of animals and birds in Roman art was quite often metaphorical in intent, reflecting the social and cultural mores of society, but this usage nevertheless suggested a society comfortable enough in its relationship with the natural world to embrace such concepts. Some of these images though were stereotypes, even if the stereotype itself often contained some degree of nuance or scintilla of difference. In the case of animal attributes these both described and classified the gods and informed or reminded the viewer of the qualities of individual deities. Some animals depicted on their own were probably in certain contexts intended to be mnemonic markers or signs that would stimulate the knowledgeable viewer to thoughts of the appropriate god or goddess for whom the beast was an attribute. For the less knowledgeable, in such circumstances it was simply an image without meaning beyond its primary physical form. In the case of apotropaic beasts, normally the most fearsome of Nature's or mythology's creatures, it was the qualities of the animals themselves that were being invoked. In the animal symbolism associated with Jesus the metaphors were going to be equally complex and were to relate to both the divine and the human, in the person of Christ, none more so than his image as the good shepherd (Plate 88).

That gods could have been thought to sometimes appear in the guise of animals, and possible reasons for such subterfuge, will be considered in a subsequent chapter, as indeed will be the question of how metamorphosis can be viewed as a conceptual opening up of inter species relationships rather than a closing door on the human condition. In the next chapter we will see how animal sacrifice was one of the central rites of the Roman state religion and also important in the private sphere.

7

Wise Blood

Blood Simple

Having previously discussed the inter-relationship between individual Roman gods and animals in terms of animals as metaphorical attributes, in this chapter attention will be turned to the use of animals in Roman sacrifice and to various other aspects of Roman religion, including augury, religious festivals, and funerary symbolism.

Sacrifice as a rite, a ritual act, gave the sacrificial animal a social meaning but one which reduced it to a victim or quite literally a piece of meat. Its intermediary role between men and gods was purely symbolic. However, it must also be remembered that the sacrifice in Roman times need not necessarily and always have been of an animal. Sacrifices of wheat and wine, what some have termed 'vegetarian sacrifices', also took place and were accorded a significance and importance of their own.

In Roman society the most common public sacrifices were of individual animals, with the sacrifice of cows or bulls being the highest status, because of the cost of the animals.[1] Sheep and pigs were the next most common sacrificial victims. Goats could also be sacrificed, as could chickens, and in the case of bird sacrifices to Isis their decapitated bodies were burned on the altar afterwards. There are also references to purification rituals involving piglets. Most prestigious of all though were the great public sacrifices known as the *suovetaurilia*, the triple sacrifice of a bull, a sheep, and a pig, which became firmly associated with the person of the emperor in Roman state religion. Each emperor's participation in the numerous and regular processions and sacrifices associated with the operation of the state religion provided them with a process by which they could regularly reassert their relationship with the Roman people through humble obeisance to the gods. Private sacrifices also took place but we know less about these because of their very intimate nature.

The importance of sacrifice as an imperial rite cannot be overstated. It was one of many ways to demonstrate the necessary qualities of an emperor's character – in this case *pietas,* or piety. It would seem that there was a strong narrative of sacrifice to which all emperors would be expected to more or less adhere. It has been suggested that the rite of sacrifice, which had its origins way back before the imperial age, was in fact hijacked by many emperors for their own ends and that in the process came to be simply a signifier of imperial authority and power when it appeared in the form of an image on imperial monuments. The origins and nature of that narrative will now be considered.

The sacrifice as a rite would have involved the selection of appropriate animals, their herding, a procession, followed by the act of killing itself. Butchery and disposal of the animal corpse and the eating of its meat would have followed the actual formal rite itself. Numerous images of scenes of imperial sacrifice have come down to us on imperial monuments throughout the empire, many of these scenes being quite generic. Mention has already been made in Chapter Five of the Hadrianic sacrifices on the *tondi* reused on the Arch of Constantine. Discussion here then will concentrate on sacrificial scenes on the *Ara Pacis Augustea* and the Arch of the Argentarii, both in Rome, as presenting good examples of the rites.

Of course the *Ara Pacis,* or Augustan Altar of Peace, dedicated in 9 BC, represented the first major public monument of the Roman imperial era and, as such, its artistic scheme has been endlessly analysed for clues as to how the ideological aspects of Augustus's political programme were reflected on it.[2] There were no direct references to war, victory and military might but rather an underlying theme of peace and stability pervaded, though even the most casual contemporary viewer would have been aware that the great, much-trumpeted Augustan peace had been brought about by the relentless pursuit of war. Harmony and peace were presented as contemporary realities, and family and lineage were put forward as part of a guarantee of stability and continuity set in train by Augustus. Here also, for the very first time, animal sacrifice was overtly presented as a religious duty for the pious Augustus and, by implication, for those emperors who followed him.

On the *Ara Pacis* altar itself, inside the precinct walls, is an image of a sacrificial procession, in a very different size and style to the wall friezes, with, in the main section, two cattle and a sheep being led to sacrifice accompanied by twelve bare chested *victimarii* who variously carry trays, a sacrificial knife, a club and a laurel branch (Plate 89). At the head of the procession is a priest and two attendants carrying rods. Other processing figures are also represented, including the Vestal Virgins. The inner walls of the surrounding precinct are decorated with carved sacrificial garlands, hung with *bucrania,* or ox skulls, just as real garlands and real ox skulls would have been used at the site of a sacrifice. While the very nature of the presentation of the sacrificial procession appears almost secondary to the processional scenes involving the new imperial family and their acolytes on the upper outer long walls, its ideological significance was intended to have been equally important.

The importance, indeed the lineage, of animal blood sacrifice was made very clear to the viewer of the monument by the placing of a frieze depicting Aeneas sacrificing to the *Penates*, the household gods of the Trojans, in a prominent place on the upper, outer wall of the precinct on its main facade. The older Aeneas, with draped head to indicate that he was carrying out a religious rite, is shown pouring a libation onto an altar. On the other side of the altar stands an attendant holding a tray bearing food offerings in one hand and a jug in the other. Behind him is another attendant leading a sow to the altar for sacrifice. The presence of this scene was intended to link Augustus and his family with the legendary Trojan forebear from whom he claimed descent and to establish a continuum in terms of obeisance to the gods and the importance of the rite of blood sacrifice. Contrasted with the Roma/Tellus frieze panel on the monument, on which a cow and sheep and other creatures sit at rest in harmony around the female deity or personification, in the sacrificial scenes on the altar itself and in the Aeneas panel we are presented with a jolting schism with Nature, which is put forward as a necessary corollary for peace in the Roman world. Through blood sacrifice, for which the viewer could assume a metaphor for war, peace could be achieved and maintained.

That Augustus had set a precedent to be followed in terms of making religious rites, and specifically animal sacrifice, an integral part of imperial ideology, responsibility and practice, can be seen by the present day visitor to the *Ara Pacis* museum. Here are displayed casts of fragments of two reliefs, known as the Della Valle – Medici slabs, from a Claudian altar, the *Ara Pietatis* to the *Ara Reditus Claudius*, dedicated following the triumphant return of the emperor Claudius after his successful invasion of Britain in AD 43. The originals are at Villa Medici in Rome. These slabs depict in one case a bull about to be sacrificed outside what is thought to be the Temple of Mars Ultor, the animal's head being held down ready for the stunning blow to be struck, and in the other a garlanded bull arriving outside what may be the Temple of the Magna Mater on the Palatine Hill with a *victimarius* and and a *popa*, or priest's assistant, holding an axe (Plate 90). Such imperial rites carried on for centuries in direct lineage from Augustus.

The Arch of the Argentarii, in the Forum Boarium, the old Roman cattle market, was dedicated in AD 204 to Septimius Severus and Julia Domna. On it can be found a number of pairs of small friezes, including ones depicting the herding of cattle and a sacrificial procession of a bull accompanied by a *victimarius* and a *popa* bearing an axe.[3] Pendant scenes show the sacrificial slaughter of the bull – the *immolatio boum*. Sacrificial implements appear on another frieze. The choice of the sacrifice of a bull in the imagery was probably quite deliberate and was made because of the locational siting of the arch in the great old cattle market, a busy, bustling and noisy hub of economic activity from early Roman times up until the area's function changed. However, the arch did have a second theme alongside sacrifice and its link to imperial ideology – that of triumph over barbarian enemies of Rome, in this case the Parthians who were defeated by Septimius Severus in the 190s AD and AD 203. This latter theme is pursued by images of victories and of Roman soldiers escorting bound male prisoners. Here again we are seeing the comparative use of images of prisoners/slaves and captive animals as we have seen used elsewhere.

It is remarkable how insistent the sacrificial imagery on this otherwise profane monument dedicated to a Roman emperor was. Even though it was to some extent a private monument, paid for and dedicated by a guild of silversmiths or the like, nevertheless it presented an imperial narrative in a public place and one that stressed the significance of sacrifice in Roman life in general, in political ideology in particular, and in this specific locality. Nearby stood the sacred precinct of Hercules. The writer Posidonius referred to banquets here as 'almost Herculean': 'Honeyed wine flows and the food consists of large loaves, boiled smoked-meat and roasted portions from the freshly sacrificed victims in abundance.'[4]

On both the *Ara Pacis* and the Arch of the Argentarii we have noted the presence of images of *bucrania,* or ox skulls. Such skulls represented the remains of previously sacrificed bulls or cattle, the skulls having been defleshed and the bone cleaned to allow the skulls to be used for decorative purposes in religious establishments or at religious rites, these relics of sacrificial beasts still being assigned some kind of remnant emotional currency and importance resulting from their previous use. Arising out of the use of actual cattle skulls these physical items also became transformed and commodified into artistic images, often connected by carved floral or drapery swags or garlands. Just as they had been common images in earlier Greek temple art, so these indeed became common tropes in Roman ideological art as signifiers of power, of imperial or military might. Some *bucrania* images even occurred as decoration on the outside of the Tomb of Caecilia Metella on the old Via Appia just outside Rome, one of the greatest surviving tomb monuments from the Republican period. On part of the entablature of the temple of Vespasian and Titus in the Roman Forum appeared a *bucranium*, with various sacrificial artefacts and paraphernalia, including an *aspergillum* or whisk for flicking liquid – wine or water – onto the sacrificial animal's head, a mallet for stunning it, an axe for the sacrificial kill, a knife for butchering the corpse, a wine jug, a patera and priest's headgear. They also appeared on other items such as altars and even cinerary urns.

These images of gruesome relics from animal sacrifices were much much later to become part of the language of Renaissance and later classical revival architecture, a form of classical reception which quite obviously had divorced origins from reality.

In the Roman religious calendar far more unusual was the sacrifice to Mars of what is known to ancient historians as the October Horse, a unique rite that took place annually on 15 October in the Campus Martius in Rome, following a meeting of ceremonial chariot racing.[5] This curious rite was described by a number of ancient authorities, including Polybius, Plutarch, Marcus Verrius Flaccus and Festus.[6] The right-hand horse of the pair of horses from the winning chariot racing team was selected for sacrifice by spearing and the slitting of its throat, rather than being dispatched with the usual mallet or sacrificial axe. Its head and tail were then cut off, the head to become a contested trophy between the neighbourhoods of Subura and Sacra Via and the bloody tail to be taken to the Regia in the Forum Romanum where horse blood was dripped on the altar. There is no indication that the beast's carcass was butchered and portioned for feasting, if we are to take Tacitus's comments about a Roman abhorrence of horseflesh as a universal truth.

The earliest reference to this curious event dates to the third century BC, while records show that it continued to take place as late as AD 354. The rite is thought to have been performed in thanks for a successful harvest, as represented by the loaves of bread that were used to garland the severed head of the sacrificial horse, though in most Roman agricultural or fertility rites a bullock would have been seen as the more appropriate animal sacrifice. Its origins though are not quite so clear. Perhaps it had been an early military or battlefield rite. The *equirria*, two other festivals dedicated to Mars, which took place on 27 February and 14 March, also involved chariot and horse racing, the March date marking the start of the military campaigning season, but no equine sacrifice took place on those particular occasions. In spring, on 21 April, at the *Parilia* festival, the Vestal Virgins are recorded as providing the blood of a horse, presumably again a sacrificial animal, to be mixed with the ashes of an unborn calf ripped from its mother's womb at the *Fordicidia* festival six days earlier. The resulting mix was then thrown into a fire of bean straw as a fumigant. Dog sacrifice also took place in early Roman times.

Festival Rites

Even when exotic animals were routinely transported to Rome for the games in the arena and the value of these creatures might have been considered greater than that of a domestic farm animal such as a bull, sheep, or pig, there is no record of such animals being considered as appropriate for sacrifice to the gods. It is likely that sacrifice was so closely linked to feasting that food animals were preferred.

There is evidence to suggest that certain religious organisations owned their own herds and flocks of animals for sacrifice. It would seem that animals from regular farms were divided up into functional categories quite soon after birth, with some being designated as food animals or for breeding stock, some being considered suitable for training up as a traction animal in the case of cattle, and some being considered appealingly suitable enough to be bred for eventual sacrifice.

In this veritable world of gods people were still required to adhere to the established rituals and traditions associated with both public worship and private rites. A religious calendar of festivals determined the very rhythm of the Roman year. Public ceremonies, often overseen by the emperor in his role as *Pontifex Maximus,* or chief priest, provided a forum for honouring the great gods, such as the Capitoline Triad, while private worship was more tied in to veneration of the household gods known as the *penates* or to the honouring of the *Genius,* or guardian spirit, of a particular place.

As we have seen, blood sacrifice lay at the heart of Roman public religion and of the state religion, along with the vow and the giving of other gifts to the gods. The question of regional variations in the importance of blood sacrifice, and chronological ones, must be borne in mind, though it cannot really be discussed at any length here. Worshippers would sponsor an animal sacrifice in order to ask the gods for help in some way, or to thank the gods for having received help, or simply to honour the god and prolong good fortune. Usually a cut of meat from the slaughtered animal or animals would be offered to the gods by burning it on an altar.

The rest of the meat would be retained for subsequent events. Very often the eating of the rest of the meat from sacrificed beasts in a formal feast would be part and parcel of an event, the cementing of the social fabric following the ritual.

There are numerous depictions of sacrifices in Roman art, which tell us something about the more formal aspects of the sacrificial ceremony (Plate 91). It has been suggested that depictions of the actual animal sacrifice taking place are rare, both in early times and in late Roman art, with the obvious exception of Mithraic art. A frieze of cupids slaughtering cattle from Pompeii is an anomalous depiction of what was otherwise quite rightly depicted as a sombre, serious rite (Plate 92). That the sacrifice on each occasion it took place had to be conducted in an appropriate manner to satisfy the gods is clear in the repetitious nature of so many of these images. Roman emperors were commonly portrayed at the sacrifice, this being seen as one of their most significant duties, and indeed images of imperial sacrifice to some extent came to represent the idea of duty rather than necessarily being an image simply of religious observance. It is difficult though to get to grips with the sheer number and scale of such events, given the regularity of religious dates in the Roman calendar.

The idea of animal sacrifice and the practical aspects of the rite itself at Rome constituted an amalgam of Greek and Etruscan influences, at times also intermixed with elements borrowed or bastardised from foreign cults such as those of Isis, Cybele, and, to a lesser extent, Mithras. As we are concentrating on the role of the animals used in sacrifice it is not really the place therefore to discuss the mechanics of the sacrificial rites here in full. Those of a delicate disposition are advised to skip the rest of the following paragraph.

We can only imagine the distress of the animals led in processions to the site of public sacrifices. Accompanied by distracting music to ward off any evil spirits that might have been present, the animals probably did not comprehend or at least were irritated by the preparatory consecration rituals. They would have been sprinkled with salted flour or wheat grains, according as to whether the 'Roman rite' or the 'Greek rite' of sacrifice was being followed on a particular occasion, and wine or water would have been poured on their heads. Larger sacrificial animals such as cattle would have been tethered with a restraint, as probably would have been any smaller, agitated sheep or pigs, prior to the animals being stunned with a blow from an axe or hammer, before their jugular veins were slit open with a knife. The dead creatures were then turned over to lie on their backs, and their stomachs were slit open to enable a *haruspex* to inspect their still warm intestines in order to confirm that the sacrifice had been conducted in an acceptable way for the overseeing deity or deities. If it was decided that something was not right with the sacrifice, another animal would then be required to be slaughtered, suggesting that understudy animals were usually kept waiting in the wings in case of just such a scenario. The role of the *haruspex* will be considered further below.

Once clearance had been gained from the *haruspex,* the animal was butchered and its meat divided up for a number of different purposes. Most commonly the entrails were cooked, cut up, sprinkled with salt and wine as the live beast had been, and then burned on the altar as the god's rightful portion. Variations on this basic rite involved the burying of the god's portion or casting it into water. The majority of the carcass was now formally deconsecrated by a gesture from the sacrificer and could then be cut up, cooked and eaten at a feast – or even sold at the market, in some cases.

Of great interest in this respect are the ninety-six detailed inscriptions, the *Acta Arvalia,* found in their sacred grove near Rome and forming records of the rituals, rites and sacrifices made by the religious college of priests known as the *Arvales Fratres,* the Arval Brethren or Brothers. This group of twelve priests was dedicated to the protection of fertility and abundance, and its origins as a body went back to the mytho-historical time of Romulus, if not before.[7] Although the college lost its standing and significance towards the end of the Republic, it received a much-needed boost through the patronage of Augustus and subsequent emperors such as Marcus Aurelius.

Given the college's link to Dea Dia and Ceres, female agricultural deities, animal sacrifice was deemed pre-eminent in its rites, often on a large scale, which helps put the wider significance of Roman animal sacrifice into a broader context. An inscription dating to AD 183 meticulously details the rationale and procedures of sacrifices of forty-nine animals:

> Under the consulship of Lucius Tutilius Pontianus Gentianus, on the sixth day before the Ides of February (the 8th), the magister Quintus Licinius Nepos sacrificed adult suovetaurilia, in order to begin the work of digging out a fig tree that had grown on the roof of the temple of dea Dia, and in order to repair the temple; he also sacrificed, close to the sanctuary, two female cattle to dea Dia, two rams to father Janus, two sheep with abundant wool to Jupiter, two rams with abundant wool to Mars, two ewes to the Juno of dea Dia; two ewes to the God-or-Goddess, two ewes to the divine Virgins, two sheep to the divine Servants, two sheep to the Lares, two ewes to the God-or-Goddess who protects this sacred grove and place, two sheep to Fons, two ewes to Flora, two ewes to Vesta, two ewes to mother Vesta; he also sacrificed two ewes to Adolenda Conmolanda Deferunda. Also (he sacrificed) before the Caesareum sixteen sheep to the sixteen divi.

Like the rites of the Arval Brethren, the origins of many of the religious festivals celebrated annually in Rome probably lay far back in the city's past and it is likely that though their full meaning might have been lost to many of the revellers on these occasions, they nevertheless continued to be celebrated almost in the manner of heritage folk events. Two of those festivals, the *Lupercalia* and the *Cerealia,* will now be considered briefly. The *Lupercalia* was celebrated each year on 14 February. On this occasion young men, mainly from the upper classes of Roman society, ran through the streets naked, striking watchers and bystanders with a goat-skin thong which hung from the end of a short stick. Many women in the crowds would openly and freely proffer their hands for striking in the hope that this action would somehow help them to become pregnant, particularly those who had already had problems in conceiving naturally. The significance of this event in the Roman calendar can be gauged from the fact that in 44 BC one of the naked running 'wolf men', the *Luperci,* was none other than Mark Antony. Sacrifice of goats and even dogs is recorded as being part of the rites of the early *Lupercalia.*

The *Cerealia* festival was held over seven days in mid to late April and, as the name implies, was dedicated to the celebration of Ceres, the goddess of grain, agricultural fertility and, by association, human fertility. Along with the sacrifice of pigs and piglets, one of the most bizarre elements of this celebration involved, according to the Roman poet Ovid in his *Fasti*,[8] live foxes being released into the Circus Maximus with burning torches tied to their tails; the poor creatures then suffering a terrible end by being burned to death as they publicly struggled to shake off the torches. White-clad young girls carrying torches would also re-enact the search for Ceres's abducted daughter Proserpina, who had been carried off by Hades to the underworld and raped and imprisoned there.

Every single festival in the Roman religious calendar, from the major *Saturnalia* to minor or niche events, would have involved animal sacrifice on some scale and feasting on sacrificial meat as part of the rites. For instance, Ovid noted that goats and hares were hunted in honour of the goddess Flora during her games each May.[9] Such pagan festivals were celebrated well into the late Roman period and in some cases into the formally Christian era; people would still take the opportunity to party on these occasions as if it was AD 99.

Early Roman human and dog sacrifice also needs to be discussed through an examination of another such ancient agricultural festival with its roots deep in the pre-Roman Italic past, the *Robigalia*. This religious festival, celebrated each year on 25 April, was held from the sixth century BC onwards and involved both sacrifice and games for young boys and adults. The festival was not held in Rome itself but outside, near the fifth milestone on the Via Claudia. According to Ovid's eyewitness account, the entrails of both a sacrificed dog and a sheep were burned, or rather offered on an altar, to help ward off mildew on the crops.[10] A number of other occasions for dog sacrifices are also attested, in one case involving the very specific requirement for the sacrificial dogs to have red coats.[11]

Excavation at the mid-fifth century AD infant cemetery at a villa at Poggio Gramignano, Lugnano-in-Teverina, Umbria in Italy, has revealed a most curious pattern of dog burial alongside the children buried there.[12] Four immature dog pups, of around five months of age, were interred near and among the infant graves. One of these four dogs had been decapitated and cut in half across its middle, being then buried in two holes some distance apart. More fragmentary remains of at least a further eight dogs were also found at the site, most of these again being immature creatures, and some displaying signs of decapitation and post-mortem butchery.

The excavators sought specific meaning in the dog sacrifices made at the site and suggested these were linked to the chthonic deity Hecate, a shadowy figure associated with boundaries, entrance-ways, the dead, particularly deceased children, and so on, and often accompanied by dogs, her attribute animal, as has already been noted above in Chapter Six. Sacrifice of dogs to Hecate was once an accepted practice, but by this time might not have been expected to have still been carried out. Dogs, and young dogs in particular, were thought to have potent powers, often associated with healing the sick or attending birthing mothers, and with purification, in some cultures. If the population of the Poggio villa had been affected by some rampant outbreak of disease, leading to sudden mass deaths there, particularly among the more vulnerable infants at the villa, then animal sacrifices to Hecate undertaken according to old traditions involving beheading, severing, and burial of young dogs, might have been viewed as not only protecting the recent dead but also the survivors at the site who might have needed to seek divine protection for themselves against the uncontrolled spread and circulation of disease, possibly malaria. What would appear to have been recourse to magic solutions to concrete problems was also reflected in a number of other indicators at the site, including the burial of an upside-down pottery cooking vessel, the presence in one child's grave of part of a bone doll, and the burial of a raven's claw.

The partial bone doll from one burial here, represented by just the head and torso, may have been a marker of the rite of passage into adulthood missed by the prematurely deceased girl buried with it, if it did not represent an artefact associated with magic practice. In support of the latter explanation reference can be made to a *kline,* daybed, funerary monument in the J. Paul Getty Museum in Malibu, California, which is in the form of a reclining girl, the deceased, petting her small dog. Two toy dolls lie against the backrest of the couch on which she lies. The hairstyle of the girl suggests the monument dates to the Hadrianic period, *c.* AD 120–140. The juxtaposition here of doll and dogs in a funerary context is of great interest too. The question then arises as to whether these dolls were toys or whether, like the Poggio Gramignano doll, they were somehow more complex in their meaning. Play and ritual need not be mutually exclusive in any particular society and it is now widely recognised that dolls in some contexts can help in establishing value systems and in constructing individual or group identities. The excavators of Poggio have suggested that the villa owners, or whoever was responsible for burying the infant children there, at a time of great crisis, sought some kind of solace in old rural pagan rituals rather than in the dominant Christianity of the time.

It might be thought that animal sacrifice played a highly significant role in the practice of Mithraism, an eastern mystery cult exclusively for men that once established in the west became highly popular among aristocratic Romans, senior military officers and bureaucrats in Rome, Italy and across the western empire.[13] However, it has been suggested that the central importance of the so-called bull slaying scene in Mithraic iconography was not reflected in the direct archaeological evidence that we have for the actual practice of the religion. It would seem more likely that ritual meals, of 'roosters, piglets, fish, and lamb, with a low occurrence of cattle bones', were eaten inside the generally small Mithraic temples. The depiction of the slaying of bulls would appear to have been both metaphorical and, at the same time, symbolic of the power of the god over life and death, over creation and destruction, while offering salvation to the adherents of the cult, through these not necessarily diametrically opposed forces.

Animal blood sacrifice and human blood sacrifice were metaphorically linked in the case of some sources describing the politically motivated murder of Tiberius Gracchus in 133 BC. For Christians, sacrifice became a totally metaphorical notion. From the reign of Constantine onwards, Christian intolerance of the idea and actuality of blood sacrifice was ramped up to almost obsessive levels and the practice was equated with madness and superstition. But animal blood sacrifice had, in any case, probably peaked in the Severan era, long before overt Christian protests against the practice. Certainly a quite dramatic fall-off in the number of depictions of animal sacrifices in Roman art from that time onwards, and a concentration on depicting scenes of what might be called vegetarian sacrifice through plant food offerings and poured libations of wine, can be ascertained. It might be that the ideology of sacrifice, and likewise its depiction, had changed. It might be that the public and private depiction of animals sacrificed or of their actual sacrifice was no longer generally acceptable.[14]

Funerary Contexts

Certain animals were commonly associated with funerary contexts in the Roman world, either appearing as images on funerary monuments, as images on items buried with an individual, or in the form of animals buried in graves, either alone or accompanying a human burial. These motifs used to be thought of as having been exclusively signifiers of belief in an afterlife but now they are generally considered to be appropriate to both the funerary context and to the reflexive commemoration of the deceased in terms of reflecting his or her status. We have already considered the symbolic value of dolphin motifs in Roman funerary art and the burial of beloved pets in earlier parts of the book. Images of pet dogs, however, could also simply have been images of fidelity, as could images of other pets in such contexts. Reference has also been made to the role of images of certain apotropaic or protective beasts guarding a tomb or grave, such creatures including lions, dogs, griffons, and sphinxes. Animals associated with the underworld were also commonly portrayed and in this category can be included dogs again, as well as cocks and chickens. Small birds catching insects, grubs or even lizards occurred as images on first and early second century AD ash chests, and birds drinking from a *cantharus* was also a popular motif, representing the soul in flight or simply acting as decoration to enhance the images of garlands that they regularly appeared with. Images of nesting birds feeding their young might have alluded to the piety of the deceased towards their children and family.

A relatively common motif in Roman sculpture was the figure of a sleeping child, sometimes in the form of a winged Eros, sometimes with attributes depicted as markers of identity. Many of these statues might have been set up as funerary monuments, particularly those that featured a lizard as an attribute. The lizard was often an attribute of certain gods or underworld figures, such as Sabazios and Mithras, while it was also seen as a symbol of hibernation and resurrection, of sleep and death, thus making it an altogether appropriate creature in a funerary context. In the art of Egypt and Greece the lizard was often used as a symbol of power and a portent of pending crisis or emergency. It has been suggested that a lizard in some Roman funerary contexts could have represented a pet kept by the now-dead child in life. This might have been so in one or two instances perhaps, but I find it highly unlikely as an explanation across the board for this common trope.

Ash chests, cinerary urns, and altars, popular in the Republican and early imperial period, gave way to stone sarcophagi, which provided an altogether larger field for decorative statements and sometimes decorative excess. With this change, a move away from emblematic imagery to a preponderance of mythological narration and expression occurred, introducing many common themes that included the depiction of animals: the Indian Triumph of Bacchus, other types of Bacchic scenes, chariot racing, hunt scenes such as the pursuit by Meleager of the Calydonian Boar, the Labours of Hercules, and so on.

Reference has already been made in Chapter Five above to the enormous popularity of chariot racing and to the popular accolades paid to the principal racing teams, to individual drivers and even to the best or most popular horses in the chariot teams. It is easy to see how racing could have been employed as a metaphor for a race through life towards death, and how fortune, victory, success, fate, luck and bad luck in racing could easily be transposed by individuals by association to allegorically identify themselves with the sport. This would account for the quite common occurrence of chariot racing images, motifs or allusions in Roman funerary art.[15]

Chariot racers were also commemorated, in the case of the most celebrated drivers, with impressive monuments. One example is that of the charioteer Publius Aelius Gutta Calpurnianus, a funerary inscription to whom was found on the Via Flaminia, just outside the Porta Flaminia in Rome where the remains of a grand decorated tomb were found that logic dictates must probably have been his. The front of the tomb was decorated with large reliefs depicting three chariot teams, each of four horses, racing. It is possible that a free-standing statuary group of Calpurnianus and his horses and chariot could have been set on top of the tomb. The tomb was subsequently demolished and parts of it became incorporated into the fabric of the Porta Flaminia gate itself.

A rather different explanation needs to be offered for the racing scene at the bottom of the grave altar of Titus Flavius Abascantus, a significant imperial freedman who had served as clerk of the courts in the late first century AD. The altar is now in the collections of the *Museo Lapidario* in Palazzo Ducale, Urbino, Le Marche. While a reclining figure at the top of the altar represents Abascantus himself, appearing with a winged figure with a torch and a child slave crowning him with a wreath, as the lengthy inscription makes clear the charioteer depicted with the victor's wreath and palm branch at the base is none other than the famous *miliarius,* thousand plus race winner, Flavius Scorpus in his chariot pulled by his team of four horses, also named in the inscription on the altar, *Ingenuus, Admetus, Passerinus* and *Atmetus.* Either Abascantus and Scorpus were somehow related or perhaps friends, both of which are unlikely, or Abascantus had been some sort of obsessive fan who wished to be associated with Scorpus in death, or Scorpus's image represented in its association with achievement and heroic exploits something that provided solace or even salvation to Abascantus or his wife and heirs who had set up this altar in his memory.

Images of chariot racing were also common on Roman children's sarcophagi, with cupids or *putti* taking on the roles of the human charioteers. Such images both testify to the sheer popularity of the sport across all age groups in Rome, and indeed across all social classes, and the sheer power of the racing metaphor in the Roman imagination.

Animal figures, in terracotta or metal, and pottery and glass vessels decorated with animal motifs such as hunt or chase scenes, were common grave-goods throughout the Roman empire. Interestingly, there would appear to have been a minor trend for some late Roman infant burials in Roman Britain to be accompanied by images of bears, what one scholar has called nurturing bears, on coin reverses or in the form of carved jet figures.[16] These are thought to have offered the deceased child motherly and physical protection on its journey to the underworld.

Augury and Divination

Like blood sacrifice, divination was another religious practice in which animals could play an intermediary role between humans and the gods. In addition to more organised religious practices, there was also a considerable folk religion that, to all intents and purposes, constituted a body of superstitions – yet which too became bound into the cultural and political fabric of Roman life and which flourished and gained power through its institutionalisation. Very serious attention was paid to the pronouncements of augurs who would determine good or bad omens from observing the song, and particularly the flight, of birds and, to a much lesser extent, unusual behaviour of certain mammals such as horses, or *haruspices* who would examine the entrails and livers of sacrificial birds and animals for signs. Such divination linked to animals again gives a lie to the idea that Roman religion was divorced from the natural world around.

Roman augury[17] would appear to have had its direct origins in Etruscan and early Italic societies, possibly influenced by Greek practices, if we are to believe Pliny the Elder's attribution of the invention of augury to Tiresias of Thebes, though earlier instances of prophecy linked to avian behaviour patterns are attested in Egypt and a number of other places. In *Antigone* by Sophocles the seer Tiresias carries out a sacrifice, and observes unusual bird behaviour, the failure of both of which he puts down to the poisoning of the food-chain by the carrion carried off by birds from the unburied, rotting, and putrid corpse of Polynices, something he blames on King Creon. This constitutes a remarkable tale of ecological consequences and the potential for the disruption of the political world by ripples or ructions in the natural world, something of which both the Greeks and Romans were evidently aware.

The significance of the practice of augury to the Romans is underlined by the centrality of augury in the mythico-historical account of the founding of Rome when Romulus and Remus resorted to the observation of the presence and flight of birds in order to choose either the Palatine Hill or the Aventine Hill for their defensible enclosure there. Romulus spotted twelve birds and Remus six, thus suggesting that the Palatine Hill represented the most propitious site, though Remus refused to acknowledge this result and broke with his brother at this point.

The role of the *augures*, the state's own augurs formed into a *collegium* or college, became enshrined in Roman civic and military life, though it must also be remembered that day to day superstitions among the plebeian classes and country dwellers existed outside this more formal system. While an augur could pronounce on the signs they had observed, it was officially up to a Roman magistrate to decide on a course of action related to the interpreted omens.

Sometimes public portents in ancient Rome were read by observing the behaviour of sacred chickens, which were bred and kept for this very purpose and overseen by an appointed official called a *pullarius*. There were different kinds of omens to be read from them feeding, or from their lack of appetite, and from their general mood and behaviour. A highly-decorated altar known as the Vicus Sandalarius Altar, dedicated to the *Lares Augusti* by the *vicomagistri* of the Vicus Sandalarius in Rome, and which is now in the Uffizi Gallery in Florence, on one face carries a depiction of Augustus acting as an augur, holding the *lituus,* or curved augury wand, in one hand while one of the sacred chickens pecks around on the ground at his feet. To one side of Augustus stands Gaius and on the other side is Livia, holding a patera for a libation.

Cicero makes us aware of a remarkable true or apocryphal incident that occurred during the First Punic War, at the Battle of Drepana in 249 BC. The Roman commander Publius Claudius Pulcher was said to have tired of the sacred chickens carried in cages on board his ship refusing to eat. He had them thrown overboard, with the words 'if they would not eat, then let them drink'. Such arrogant behaviour was, of course, blamed for the Roman defeat in battle that was to follow.[18]

The role of the *haruspices* has already been mentioned in relation to their role in examining and reading the entrails of sacrificed animals. The opportunity will be taken here to look at the history of the practice, the rationale for its widespread use in Roman rituals, and the mechanics of its application in practice.[19] Despite there being some evidence for a formal system of Roman haruspicy quite early on, derived from the Etruscans in all probability, unlike the *augurs*, the *haruspices* did not belong to a formal college of the craft's practioners until the late Republic. To some accusers their practices were tinged with un-Roman elements that left them open to question.

The famous Etruscan bronze Liver of Piacenza is both part of a map of a body and a map of the heavens.[20] It helps provide remarkable insights into the ideas that probably helped shape and form Roman divination and, at the same time, adds information about the practicalities of its practice. This life-size model of a sheep's liver, found near Gossolengo in Piacenza province in the nineteenth century and now in the *Museo Civico* in the Palazzo Farnese in Piacenza, probably dates to the late second to early first century BC. The liver is flat, with three protuberances that correspond to the gall bladder, the portal vein (posterior vena cava), and the caudate lobe, and is inscribed on its upper surface – the visceral side of the liver. A small amount of writing is also etched on the underside of the liver. The upper surface is divided by incised lines into sixteen areas or zones, each of which bears an Etruscan god's name, or sometimes names, and each zone is further sub-divided and labelled, giving forty individually annotated units. The sixteen main zones probably corresponded to the sixteen zones of the heavens as defined by the Etruscans, each the home of particular deities. Thus observations of areas of disease, discolouration or enlargement taken on the warm, probably still throbbing, liver of a dead sheep would be viewed within this preordained grid system and then transposed onto a grid of the skies and interpreted in cosmic terms for their relevance to contemporary life and events.

It is possible that the Piacenza Liver could have been a teaching aid of some sort, used in the training of divinators or as an aide memoire for a trained operative. It is also possible the object was actually used on the spot during an examination of a sacrificed beast's organ as a reference tool. In whichever of these scenarios it was used, its very existence tells us that the system of divination, no matter how much hocus pocus we might think was attached to the practice, was formally codified and when readings were given on the spot these were somehow informed by a system of knowledge, however flawed or arcane. While the Liver of Piacenza is a unique object, a similar item is in fact represented being held in the hand of a reclining man, probably himself a *haruspex*, adorning the lid of a second-century BC alabaster cinerary urn from the Etruscan necropolis at Volterra, and now in the *Museo Etrusco Guarnacci* there. This suggests such models were perhaps commonly in use among the ritual groups performing divination in Etruscan society and maybe subsequently Romanised versions of these models were produced and used. Other depictions of *haruspices* are known. A relief from Rome, now in the *Musée du Louvre* in Paris, is almost unique in carrying a depiction of the immediate aftermath of the poleaxing of an oxen at a sacrificial ceremony. The beast lies on the ground, turned on its back while a man leans over it, presumably to open up its stomach with a knife to allow its entrails and organs to be inspected by a *haruspex*, who stands by to one side. At Ostia, a mid-first-century BC votive relief to the hero god Hercules was dedicated by the *haruspex* Caius Fulvius Salvis.

Magic

Animals or their body parts also sometimes featured in rites connected to Roman popular superstition, magic and folk medicine, as in many cultures.[21] For instance, certain magical texts tell us that lizards, often seen as creatures connected with omens and portents, were burned over a fire as part of a love ritual in both Greek and Roman magic. Pliny in his *Naturalis Historia* lists many animals or animal parts that could be used beneficially or in a malign way, as indeed he does for plants. He notes the supposed efficacy of many odd eaten cures such as snake's heart, mice, live snails in vinegar, roasted ferret and so on. He tells of dozens of cures that could be achieved by the use of hyena body parts and even, in a few cases, its urine or faeces.[22] Numerous other strange cures involving animals can be found in other writers' works. Puppies, associated with Hecate, could be sacrificed and their bodies used in conjunction with binding spells, as one example written on lead curse tablets from Gaul demonstrates. The evolution of the complex lore that led to the codification of boar's semen being a cure for ear-ache (collected during mating as it comes out of the sow and before it hits the ground) and other such arcane cures and curses must be considered to have taken place over centuries.

Animal figurines or images may sometimes have been used in binding spells and rituals: a horse inscribed with names may have been a curse against a particular charioteer and his horses. Indeed, at Antioch a cache of nine horse figurines has been found, each inscribed with a human and animal name, and each probably linked to an act of malign magic.

In the vast rural tracts of the Roman and Italian countryside agricultural magic would also have been commonly practiced. We have already seen how pet animals may have been presented by their doting owners at healing shrines to seek a cure for their illness, and indeed how at many shrines valuable agricultural animals may also have been regularly presented to the gods for curing through economic necessity and crisis.

Among the remarkable and fascinating finds from the site of the Fountain of Anna Perenna at Piazza Euclide in northern Rome, discovered relatively recently in 1999, are some items suggesting links between animals and superstition even as late as the fourth century AD, though activity at the site started much earlier.[23] In the cistern of the fountain were found numerous coins, many oil lamps, pine cones and egg shells, a bronze cauldron, a group of *defixiones* or curse tablets in lead or copper alloy, and sealed cylindrical containers associated with malign magical practices in the latest phase of activity there. Eighteen of these containers were made of lead and three of terracotta with lead lids. Six of these containers housed crude human figures, known as poppets, crafted from organic materials, which detailed scientific analysis has shown to include 'wax, flour, sugars, herbs and liquid substances such as milk'. X-rays showed that each poppet was formed around a small piece or sliver of animal bone; over time, as the organic material partially decayed, two of these central bones had fallen out of their respective poppets to allow the archaeologists to discover that each bone was inscribed. Thus the person represented by the poppet was both contained or trapped and at the same time cursed. Presumably the pieces of bone used in the construction of the poppets had their own individual emotional currency and may have been imbued with particular significance for this role by coming from a specially sacrificed animal. Where images were drawn on the curse tablets or cylinders, these too sometimes were of animalistic daemons or gods – a writhing fanged snake, a cock-headed deity, and a birdman.

While public sacrifice has been discussed at length, as has sacrifice as part of the practice of various religious sects in the Roman world, sacrifice would also have taken place in private contexts, sometimes as part of magic rituals. For instance, a Gallic puppy sacrifice is referenced on two later second century AD lead tablets from a burial in Aquitaine, between Villepouge and Chagnon in France.[24]

> I denounce the persons written below, Lentinus and Tasgillus, in order that they may depart from here for Pluto and Persephone. Just as this puppy harmed no one, so (may they harm no one) and may they not be able to win this suit; just as the mother of this puppy cannot defend it, so may their lawyers be unable to defend them, (and) so (may) those (legal) opponents be turned back from this suit; just as this puppy is (turned) on its back and is unable to rise, so neither (may) they; they are pierced through, just as this is; just as in this tomb animals/souls have been transformed/silenced and cannot rise up, and they (can) not...

Along the same lines, of particular interest here is the idea of *voces magicae*, voices in which magical incantations or spells could be uttered during a ritual. It is known from a number of magical papyri and *tabellae defixionis* that in some contexts it might have been thought appropriate to imitate or spell out onomatopoeically the sounds and vocalisations of particular animals, imbuing animal calls with a communicative value that transcended the natural world and thus which created or channelled power through its very mystery and otherness.

Condemnation and Indifference

Just as there was no coherent, extended condemnatory tract against the cruelty of animal spectacles in the Roman arena, so it was also the case with animal sacrifice, though it can be suggested that from the early Hellenistic period up to the fourth and fifth centuries there were many individual intellectuals and philosophers opposed to the practice of blood sacrifice. The anti-blood sacrifice stances of the

Greeks Aristotle and Theophrastus can be found echoing through the writings of Porphyry many hundreds of years later.[25]

The Christian, and indeed Jewish, view of the relationship between man and animals can be found in the creation stories in Genesis in the Bible. Man is placed at the apex of the natural world and, after the Flood, is granted permission to eat the flesh of animals. In the New Testament much is made of the opportunity to utilise various creatures of the natural world in metaphors and allegories that reflected both human and animal relationships and Christian relationships with God, mediated through the person of Jesus or his disciples: fishermen as fishers of souls; shepherds looking after flocks, that is Christians; Jesus as the good shepherd or as the lamb of God; and so on. Christian and Jewish opposition to animal sacrifice was in reality opposition to pagan practice and not an opposition necessarily always based on sympathy for animals. It was to all intents and purposes a cultural rather than a moral opposition.

Against Nature

To Be a Man

In this chapter an examination will be made of the idea of human and animal transformation or metamorphosis, and the concept of Nature and the natural world as filtered through the Roman male gaze and male experience, and how this may have impacted on various manifestations of apparent cruelty to animals. This is not to neglect female experience but rather to investigate how hyper-masculine display through the exercise and manipulation of power at various levels within Roman society often involved a synchronic (male) human/animal identification.

We will also examine what appears to have been a deep-seated need to conjure forth monsters and mutations that both reflected a fear of certain aspects of the wildness of Nature and yet, at the same time, also an admiration for vital animal qualities which might have been seen as lacking in contemporary society and its citizens. In Roman society fear and the monster fed off each other in a way that was not mutually exclusive. This occurred on many levels: the wild beast was simultaneously a dangerous animal, a (sexual) predator, and an annoyance because it defied easy and permanent categorisation, slipping from one role to another easily and regularly. Truly threatening, sinister and cunning, all at the same time, yet fear of such a beast could be almost immediately dispelled by its containment, confinement and taming, by being framed as an image or metaphor.

Violence of certain kinds blurred any distinction between animals and humans and to a certain extent accounted for the equation of human violence with bestial violence in the works of so many Greek poets, writers, and dramatists from Homer and Aeschylus onwards into Roman times. But animal images do not always necessarily mean something: we have only to think about the ubiquity of cat images on the internet today, which ultimately symbolise absolutely nothing, yet represent a genuine contemporary pop-cultural phenomenon. We can start this discussion by considering the rebus – an image with hidden meaning, beginning with the Roman imperial eagle and other imperial attribute birds.

The Roman imperial eagle, equating the male emperor with Jupiter, the greatest and most powerful of the gods, came to symbolise the power and authority of the emperor and of the Roman army; indeed, it had been a military emblem, one of a number of legionary animal symbols, before its usurpation as an exclusively imperial indicator. In many ways the Roman eagle served the same purpose as the Chinese imperial horse, dragon or lion, although its connotations were largely confined to symbolising individual male power and strength or dynastic power through the male blood line or through the Roman system of imperial adoption of male heirs.

The mythical phoenix came to be used as a symbol embodying Roman imperial power, its death, regeneration, and rebirth highly suitable as a metaphor for imperial deification and dynasty, particularly from the reign of Hadrian onwards. Later, it also suited Christian ideas of resurrection. The stork too became a bird occasionally linked to the person of the emperor and to some of the legions. To the Romans it would appear that the stork represented exceptional filial piety by reason of its natural instinct to return to the same nest year after year, and the bird thus became associated with the Roman concept of *pietas*, a quality associated in the Republican period with men in public office and in the imperial period almost exclusively with the person of the emperor. Early examples of the phenomenon and its propagandistic value can be seen on the 77 BC coin issue of Metullus Pius where the bird appears next to the personified figure of *Pietas* and on Mark Antony's issues of 41 BC where a stork accompanies the legend *Pietas*. The doubling up of bird image and legend was still appearing much later, on some of the coins of Gallienus, for example. Prominent and probably allusive images of storks also appeared on two of the silver cups from the magnificent Boscoreale Treasure, probably buried in AD 79 at the time of the eruption of nearby Mount Vesuvius. In one case the storks are feeding their young with crabs and snakes and in the other driving away an intruder. On a pair of gladiator's greaves from Pompeii an image appears of storks attacking snakes. Most significantly, the fourth century AD *Cataloghi Regionari* or Regionary Catalogues of Rome record a monument, or possibly two monuments, known as the *ciconiae nixae*, presumably a statuary group of storks set up in the Campus Martius. This could have been associated with an altar to *Pietas* dedicated by the emperor Hadrian to his deified wife Sabina who died in AD 136.

Another type of animal statue associated almost exclusively with aristocratic men and emperors in Roman times was the equestrian statue. The Romans were not particularly famed as horsemen or horsewomen and it is therefore of great interest to consider the information that can be gleaned from a consideration of equestrian or rider statues from Rome and more widely in the empire (Image 93).[1]

However, it is known that an equestrian statue of the semi-legendary heroine Cloelia once stood at the top of the Via Sacra. Cloelia, a Vestal Virgin, the College of the Vestals being highly significant in maintaining ancient Roman historic religious rites and tradition, was linked to Rome's semi-mythic deep past. The one-time existence of the equestrian statue of Cloelia, verified by ancient sources, is of particular interest, given that equestrian statues in the Roman world were otherwise almost exclusively associated with male subjects. As part of the peace treaty that ended the war between Rome and Clusium in 508 BC male and female hostages were handed over to Lars Porsenna by the Romans. An escape of the Roman women hostages was led by Cloelia, who was said to have bravely crossed the seething River Tiber on horseback on her way back to the city. However, the Romans were forced to comply with the terms of the treaty and returned her to Porsenna. He allowed her to pick other hostages to be freed in recognition of her courage and, in keeping with her patriotism, she chose young male hostages who could eventually mature to fight for Rome in the future. She was eventually freed herself and came back to Rome where her exploits were honoured with the dedication of the equestrian statue.

In the course of the first century BC the equestrian male statue type became most associated with the Roman senatorial class and their need to enhance their status through propagandistic grand gestures such as this, eventually to become the sole preserve of the imperial family, beginning with a series of equestrian statues of Augustus, as depicted on coins. In excess of 200 equestrian statues are recorded by historical and literary sources in the classical world, while the *Cataloghi Regionari* record the presence of twenty-two imperial equestrian statues in Rome itself, some of which are referred to as being '*equi magni*', presumably a reference to their larger than life-size. Perhaps the most significant imperial equestrian statue to have survived is that of Marcus Aurelius, which stood for many years in the centre of the Campidoglio in Rome before being brought inside the *Musei Capitolini*. Equestrian statues can be expected to have been present in many, or even most, of the cities and towns of Roman Italy at this time.

If much imperial iconography had its origins in the Augustan court, perhaps an exception can be claimed for the imperial equestrian statue or image, even though the cult of Alexander the Great, and thus Bucephalus, fed into image creation at this time. The horse became an almost symbolic companion of the subsequent emperors, probably starting with Domitian, in what has been called the theology of victory. Under Constantine and his successor emperors this whole system and process became Christianised. Constantine in stages rode the horses of the *cursus publicus* from Nicomedia to York in Britain to escape from Galerius. He had the mounts killed as he went to prevent, hinder or delay pursuit. Proclaimed emperor in York, the blood sacrifice of these horses took on an almost divine aspect. Victory at the Battle of the Milvian Bridge tellingly came as Maxentius perished with his horse, another equine pseudo-sacrifice. Fittingly it was thought, an equestrian statue of Constantine was set up in the Forum Romanum in AD 334.

That is not to say that no equestrian statues of Augustus existed. A large fragment of an equestrian statue of the emperor, including the head and upper body and part of one leg is in the National Archaeological Museum in Athens. A more recent find in 2009 of a wonderful gilded bronze horse's head and a rider's foot from a well at a site near Waldgirmes, Hesse, central Germany, has been assigned an Augustan date by the excavators on stratigraphic and stylistic grounds but the absence of any of the rider's face or head urges great caution in identifying the emperor it portrayed.

Some art historians have seen the influence of depictions of the Thracian rider god on the development of relief images of cavalry soldiers in the Roman army and possibly also of certain mounted emperors. *Reitertyp* military tombstones of the first and second centuries AD, as they are known, may well have had their origins in the Thracian east and became a popular way for auxiliary soldiers to commemorate themselves or for their fellow soldiers to commemorate a fallen comrade. The closest imperial parallel stylistically is a relief of the emperor Trajan on horseback trampling enemies, which was originally conceived as part of the rolling narrative of the Great Trajanic Frieze which probably stood at the north end of Trajan's Forum. By the early fourth century the frieze had been taken down for some reason and probably placed in storage. From there the panel containing this scene was selected for reuse in the Arch of Constantine.

Thus the image of the rider came to be associated with men in Rome and Italy, initially mostly aristocratic men and later almost exclusively emperors, often in the form of hyper-masculine imagery. One wonders how some viewers would have dealt with depictions of the female rider deity Epona, so popular in Gaul and some other parts of the western empire.

In bringing this discussion of horse riding to a close it is worth briefly noting the existence of a minor image on the frieze around Trajan's Column in Rome, showing a messenger falling off a donkey. This scene must have been intended as humorous, and indeed represents the only moment of light relief on a monument otherwise concerned with celebrating the exercise of Roman military might and of Trajan's conquest of Dacia.

Hyper-Masculinity and Nature

There was no more hyper-masculine role for the Roman, Italian, or provincial male than to serve in the Roman army. Subsuming his individuality within a corporate whole he would have become defined by his uniform and equipment, by the very vocabulary and grammar of the official language of command, by the signs and symbols by which each cohort or legion identified itself and by universal military symbolism that represented the army as a whole and situated its position in the broader Roman world. Many Roman military insignia were representations of animals. Originally each unit would have a standard with either an eagle, a wolf, a Minotaur, a horse, or a boar. The eagle later became an exclusively legionary symbol. Some of the other animal symbols either fell out of use or were replaced or used alongside signs of the zodiac, which of course also included some animal images such as the goat for Capricorn.

Along the Antonine Wall in Scotland, the short-lived, most northerly of the Roman empire's frontiers, a series of large inscribed and sometimes decorated marker stones was set up to record the building works of each legion that helped in the construction of the wall and its forts. Known as legionary distance slabs, together these constitute a unique record of Roman military endeavour and building and engineering skills. They also can tell us a great deal about military pride and the forging of military identities among the soldiers, and about competition between different army units, as exemplified by the use of unit names in inscriptions and unit symbols for decoration. The Second Legion was represented by a Capricorn and a winged horse, or Pegasus, and the Twentieth Legion by a wild boar, sometimes shown in juxtaposition with a tree. For some unknown reason, the Sixth Legion did not use an animal symbol on its slabs here, though on monuments elsewhere it used a bull.

All army standard bearers wore animal skins over the top of their otherwise standard uniforms. To some this must have summoned up thoughts of the lion-pelt-wearing hyper-masculine hero god Hercules, whose image appears so often in Roman military contexts, although it was not as common as images of Mars, the Roman god of war.

The hero god Hercules was sent by Apollo to serve King Eurystheus of Mycenae who assigned him twelve labours or tasks to free himself of his all-consuming guilt after killing his wife and children when sent temporarily mad by the vengeful goddess Juno (Hera). Many of these labours involved fearsome animals and tell us something about both the fear and admiration of the exotic and unusual in the Greco-Roman psyche. It is those particular labours that will be discussed here. Depictions of the twelve labours together, or of individual labours, were hugely popular subjects in classical art, as was the retelling and embellishing of the myth in classical literature.

The first labour involved the slaying of the Nemean Lion. Subsequently Hercules was to wear the protective pelt of this great beast which became, like his club, one of his trademark attributes. Next, he killed the many-headed Lernaean Hydra, a hideous creature created by Juno to thwart the hero god. In his next task Hercules was up against a less fearsome creature. The Ceryneian Hind possessed extraordinary speed, including the ability to even outrun arrows, and in setting the task it had been assumed that it would therefore be impossible to catch. After a year of pursuit throughout Greece Hercules captured the hind and took it back to Eurystheus who wished to add it to his menagerie. However, Hercules had promised Diana (Artemis) that the stag would eventually be set free and tricked the king into allowing the hind to escape before it could be locked up in a cage or secure enclosure. Hercules was then despatched to capture the legendarily savage Erymanthian Boar alive, according to the rules of the fourth labour, and Hercules, following advice, achieved this by driving the boar into a deep snowdrift where he was able to subdue and bind the trapped beast. When he brought the trussed boar to Eurystheus the king found it so uncontrollable that he decided to give it its freedom.

The fifth task was relatively mundane and was intended to humiliate Hercules, in that he was tasked to clean out the Augean Stables, where thousands of cattle were housed. Uncleaned for years, the task seemed impossible until Hercules decided to divert the rivers Alpheus and Peneus to flush out the stables in a torrent of clean water. The Stymphalian Birds, with their metal beaks and

1. Detail of ibises on Nilotic mosaic. House of the Faun, Pompeii. Late second to early first century BC. *Museo Archeologico Nazionale di Napoli.* (Photo: Author).

2. Personification of the Nile. Note the crocodile towards his feet. Rome. Second century AD. *Musei Vaticani*, Rome. (Photo: Author).

3. The Nile Mosaic, Praeneste/Palestrina. First quarter of the second century AD. *Museo Archeologico Nazionale, Palestrina.* (Photo: Author).

4. Detail of the Nile Mosaic, Praeneste/ Palestrina. First quarter of the second century AD. *Museo Archeologico Nazionale, Palestrina.* (Photo: Author).

5. Detail of the Nile Mosaic, Praeneste/ Palestrina. First quarter of the second century AD. *Museo Archeologico Nazionale, Palestrina.* (Photo: Author).

6. Detail of the Nile Mosaic, Praeneste/ Palestrina. First quarter of the second century AD. *Museo Archeologico Nazionale, Palestrina.* (Photo: Author).

7. Detail of the Nile Mosaic, Praeneste/ Palestrina. First quarter of the second century AD. *Museo Archeologico Nazionale, Palestrina.* (Photo: Author).

8. Dolphin grave marker. First half of first century AD. *Museo Archeologico Nazionale di Aquileia.* (Photo: Author).

9. Small bronze mice, one a lid to an oil lamp. Italy. First century AD or earlier. British Museum, London. (Photo: © Trustees of the British Museum).

10. Detail of the wall painting in the Garden Room of the Villa of Livia at Prima Porta. Second half of first century BC. *Museo Nazionale Romano, Palazzo Massimo alle Terme*, Rome. (Photo: Author).

11. Detail of the wall painting in the Garden Room of the Villa of Livia at Prima Porta, showing caged pet bird. Second half of first century BC. *Museo Nazionale Romano, Palazzo Massimo alle Terme*, Rome. (Photo: Author).

Above left: 12. Mosaic of doves drinking out of a cantharus. Hadrian's Villa, Tivoli. Second century AD. *Musei Capitolini,* Rome. (Photo: Author).

Above right: 13. Mosaic panel of a dog on a leash. First century BC. Pompeii. *Museo Archeologico Nazionale di Napoli.* (Photo: Author).

14. Guard dog with *Cave Canem* (Beware of the Dog) inscription. House of the Tragic Poet, Pompeii. 63-79 BC. (© Eufrosine, Wikimedia Commons).

15. Metal workshop scene; a dog lies on a bed to one side. First century AD. Pompeii. *Museo Archeologico Nazionale di Napoli.* (Photo: Author).

Above left: 16. Statues of baying dogs. First century BC to first century AD. Pompeii. *Museo Archeologico Nazionale di Napoli.* (Photo: Author).

Above right: 17. Statue of dog washing. First century B.C. to first century AD. Pompeii. *Museo Archeologico Nazionale di Napoli.* (Photo: Author).

Above left: 18. A Molossian hound. Roman copy of Hellenistic original. *Musei Vaticani*, Rome. (Photo: Author).

Above: 19. Townley Greyhounds. Monte Cagnolo, Latium. First to second century AD. British Museum, London. (Photo: © Trustees of the British Museum).

Left: 20. Epitaph of dog called Margarita. First to second century AD. British Museum, London. (Photo: © Trustees of the British Museum).

21. Dog on funerary altar of Caius Vitullius Priscus. First century AD. *Museo Archeologico Nazionale di Aquileia*. (Photo: Author).

Right: 22. Dog on lid of decorated cinerary urn. First century AD. *Museo Archeologico Nazionale di Aquileia*. (Photo: Author).

Below: 23. Funerary relief of Ulpia Epigone. Rome. Late first or early second century AD. *Musei Vaticani*, Rome. (Photo: Author).

24. Kline sarcophagus bearing scenes of cock fighting and a small lapdog on its lid. Fourth century AD. *Museo Nazionale Romano, Palazzo Massimo alle Terme*, Rome. (Photo: Author).

25. Mosaic panel of cat at a bird bath. Santa Maria Capua Vetere. Late second to early first century BC. *Museo Archeologico Nazionale di Napoli.* (Photo: Author).

26. Mosaic panel of cat and birds. House of the Faun, Pompeii. Late second to early first century BC. *Museo Archeologico Nazionale di Napoli.* (Photo: Author).

Above left: 27. Mosaic emblema of cat and birds. Third century AD. *Museo Nazionale Romano, Palazzo Massimo alle Terme*, Rome. (Photo: Author).

Above right: 28. Ceramic oil lamp with image of an entertainer with a monkey and a cat climbing a ladder. *c.* AD 30–70. Italy. British Museum, London. (Photo: © Trustees of the British Museum).

Above left: 29. Funerary altar for five-year-old Aulus Egrilius Magnus, carrying image of a boy and goat. Ostia. Mid-first century AD. *Museo Ostiense*. (Photo: Author).

Above centre: 30. Votive statue of child holding animal. Sources de la Seine, Burgundy, France. First to third century AD. *Musée Archéologique Dijon*. (Photo: Author).

Above right: 31. Votive statue of child holding animal. Sanctuary of Tremblois at Villiers-le-Duc, Côte-d'Or, France. First to third century AD. *Musée du Pays Châtillonnais, Vix*. (Photo: Author).

Below: 32. The Dominus Julius Mosaic. Carthage. Late fourth century AD. *Musée National du Bardo, Tunis*. (Photo: © *Agence de Patrimonie Tunisie* and the *Musée National du Bardo*, Tunis).

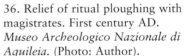

Above left: 33. The Roma/Tellus panel on the *Ara Pacis Augustae*, Rome. (Photo. Author).

Above: 34. A bronze of a ploughing team. Piercebridge, County Durham, England. First–third century AD. British Museum, London. (Photo: © Trustees of the British Museum).

Left: 35. Relief of bullock cart carrying wineskins. Third century AD. Rome. British Museum, London. (Photo: © Trustees of the British Museum).

36. Relief of ritual ploughing with magistrates. First century AD. *Museo Archeologico Nazionale di Aquileia.* (Photo: Author).

37. Relief scene of ritual ploughing outside a city. Via Salaria, outside Rome. Antonine. *Museo Nazionale Romano, Palazzo Massimo alle Terme*, Rome. (Photo: Author).

38. Sarcophagus fragment with depiction of donkey mill. Via Appia, Rome. A.D. 225-250. *Musei Vaticani*, Rome. (Photo: Author).

Right: 39. Depiction of donkey mill on cinerary urn holder of Publius Nonius Zethus. Ostia. First century AD. *Musei Vaticani*, Rome. (Photo: Author).

Below: 40. Mosaic image of mules being readied for cart. Baths of the *Cisarii*, Ostia. Hadrianic. (Photo: Author).

Above left: 41. Relief depicting camel driver. Rome. First Century AD. *Musei Capitolini*, Rome. (Photo: Author).

Above right: 42. Messenger falls off a donkey in Scene IX, Trajan's Column, Rome. (Photo: Author).

43. Funerary relief of horse trader. First century AD. *Musée Archéologique de Dijon*. (Photo: Author).

44. Relief depicting a triumph. First half of second century AD. Praeneste/Palestrina. *Museo Archeologico Nazionale, Palestrina*. (Photo: Author).

45. The Alexander Mosaic. House of the Faun, Pompeii. Late second to early first century BC. *Museo Archeologico Nazionale di Napoli*. (Photo: Author).

46. Dead horses in Scene XVI, Column of Marcus Aurelius, Rome. (Photo: Graham Norrie after Petersen *et al.* 1896 *Die Marcus-Säule auf Piazza Colonna in Rom.*).

Left: 47. Ivory diptych showing elephants in scene of apotheosis of Antoninus Pius or Julian. Late fourth or early fifth century AD. British Museum, London. (Photo: © Trustees of the British Museum).

Above: 48. Relief of interior of butcher's shop. Rome. Second century AD. Ashmolean Museum, Oxford. (Photo: Author).

Below: 49. Mosaic still life of fish and birds. House of the Grand Duke of Tuscany, Pompeii. 80–70 BC. *Museo Archeologico Nazionale di Napoli.* (Photo: Author).

Above left: 50. Statue of child on horseback holding game animals. Tomb of Julia Procula, Isola Sacra, Ostia. Second century AD. *Museo Ostiense*. (Photo: Author).

Above right: 51. Personification of winter with hunted game animals. Third century AD. *Museo Archeologico Nazionale di Aquileia*. (Photo: Author).

52. Mosaic of the Unswept Floor. First century BC to first century AD. *Museo Archeologico Nazionale di Aquileia*. (Photo: Author).

53. Detail of Mosaic of the Unswept Floor. First century BC to first century AD. *Museo Archeologico Nazionale di Aquileia*. (Photo: Author).

Left: 54. Mosaic of fish trader. *Taberne dei Pescivendolo*, Ostia. Third century AD. (Photo: Author).

Below: 55. Mosaic panel of Mediterranean seafish. House of the Geometric Mosaics, Pompeii. First century AD. *Museo Archeologico Nazionale di Napoli*. (Photo: Author).

Above left: 56. Statue of an acrobat balancing on a crocodile. Rome. First century BC to first century AD. British Museum, London. (Photo: © Trustees of the British Museum).

Above right: 57. Ivory consular diptych with arena scenes. *c*. AD 400. *Musée du Louvre*, Paris. (Photo: © Genevra Kornbluth).

58. Ivory consular diptych with arena scenes. Second half of fifth century AD. Hermitage Museum, St Petersburg, Russia. (Photo: © Genevra Kornbluth).

59. Close-up
of scenes of
cock fighting on
sarcophagus. Rome.
Fourth century AD.
*Museo Nazionale
Romano, Palazzo
Massimo alle
Terme*, Rome.
(Photo: Author).

60. Mosaic panel of cock fighting. Pompeii. *Museo Archeologico Nazionale di Napoli.* (Photo: Author).

Above right: 61. Mosaic image of elephant. *Piazzale delle Corporazioni*, Ostia. Augustan. (Photo: Author).

Right: 62. Handlers carrying captured ostriches. Detail of the Great Hunt Mosaic. Piazza Armerina, Sicily. After AD 320. (Photo: © Professor R.J.A. Wilson (Vancouver)).

Below: 63. A captured elephant in transit. Detail of the Great Hunt Mosaic. Piazza Armerina, Sicily. After AD 320. (Photo: © Professor R.J.A. Wilson (Vancouver)).

64. A cart for the transportation of animals. Detail of the Great Hunt Mosaic. Piazza Armerina, Sicily. After AD 320. (Photo: © Professor R.J.A. Wilson (Vancouver)).

65. Detail of the Small Hunt Mosaic. Piazza Armerina, Sicily. After AD 320. (Photo: © Professor R.J.A. Wilson (Vancouver)).

66. The Magerius Mosaic. Amphitheatre, Smirat, Tunisia. Mid-third century AD. Sousse Museum. (Photo: © Professor R.J.A. Wilson (Vancouver)).

67. Detail of the amphitheatre mosaic, Zliten villa, near Leptis Magna, Libya. First half of the second century AD. Archaeological Museum, Tripoli. (Photo: © Professor R.J.A. Wilson (Vancouver)).

Right: 68. Mosaic of four charioteers and their horses. Villa of the Severans, Baccano. Third century AD. *Museo Nazionale Romano, Palazzo Massimo alle Terme*, Rome. (Photo: Author).

Below: 69. Chariot racing relief. Rome. Second to third century AD. *Musei Vaticani*, Rome. (Photo: Author).

Above: 70. Altar to Mars and Venus with scene of *putti* and chariot horses. Ostia. A.D. 120s. *Museo Nazionale Romano, Palazzo Massimo alle Terme*, Rome. (Photo: Author).

Below: 71. *Opus sectile* mosaic of magistrate in chariot accompanied by riders from the four chariot factions. Basilica of Junius Bassus, Esquiline Hill, Rome. AD 330s. *Museo Nazionale Romano, Palazzo Massimo alle Terme*, Rome. (Photo: Author).

72. Front of child's sarcophagus decorated with cupids racing in chariots, Rome. Third century AD. *Musei Vaticani*, Rome. (Photo: Author).

Above left: 73. Two of the Hadrianic hunting *tondi* reused on the Arch of Constantine, Rome. (Photo: Author).

Below left: 74. Small hunt sarcophagus. Via Appia, Rome. Third century AD. *Musei Capitolini*, Rome. (Photo: Author).

Above right: 75. Relief of slaves and captured wild animals. Smyrna/Izmir, Turkey. *c.* AD 200. Ashmolean Museum, Oxford. (Photo: Author).

Below right: 76. Mosaic of owl. Rome. AD 130–140. *Museo Nazionale Romano, Palazzo Massimo alle Terme*, Rome. (Photo: Author).

Left: 77. Relief of Bacchus and panther. Pompeii. First century AD. *Museo Archeologico Nazionale di Napoli*. (Photo: Author).

Above: 78. Sarcophagus with Bacchic procession. Palazzo Firenze, Rome. End of second to third century AD. *Museo Nazionale Romano, Museo alle Terme*, Rome. (Photo: Author).

79. Sarcophagus depicting the Indian triumph of Bacchus. Third century AD. *Musei Capitolini*, Rome. (Photo: Author).

80. Panel relief of Silenus on a donkey. Pompeii. Second to first century AD. *Museo Archeologico Nazionale di Napoli*. (Photo: Author).

Above: 81. Mithras slays the bull. Second half of second century AD. *Museo Archeologico Nazionale di Aquileia*. (Photo: Author).

Below: 82. Laocoon and his sons struggling with the serpent. Esquiline Hill, Rome. 40–30 BC. *Musei Vaticani*, Rome. (Photo: Author).

Above: 83. Statue of Pan ravishing a goat. Villa of the Papyri, Herculaneum. First century BC to first century AD. *Museo Archeologico Nazionale di Napoli.* (Photo: Author).

Left: 84. Relief of Antinous in the guise of Silvanus with his dog. Torre del Padiglione, Lazio. AD 130–138. *Museo Nazionale Romano, Palazzo Massimo alle Terme*, Rome. (Photo: Author).

85. Funerary statue of Omphale wearing the lion skin of Hercules. Rome. A.D. 210-220. *Musei Vaticani*, Rome. (Photo: Author).

86. Altar to Mars
and Venus with
scene of Romulus
and Remus and the
she-wolf, Ostia.
AD 120s. *Museo
Nazionale Romano,
Palazzo Massimo
alle Terme*, Rome.
(Photo: Author).

87. The Capitoline Wolf. Early fifth century BC or much later. Figures of Romulus
and Remus added later in Renaissance. *Musei Capitolini*, Rome. (Photo: Author).

Left: 88. Statue of the
Good Shepherd. Catacomb
of Domitilla, Rome. c.
300 AD. *Musei Vaticani*,
Rome. (Photo: Author).

Below: 89. Sacrificial
procession on the *Ara
Pacis Augustae*, Rome.
(Photo: Author).

Above: 90. Cast of Della Valle-Medici relief depicting sacrifice. Original mid-first century AD. *Ara Pacis* Museum, Rome. (Photo: Author).

Right: 91. Bull being led to sacrifice. Rome. First century AD. *Musei Vaticani*, Rome. (Photo: Author).

Below: 92. Frieze of Cupids slaughtering cattle. Pompeii. First century B.C. to first century AD. *Museo Archeologico Nazionale di Napoli*. (Photo: Author).

Above: 93. Equestrian statue of Marcus Nonius Balbus. Forum, Herculaneum. Second half of first century BC. *Museo Archeologico Nazionale di Napoli.* (Photo: Author).

Below: 94. Relief of Europa and the bull. Second century AD. *Musei Vaticani, Rome.* (Photo: Author).

Right: 95. Relief of Maenad and goat, *Horti Lamiani*, Rome. A.D. 117-138. *Museo Nazionale Romano, Palazzo Massimo alle Terme*, Rome. (Photo: Author).

Below: 96. *Opus sectile* mosaic of a tiger attacking a bull. Basilica of Junius Bassus, Esquiline Hill, Rome. AD 330s. *Museo Nazionale Romano, Palazzo Massimo alle Terme*, Rome. (Photo: Author).

Above: 97. Detail of hippopotamus on Nilotic mosaic. House of the Faun, Pompeii. Late second to early first century BC. *Museo Archeologico Nazionale di Napoli*. (Photo: Author).

Below: 98. The Owl Mosaic, El Djem, Tunisia. Archaeological Museum, El Djem. Third century AD. (Photo: © Professor R.J.A. Wilson (Vancouver)).

protective metallic feathers were terrorising the countryside around their lakeside home. Hercules killed a number of the birds in flight with his bow and arrow and sent the rest flying away from the area in terror. In his seventh task Hercules successfully captured the Cretan Bull alive, another creature that was released by Eurystheus because of its uncontrolability. Sent next to Thrace Hercules bound shut the mouths of the human flesh eating Mares of Diomedes and returned home with the calmed animals to Eurystheus. In his tenth task Hercules captured the Cattle of Geryon, slaying the ferocious two-headed dog Orthrus en route. Juno tried to prevent his return with the cattle by plaguing the herd with flies and flooding a river to make it uncrossable. Hercules was not to be diverted from his task and herded the cattle safely back home where they were sacrificed to Juno. It was probably the association of Hercules with cattle in this task that led to the dedication of a temple to the god next to the Forum Boarium or cattle market in Rome.

The twelfth and final labour was deemed by Eurystheus as being completely impossible, despatching Hercules to capture Cerberus, the three-headed dog who guarded the entrance to the underworld. The god Hades agreed that Hercules could capture the dog only if he did so with his bare hands, a task that was completed successfully. Once more, Eurystheus was terrified by the captured Cerberus and bade Hercules to return him to the underworld.

In many ways most of the tasks involved hunting and it is no coincidence that Hercules was thus linked to this most manly of pursuits, as it was seen in the ancient world. However, in one part of the Hercules myth the god's masculinity was openly brought into question. Omphale, the queen of Lydia who ruled alone after the death of her husband Tmolus, entered the mythological canon through her purchase of the god-hero Hercules as a slave, after the disgraced and repentant hero had submitted himself to life as a slave in punishment and mitigation for his treacherous slaying of Iphitus, king of Oechalia. As might have been expected in the circumstances, Hercules served Omphale well during his period of servitude and in this time performed many heroic deeds on her behalf and to the benefit of her kingdom. It would appear that the queen wished to both dominate Hercules and humiliate him, almost emasculate him, while at the same time making use of his manly superhuman strength, courage, and indomitable nature. As part of his ritual humiliation the queen is said to have dressed up in the hero's trademark lionskin and brandished his wooden club, while Hercules was required on occasions to wear women's clothing and in this guise to help the women of the household with their tasks, including spinning.

It surely does not require the help of a psychologist to get to the bottom of these acts of gender inversion and role reversal, and to expose this link between power and sexual submission. That Hercules had sired a child with Omphale before being set free comes altogether as no great surprise. If the figure of Omphale wearing Hercules's lion skin pelt was seen by many male Roman patrons as an appropriate subject for depiction in the artworks they were commissioning until possibly as late as the end of the second century AD then it was as an image of eastern decadence, of a dangerously powerful woman, a warning to other men to beware. Yet after this time she became a figure whose image would occasionally adorn funerary sarcophagi, or in whose guise Roman elite women would appear in portraits, the best known example of the latter phenomenon being a statue of around AD 200 now in the collections of the *Musei Vaticani* in Rome. The full length statue is of an almost naked Omphale, her modesty only just retained by being partially covered by the end of the lion pelt she holds over her nether regions and which covers her head and is draped over her shoulders and down her back. In her other hand she holds Hercules's club. To some viewers today there is an air of Camp about the Vatican Omphale statue, for, as Susan Sontag has written, the essence of Camp can be defined as 'its love of the unnatural: of artifice and exaggeration', something that well describes this particular artwork.

The image of the hero or of certain male deities battling or working against Nature could often be used in a way to enhance or support ideas centred around the concept of Roman hyper-masculinity and the most obvious example of this must be the depiction of the Labours of Hercules, as we have just seen. Less obvious was the use of the figure of Orpheus, a god whose significance in the Roman world increased in the third and fourth centuries AD as salvation cults dramatically grew in popularity.

One of the most striking depictions of Orpheus at this time occurs on a fourth-century AD Romano-British mosaic pavement from a villa at Woodchester, in Gloucestershire, south-west England where it still remains buried in situ. Indeed, what are known as Orpheus pavements would appear to have been a design speciality of a mosaicists' workshop probably operating out of the nearby town of Corinium – Cirencester – at this time.

Towards the centre of the Woodchester pavement stands Orpheus, immediately identifiable by his holding a lyre and his wearing of an eastern or Phrygian soft cap. He is accompanied, as usual, by his dog. In concentric circles, leading towards the centre, pace a number of animals and birds charmed by the music of Orpheus's lyre. The god and his music have tamed wild Nature and tamed ferocious beasts such as the lion and tiger. He was offering the viewer hope, of salvation in particular. He stands at the still centre while all around him churns the unpredictable natural world. This is also the figure of a man taming wild Nature, which perhaps here can also be read as a feminised space and place. He was also perhaps meant to represent the person of the *dominus* of the grand villa at Woodchester and of its estate, overseeing and controlling his family, servants, and workers. Orpheus pavements, with Nilotic mosaics and wall paintings, represented instances in which ferocious and dangerous exotic animals were depicted in an almost benign manner. These creatures were not being depicted being slaughtered, as in the more common arena scenes. It is highly significant that these works were presenting a version of reality that questioned the more dominant contemporary narrative, which suggested that the interest of these animals lay solely in their value as a tradeable commodity. Sadly, the Great Orpheus pavement at Woodchester now lies under part of the present-day churchyard and is covered over. At one time the mosaic was re-exposed every ten years or so until conservation considerations precluded this. I was lucky enough to view the mosaic there the last time it was uncovered in 1973, the summer before I started at university.

The World Turned Upside Down

In some ways animal hunts and staged contests between particular animals in the arena allowed the games' patron, that is a male aristocrat or emperor, to organise Nature, to oversee its manipulation in a totally artificial way, like Orpheus. Some combinations of animals fighting together there were totally artificial, in that they would never otherwise have encountered each other in their different natural habitats. This represented a powerful statement about Rome the cosmopolis, in the same way that slaves from all around the empire could be found here as well as looted artworks and artefacts, which added to the creation of a cultural free-for-all mediated by Roman power and controlled assimalation. This degree of control was highly unusual, but was akin to the way in which Rome brought together in its streets, houses and public places, peoples from different provinces of the empire, many of them slaves. This easy manipulation of natural space and environment was a cultural indicator of Roman power and its articulation.

The idea of 'a world turned upside down', in other words of things not being as they were or as they should have been, was to some extent an appealing and pervasive idea throughout much of the ancient Mediterranean world, and indeed found its most noteworthy expression in the accepted, and indeed encouraged, chaotic informality and strange characteristics of certain Roman religious festivals. This overturning of the natural order and the social order was occasionally manifested in the creation of unusual, reflective images. A strange, unsettling, and somewhat unpleasant wall painting of an ass being crowned by Victory as it mounts and penetrates a lion was made on the outer facade of a building, possibly a tavern, in Regione V in Pompeii, a work which has attracted the intellectual attention of the art historian John Clarke.[2] This painting is now in the *Museo Archeologico Nazionale* in Naples.

Clarke's almost forensic interpretation of the original context of this painting is compelling, but I cannot find it within myself to agree with his view that the image was intended to be humorous or that it 'is funny even to modern viewers'.[3] Not only do we seem to be seeing an inversion of the natural order in terms of the strong and dangerous lion being sexually conquered or violated by a much weaker and not naturally predatory beast such as an ass, but also a scene in which a male creature is penetrating another male creature. This is but one of a number of paintings adorning this building and which is therefore an integral element of a broader decorative scheme, including flanking images of Bacchus and a panther and of Mercury holding what may be an empty purse. Certainly allusions in these paintings to some kind of 'reversal of fortune' as Clarke terms it,[4] through drinking (via Bacchus) and possibly through gambling or commerce (via Mercury), might be the very subject of the otherwise difficult to interpret animal painting. If so, this would appear to be an example of what we might call negative advertising today.

Three particularly unsavoury myths concern Jupiter, kidnapping Ganymede of Troy from Mount Ida and Europa of Phoenecia, and raping them, and raping Leda, though the myths tone down the nature of these events to talk more in terms of abduction and seduction rather than rape. Taking the form of an eagle to seize Ganymede he carried him off to Mount Olympus to serve as a cup bearer to the gods and thus to be blessed with immortality. Jupiter took the form of a handsome white bull to carry off Europa on his back, swimming over the seas to the island of Crete where he revealed himself, impregnated her, and in so doing founded the Cretan royal dynasty that began with their son, the future King Minos (Plate 94). In the guise of a swan Jupiter raped Leda, daughter of King Thestius of Pleuron in Aetolia, either by directly attacking her or, according to another version of the story, by seeking protection in her lap away from a conniving, complicit Athena, herself in the form of an eagle. Once secure in her lap and held protectively in her arms the god ravished her.

All three of these rapes have an additional meaning other than representing male violence against women in two cases and against an innocent male youth in the third. The fact that in all three cases Jupiter/Zeus appeared in animal/bird disguise to carry away the abductee suggests that they were also violated by Nature itself. There is something altogether transgressive in this second meaning, indeed something against Nature. I find it again difficult to share John Clarke's interpretation of representations of these so-called abduction scenes involving Zeus/Jupiter as being partly humorous in content or intent.[5] They certainly could be bracketed with other known, quite common, bestiality scenes involving female victims, presumably intended for the male gaze.

The use of animal imagery in complex and sometimes very disturbing Roman psycho-sexual myths or narratives is well illustrated by the nature of the hybrid, part human part animal, monsters that inhabited many of these dramas. Of course, many of these mythic monsters derived from earlier Greek myths but nevertheless they were part of a shared cultural empathy between Greece and Rome and will be examined as a Roman phenomenon here.

Perhaps the most significant ancient monster was the Gorgon Medusa, together with her two sisters. The Gorgon in Roman culture has been much discussed and indeed was one of the central subjects of an extraordinary and controversial book by Carlin Barton called *The Sorrow of the Ancient Romans: the Gladiator and the Monster.*[6] The destructive gaze of the Gorgons represented an inversion of the power of the male gaze. Their fangs, snake hair, and ability to turn mortals to stone with their glare made them anathema to many men, an untamed demonic female sexual energy. Medusa in Roman art was generally shown just as a severed head, a *gorgoneion,* particularly in military contexts throughout the empire where her ferocity might have been often admired and in funerary contexts as well where, like the sphinx, she served a protective purpose. Perhaps surprisingly, images of Medusa were also popular on mosaic pavements, serving perhaps as talismanic, apotropaic protectors of the household, their ubiquity in this context being well illustrated by the fact that they occurred quite widely in the western provinces on mosaics, with at least five examples being known from Roman Britain alone. The underlying sentiment behind the use of images of Gorgons in funerary contexts went well beyond simply being trite or mawkish. Its linking of ideas of love, violence, and (female) death might appear perverse to us today, but its reflection through the male gaze at the time of its first viewings in Roman times might indeed have been as much about male status and power as it was about love between equals. It must have been more than simply a sophisticated intellectual identification with Greek myths and culture.

If the Gorgons represented the inherent dangerous wildness of women somehow personified, then a more monstrous regiment of other mythological female figures could equally be utilised in

Roman art to depict the potential of women to emasculate men and disrupt or destroy the natural order of things, that is male power and control. With the head of a woman, the body of a lion and the wings of a bird, the Sphinx commonly appeared on funerary monuments in an apotropaic or protective role, yet in mythology the creature was the bane of all she encountered and came to punish. Obviously Egyptian in origin, the Roman familiarity with the creature and its visual construction in Roman art probably came as much through Greek art as it did through the Egyptian originals. The three Sirens, the three Furies and the three Harpies were rather rarer as images. The harpies were creatures with bird bodies and talons with a woman's face, tormenting, punishing, or carrying off innocents for having somehow crossed the gods. The sirens too had bird bodies or perhaps just wings: their other-wordly sweet call was used to lure the unsuspecting or innocent down into the sea and the underworld. The furies were the fiercest and most horrendously terrifying of all, punishing family crimes and murders and coming from Hades to uphold the natural order of the world. They were usually depicted as winged figures in images that showed them with hair of writhing snakes and carrying torches and scourges. In Aeschylus's play *Eumenides* they were not winged but crawled on the ground like dogs scenting a trail and howled and whined like demented canines.

The linking of women with Nature in Roman art was not necessarily always so negative, and indeed statues of more benign female figures were incredibly common in the semi-natural but controlled environments such as house courtyards and gardens, and in Rome in the great, vast *horti* or pleasure gardens established by the city's patrician elite, at country houses and on rural estates, and in association with fountains and other water features. Thus these settings would have hosted together thousands of statues of figures such as Venus, Maenads (Plate 95), Danaids, nymphs, dancing women, muses such as Polymnia, Ceres, the goddess most linked to agricultural and horticultural fertility, and Igea, goddess of health. But these women would not be alone and these courtyards, gardens and rural settings would also have been decorated with statues of male figures equally associated with the natural world, especially Bacchus, satyrs, Pan, and Faunus, and male athletes. When male figures were equated with Nature, as was the case with Pan and Faunus, or were part male human/part animal figures again such as Pan and the centaurs, or were shape-shifting figures such as Jupiter in his various animal and bird guises, there usually seemed to be some ideas centring around virility, potency, and hyper-masculinity implicit in the phenomenon. With women and Nature, as we have seen, there was usually also danger, disturbance, or transgression.

The Roman mythological semi-human creatures, both male and female, that have been the subject of this discussion were very large in number and well illustrate the allure of tales and narratives of transformation and metamorphosis for Roman audiences, suggesting a relationship with Nature, and animals in particular, that was bound up in the overall fabric of the Roman cultural mentalité and which was buried deep in the national psyche.

The foundations of many particular Roman relationships with specific animals partly lay in the cultures and belief systems of other pre-Roman Italic societies, as we have seen in a number of instances in this book. Human and animal relationships in Etruscan and other historic and prehistoric Italian societies were often articulated and mediated through artistic expression. One of the most unusual mediums for doing this was through the creation of rock art petroglyphs or carvings in the societies of Valcamonica in northern Italy.[7] I am not claiming at all that there are direct influences on much later Roman culture to be found here. As with my discussions in this book of examples of Renaissance and modern artworks depicting animals, I am simply proposing that looking at these works can provide comparative ideas and suggest ways of interpreting and understanding.

In Valcamonica carvings of animals were almost as common and numerous as human figures at all periods from the Neolithic to the Iron Age, suggesting their cultural importance, perhaps on a symbiotic level. Images of predatory creatures such as foxes and wolves appeared, as did highly significant prey animals such as deer. Images of dogs appeared regularly, both in benign contexts and in scenes of canine sacrifice. Although images of women and looms appeared commonly, the animals from whose fleeces the weavers gathered their wool did not. A number of ploughing scenes, with the ploughs being pulled by oxen, may not simply have been illustrative but could have been linked to the expression of fertility and links with the land and natural phenomena. The construction of masculinity in this society was linked to the key activities of metallurgy, warfare and hunting, particularly in the Iron Age. Numerous hunt scenes testified to both hyper-masculine display and the importance of deer in the diet and in the cosmological beliefs of those people. Images of water birds were more often than not linked to sun symbolism and appeared to represent harbingers of future events rather than simply game birds. A small number of images of bestiality involving men and donkeys could have been intended as humorous or insulting but could equally have been intended to evoke ideas of natural fertility or even male potency and dominance. A large human but antlered phallic male figure appears on one rock with a snake, while in another image a phallic male appears to be sprouting antlers from his hands, such images possibly being of deities or shamen, though the possibility that metamorphosis was here being used to illustrate and articulate the fundamental indivisibility of human and animal in Nature cannot be altogether discounted.

Metamorphosis

For those interested in the concept of shape changing in Roman times there is no better text to examine than Ovid's *Metamorphoses*, a compendium of poems woven around the themes of transformation and bodily change, a work that to all intents and purposes was a chronological outlier of a longer Greek tradition. All the transformations described by Ovid took place through the actions or will of the gods or through internal growth, and all ultimately inspired the reader to question what it meant to be human and to consider whether it was thought that distinguished and separated humans from animals, in the same way that it allowed Romans to distinguish themselves from barbarians. Amongst other tales Ovid relates the stories of the metamorphosis of Arachne, transformed into a spider; Daedalion transformed into a falcon; Lycaon transformed into a wolf; Picus transformed into a woodpecker; Cadmus and Harmonia transformed into serpents; Perdix transformed into a partridge, and so on. These animals created by transformation were portrayed by Ovid as being no worse than humans and indeed when they exhibited negative traits these were often traits inherited from their human progenitors.

The creation of an unreal hybrid through metamorphosis was a common trope throughout Greco-Roman antiquity, as indeed it was and is in many other cultures, groups and societies. The role played by cultural transformation myths such as these, and their attendant ideologies, in helping to define Roman being through questioning the very concept of humanness, and by extension notions of masculinity and femininity, cannot be underestimated, discounted, or simply ignored. My thoughts on this subject, particularly with regard to hybrid objects rather than creatures as such, have been particularly influenced by the contemplation of a quite recent work of art in the collections of The Museum of Modern Art in New York. Dating from 1936, *Object*, also known as *Le Déjeuner en Fourrure*, variously translated as *Fur Tea Cup* or *Fur Breakfast*, was created by the female German Swiss artist Méret Oppenheim (1913–1985). It consists of a breakfast cup, saucer and spoon all covered in antelope fur. In appearance they still appear to be a cup, saucer and spoon but our eyes also tell us that they are clearly not regular or indeed functional ones. This surreal assembly works on a number of levels, being at once, on the surface, a brilliant comment on the materiality of everyday existence, as well as presenting itself as a covert statement on female sexuality, physicality, and desire. I reject the interpretation put forward of the fur representing a luxury material in contrast with the usually commonplace ceramic material of which cups and saucers are made and the metal of the teaspoon: this seems too banal. Rather, the act of transformation involved in conceiving and creating the work, from a proto-feminist and anti-patriarchal perspective, also involved conceptual questioning of human and animal bodies and behaviours. In her choice of fur as the material to cover the cup, saucer, and spoon Oppenheim introduced an element of Freud's theories of psychosexual development to the work, providing an erotic undercurrent to its meaning. The fur cup is neither an artefact or an animal: it is symbolic of both.

Just as a hybrid human/animal creature never did exist, nevertheless there was obviously a deep-seated need in Roman culture to recognise or create such creatures through visual or written images. Equally, there was a common linking of animal imagery with utilitarian items in a way that might on occasions have been intended to be similarly transformative, though purely decorative functions may more often have been intended, or of course both motives could have applied together. Roman knife handles, particularly clasp knife handles, were most commonly made of bone, though sometimes other more expensive materials such as ivory or jet were used. The carving of these handles into various forms of animals such as dogs, lions, dogs chasing hares, elephants and so on was common. That is not to say that images of other figures such as the gladiator did not appear on knife handles. It may be that the presence of the animal image on the knife handle was intended to symbolically transform the object from being an otherwise utilitarian object and to imbue it with some other quality or trait. A jet knife handle in the form of a greyhound type dog has been found during excavations at Binchester Roman fort, County Durham in northern England.[8] The item is unique. Both the material used, that is jet, and the image of the dog have chthonic associations.

But were strange creatures and hybrid monsters creations without reason, pure figments of imagination? Or was there some rational process of thought behind such irrational inventions? Was their existence a way to promote debate about the state of being human? Of some considerable relevance here is the work of Adrienne Mayor who in her strikingly original book *The First Fossil Hunters: Paleontology in Greek and Roman Times* convincingly makes the case for a return to the idea that the roots of palaeontology lay in the classical world rather than in the Renaissance period.[9] Although some might see this as somewhat of an academic straw man, nevertheless her evidence would appear compelling in terms of demonstrating that the Greeks and Romans were familiar with fossils as the remains of once-living beings and that there is indisputable archaeological evidence for fossil collecting in the ancient world.

She shows that in the Roman world collections of natural curiosities such as large vertebrate fossils were frequently recorded as being on display in temples and in other public places, citing, for instance, the early example of Augustus's museum of giant bones at his villa on Capri, and a much later display of similar 'giant bones' in Constantinople. According to Mayor, 'people brought curious objects to sanctuaries, not just as private offerings to gods, but in the spirit of creating communal museums where men, women, and children could contemplate natural wonders and try to puzzle out their meaning'.[10] It is important to note, however, that though such displays generated intense interest and speculation they were nonetheless sensationalised events, presenting exhibited natural curiosities as relics of some mythical past, the remains of giants or mythical creatures no longer walking the earth. These fossils were interpreted and presented as being 'of the past' but not of the real past; they allowed viewers to reconcile the ancient myths with contemporary life and to grapple with the concept of a physical, pre-political chronology. If Roman foundation myths helped to underpin the legitimacy of the authority of the Roman emperors from Augustus onwards, then the contemplation of the chronological scale of times past linked people to pre-foundation mythology and to the roots of a popular, oral, folk tradition. It allowed what might at first sight be an irrational world view to co-exist with the Roman imperial world view.

It is known that in 31 BC Augustus was responsible for the plundering of what were allegedly the giant tusks of the legendary Calydonian Boar from a temple at Tegea in Greece and their display as trophies in Rome. Even less convincing as genuine natural relics would have been the bodies of a giant and giantess he had displayed in Sallust's Garden in Rome. However, it is instructive to consider here the palaeoentological museum set up by Augustus on Capri. As Adrienne Mayor so convincingly puts it: 'according to his biographer Suetonius, it housed "a collection of the huge limb bones of immense monsters of land and sea popularly known as giants' bones, along with the weapons of ancient heroes."[11] This offhand statement is an important milestone in palaeontology, because it shows that Suetonius, writing in the early second century AD, was aware of the *animal* origin of the prodigious remains conventionally ascribed to humanoid giants. Thus, it may be that monsters such as the Minotaur were created in ancient times in response to fossil finds such as these.

Nature and Culture

We can find instances where Roman writers and Latin speakers made use of animal metaphors to help define or describe certain human characteristics, acts or behaviours, for example with regard to the character of barbarians or as part of the Latin sexual vocabulary.[12] The former is perhaps quite easily understood, as comparing barbarians to wild beasts fits well with general Roman political rhetoric on non-Roman peoples. The latter is more complex and is often tied in with ideas of metamorphosis and change. A highly influential study of the Latin sexual vocabulary by J.N. Adams published in the 1980s has highlighted many examples of animal metaphors.[13] The penis or phallus was occasionally identified with certain animals, of which the snake is perhaps the most obvious but not necessarily the most common, or with birds such as the dove and turtle-dove. The vague possibility of the *passer* or sparrow of Catullus's Lesbia being in fact a penis rather than a bird has already been noted in an earlier chapter. There is evidence to suggest that female genitalia could sometimes euphemistically be referred to as *porcus* or pig, a usage probably mostly by women themselves. Proverbial expressions involving animals such as hares or rabbits and even lions were sometimes given an obscene slant by writers such as Petronius and Martial. The coining of words for the sexual behaviour of animals sometimes led to the use of such words to describe human sexual activity such as 'mounting' 'climbing', or 'covering'.[14]

There was most certainly a correlation between grammatical gender and representation in Greco-Roman culture and to some degree a correlation between woman and Nature, as best represented by the goddesses Ceres and Flora. Again, one only has to think of the figure of *Tellus*, the earth, as a woman to see how powerful this idea was in cultural terms in the Roman world. Images of women could also be used to represent the seasons, though images of men were also commonly deployed to do this as well, and women were sometimes metaphorically linked in images with wild animals. Women themselves could also be portrayed as wild animals or as feral mythological forces of Nature. The employment of images of these wild animals and more monstrous creatures could have been intended as allusions to the chaos and disorder so often associated with the natural world. A Nature versus culture opposition could sometimes be created by the appearance of male and female images together. There was a continuation in Roman culture of the idea derived from Greek mythology that erotic drive and madness were often linked to death and destruction, or at least were the signs of some inner turmoil or a psychological or societal malaise. Certain types of images of female mythological monsters in Roman mythology, literature, and art may have been intended to be reflections of contemporary mortal women as a gender group.

Certain types of images of mythological women could have been seen by men in particular to have been images of apprehension. Fear of untamed women such as Medusa and the gorgons for instance placed the use and deployment of such images often in a didactic context aimed at female viewers. It was as if the appeal of such rogue and feral women could have negatively influenced ordinary Roman women and subverted individual male power and society's institutions in the process.

In Greco-Roman mythology, when a god such as Jupiter/Zeus took on the form of an animal, as he took on that of a swan, for instance, in order to rape Leda, his cunning and potency were stressed more than his bestiality. It is possible that such tales of metamorphosis and inter-species sexual encounters and acts, mostly unwelcomed as they often constituted rape as we would understand it, impacted on attitudes to actual human and animal relationships, whether they were defined as bestiality or zoophilia.

In Aelian's (Claudius Aelianus *c.* AD 175–235) book *De Natura Animalium* we find a number of reports of human and animal relationships, some of them affectionate and some of them sexual, presented in a somewhat matter-of-fact kind of way.[15] Nearly all the instances cited involved individual animals 'falling in love' with a specific human, some of them being instances of what are known as 'imprinting', that is the adoption of behavioural characteristics from a family member, usually a mother, or from an adoptive figure. His tales included the stories of the love of a dolphin and a boy, and of a snake and a boy. Most of these stories were relatively anodyne. However, the two stories in which the initiative was taken by humans, the story of Crathis the goatherd and one of his she-goats and of a groom and a mare in his care, were of an altogether different kind. Aelian converted the tale of Crathis into a religious myth by going on to report that the sexual congress between the boy and the goat produced a child, with the face of a man and the legs of a goat, the hybrid creature becoming a forest deity. As to the groom, his sexual assault of the mare was roundly condemned by the author.

The Roman male gaze and male experience may have impacted on various manifestations of cruelty to animals, above and beyond the instances associated with arena games, ritualised hunting and animal sacrifice. All three of the latter, as has been argued above, contributed towards the maintenance of the identity of the Roman and Romanised elite male in some way or another. The use of animals in warfare, as has also been discussed above, also constituted an area of Roman life in which questionable attitudes to the value of animal life were brought sharply into focus. Lucretius (Titus Lucretius Carus who lived 99–55 BC) in his extended philosophical poem *De Rerum Natura* considered in a number of passages whether humans brought unhappiness and anxiety upon themselves by unnecessarily placing animals in jeopardy through the demands of religion and particularly in battle.[16]

He asked whether indeed they were breaking some sort of contract with Nature in doing so and moving away from their own primitive origins, not necessarily some lost golden age but rather a time when humans still experienced pain and fear. The pathetic grief of a cow whose calf had been slaughtered in sacrifice was, according to the philosophy of Lucretius, herself a victim of the irrational human fear of the gods, a fear which had brought about a breach of the 'contract' of security between humans and domesticated animals. The poet's equal disdain for the needless slaughter of war, a pointless human invention as he saw it, was reflected in his description of how first horses and then elephants were co-opted by man to take part in battle. He then went on to discuss failed experiments to train and test lions, bulls and boars as combatants and the resulting mayhem when in the frenzy and tumult of battle the animals turned on their trainers and on each other. Most commentators on this particular passage are quite rightly sceptical about the historical veracity of these incidents involving lions, bulls and boars employed in warfare: Lucretius's account is lacking in specificity and there are no other known accounts of these practices. Was this simply a poetic flight of fancy or some kind of broader metaphor? Was he merely proposing that this was the kind of extreme thing humans *might* do in their thirst for power and conquest? While his argument with regard to domesticated animals was that humans had some kind of 'contract' with them, in the case of these wild beasts he was seemingly arguing that while no such contract existed with them as with domesticated animals, nevertheless forcing wild animals into situations *that were unnatural for them* was also somehow unethical.

Given his ethical concerns for animals, it is difficult to understand why Lucretius did not directly address the issue of animals being forced to fight in the arena and it must therefore be asked whether this passage could in fact have been alluding to arena *venationes* rather than to warfare as we are led to believe? Did he imagine that it was simply a small step from organising the pitting of animals against each other and against humans in the arena to employing them in warfare, something that in the not too distant future from his time was more than likely to occur? Was this what we might call today a future-shock scenario? With the sponsoring of games at Rome being so inextricably linked to elite status and identity, and political posturing, would it have been foolish, indeed dangerous, for Lucretius to directly condemn them? Yet his criticism in the poem of animal sacrifice in religious practice, which might also have been thought to have been potentially controversial in his time, was presented in quite an overt manner. Taken together, the passages on human and animal relationships in *De Rerum Natura* present a complex argument that boils down to the precept that humans needed to be mindful of their duty as civilized beings to heed and observe the patterns of the natural world.

A considerable amount of discussion in this book has focused on exotic animals, or as some academics call them 'charismatic megafauna', and on the possible reactions of people seeing such creatures for the first time, particularly in the Roman arena. One issue that has not been discussed so far and for which evidence is virtually non-existent is the Roman discovery of new (to them) species of animal in the process of the exploring and scoping out of new territories as the empire expanded or through trading contacts.

One of the most curious aspects of the Roman imperial project was that its economic programme was predicated on very conservative lines, akin to asset stripping, and expected eventual depletion and exhaustion of provincial resources, be it slaves, or mining for gold and silver, rather than being innovative and forward-thinking, building on pre-existing structures through research and development and the seizing of new opportunities. Was the finding of new and different breeds of horses, cattle, sheep and pigs in the provinces ever regarded as a means to selectively breed new and better strains of these animals?

The manner in which the European empires of the early modern period discovered and exploited, for instance, sugar, cotton, tea, the potato, coca and quinine in the most extraordinary and exhaustive way might be thought of as providing comparative data for the study of the economics of the Roman empire. However, we can find no real Roman equivalent in terms of plant or animal exploitation. Again, if Italian exploration of the New World brought aubergines, tomatoes, peppers and squashes to Italy, ingredients which we now think of as being quintessentially Italian, was there a Roman equivalent? Treating exotic animals as potential commodities, capturing them then shipping them to Rome and the other arenas of other cities around the empire at huge expense, only for them then to be summarily slaughtered, is one of the great curiosities about Roman imperial behaviour and priorities.

According to the historian Keith Thomas, by the time of the renowned Swedish botanical and zoological classifier Carl Linnaeus (1707–1778) 'the number of known plants was ten times that which had been recorded in classical antiquity and the range of known animal life had been similarly extended.'[17] If there was no audit by the Romans of the plants and creatures they encountered during their conquests and the expansion of the empire, then of course there was no balancing audit of the destruction of Nature in certain regions. This seeming lack of interest in cataloguing and then exploiting plants and animals from the provinces seems somehow perverse.

In a previous book I have examined the way in which images of barbarians in Roman art often were used in a narrative of self-representation for the Romans themselves[18] and I wonder if to some extent this was also occasionally true about exotic animals and images of animals in Roman culture. In this chapter I have explored the ways in which Roman male identity was sometimes expressed through identification with certain animals, both real and mythological, and how gender difference appears to have often been defined in terms of schismatic or transgressive female relationships with Nature: how, in other words, shifting relationships with animals and Nature played a prominent and significant role in Roman male self definition.

Lions and Shadows

The Lives of Others

In this final chapter discussion of animals and images of animals in the Roman world will be set in the broader geographical, chronological, political, religious, artistic and cultural context of the Republic and empire and of Late Antiquity. An opportunity will also be taken to consider the Roman evidence against that from other cultures, periods and locations, particularly with regard to some more theoretical studies of human and animal inter-relationships. Questions about the ecological impact of Roman imperialism on animal populations will also be raised. The reader will by now be aware that the Romans' ways of looking at animals were really quite inseparable from their perceptions of themselves.

In this book I have presented evidence about the various roles played by certain animals in Roman and Roman provincial life and in the Roman imagination. While there appeared to be significant differences in human and animal relationships and inter-relationships in different areas of the empire, and indeed variations over time, nevertheless it has been possible to discuss animals kept as household pets or in menageries or aviaries, farm and food animals, other working animals, animals drafted into warfare, animals caught and transported to fight or rather to be killed in arenas in Rome and throughout much of the empire, hunted animals, animals sacrificed in religious rites, and animals associated with the gods. Discussion of animal symbolism and iconography has been a significant part of this study, though it is recognised that visual culture was but a part of an overall Roman culture where literature was equally significant.

It will already be clear to the astute reader that there was no fixed, immutable, unchanging 'Roman' attitude towards all animals in all situations. Far from it. In earlier chapters of this book we have seen, for instance, the rightfully pragmatic attitudes of farmers raising food animals, some more exotic food animals being sought out and acquired by gluttonous voluptuaries to achieve or enhance status, sentimental pet owners, animals treated as political pawns in the arena games, certain animals being well regarded and revered in religious mythology, and others being reared specifically for sacrificial rites or ritual performances. Animals lived within the strictures of Roman and Romanised societies but were burdened by their innate lack of the ability to understand just what these were. A North African elephant in Roman times would have possessed agency in its natural environment, but once out of there it could have been subject to the needs, whims, and desires of numerous human individuals and organisations for any number of motives. The hunters capturing the beast and selling it on alive or for its ivory, the trader in such exotic creatures, and the shipper of the animal to Italy would all have seen the elephant simply as a commodity. Such a creature could have been given as a diplomatic gift to a Roman emperor, then displayed in a triumph, and afterwards consigned to the arena. In such a scenario the elephant has moved from being a valued gift intended to elicit goodwill, to a triumphal symbol of imperial power, to a largely disposable protagonist or victim in a spectacle for the public's edification. Once dead in the arena the elephant became simply its constituent parts: meat for sale, ivory for sale, and a hide and bones for sale. It might have reappeared some time later in the form of intricate and expensive ivory inlay on a piece of furniture in a senator's house in Rome.

In the very early Roman period it is likely that there was a far more symbiotic relationship between humans and certain species of working animals. As Rome's territorial ambitions grew and an empire was created, so the slave economy grew and the reliance on animal labour lessened considerably, though it certainly did not altogether disappear. This schism, this breaking of a historical bond, might well have accounted for the creation of a broad cultural sensibility in which animals were now marginalised and thus deemed less deserving of concern, paving the way for the acceptance of the kind of institutionalised cruelty that was manifested in the arena animal spectacles.

The narrative of this study has been very much driven by the structure chosen for this book when it was first planned. An alternative structure could have involved the discussion of individual species of animals one after the other – dogs, cats, exotic animals and so on, in the way that Jocelyn Toynbee chose to structure her important book on *Animals in Roman Life and Art* all those years ago.[1] A geographical theme of some sort could have been followed: either discussing animals from Europe, Asia, or Africa, or looking in detail at evidence for animals in a number of individual provinces and extrapolating from there. Yet both these methodologies appeared to me to be too restricting in certain ways, and redolent of writing an analysis of vibrant tapestries such as those at Cluny by writing individual chapters on each different coloured wool employed in the weave without analysing the tapestries as a whole.

A more theoretical structure could have dictated examination of man-animal relationships in Roman culture in terms of fascination, awe, wonder, surprise, fear, toleration, acceptance, indifference, intolerable cruelty, symbiosis, exploitation, understanding, defining, colonising and collecting.

However, within my chosen structure for this book there has been afforded room for the discussion of certain topics on a cross species basis, as well as the opportunity to consider more conceptual notions relating to human and animal relationships. Sometimes though it has been necessary to let things go, as the invitation towards endless digression afforded by the book's structure could have produced a work three times as long and probably half as readable. Thus, for instance, the irony that the role of the bee in helping in the propagation of crops and in plant fertility was evidently understood and appreciated by the Romans and yet that honey was perhaps among certain materials commonly and regularly used by Roman women in contraception, if we are to believe the medical writings of Soranus,[2] cannot other than be mentioned here when it is one of hundreds of diverting but minor topics that a rare moment of self control has forced me to omit from full discussion in this study.

It would be useful now to turn to three other studies of human and animal relationships, one concerned with ancient Greece, one with Ottoman Egypt and the other relating to medieval and early modern Britain and Europe. Certain theoretical and philosophical aspects of these studies resonate with the results of our present study, in terms of perhaps explaining certain facets of man-animal relationships in the Roman world.

It is intended here to briefly consider ancient Greek views on exotic animals.[3] Greece was certainly the first European country to which a number of exotic African and Asian species such as parrots, monkeys, camels, tigers and some other big cats, and elephants were brought for various reasons, including being given as diplomatic gifts. The domestic cat, cock, peacock, pheasant and guinea-fowl were also introduced, and thrived there through captive breeding and eventual acclimatisation. The Greeks were also familiar with many other Asian and African creatures through trading, colonisation, travel, and knowledge imparted by imported artefacts and artworks. However, the more exotic species were not imported in the numbers that would later come to Rome. Numerous Greek writers made mention of other exotic species, none more so perhaps than Herodotus whose extended descriptions of animals, such as the crocodile, sacred in Egyptian religious belief, and animals in other foreign lands such as Libya, are positively zoological, anthropological and practical compared to a later Roman writer such as Pliny the Elder, whose style was more anecdotal. Exotic animals were a source of wonder and were admired for their strangeness, rarity and worth, for their geographical origins, their physical characteristics and their innate behaviour.

Alan Mikhail's book *The Animal in Ottoman Egypt* is a fascinating and incisive study of changing human and animal relationships in Egypt between the sixteenth and nineteenth centuries, many aspects of which are directly relevant to the present exploration of Roman and animal interactions.[4] The study concentrates on the changing fortunes of livestock, dogs, and what Mikhail refers to as 'charismatic megafauna', that is elephants, lions, tigers, giraffes, hippopotamuses and certain kinds of birds. As he noted:

Egypt was not only an exporter or way station for these animals, but also became an active consumer of them as it founded multiple animal institutions that served to mediate the human experience of these large creatures. The school of veterinary medicine, the silk industry, hunting preserves, and particularly the zoo became the cornerstones of a new Egyptian relationship with charismatic megafauna – one characterized by separation, capitalist exchange, and cages.[5]

One of the key concepts of the study is how human-animal relationships could change as a result of wider social transformations and cultural currents; how the economic value of animals at the time and in that place needed to be weighed against the costs of human labour, and particularly of forced and slave labour. Integration into wider cultural networks through being part of the wider Ottoman empire also had a profound effect, which we might rightly expect to see mirrored in the case of Rome and its empire.

Just as Rome became a destination for the shipping of exotic animals from Egypt and the North African provinces in particular, so the self-same process can be seen to have occurred in the later period in the case of animals being transported from Ottoman Egypt to the Ottoman capital Istanbul, with Egypt sometimes acting as the intermediate staging port for animals traded from India. When reaching Istanbul such animals had a great deal of cultural currency and cachet, being brought by or bought by high status political figures and institutions and destined for their menageries and lion houses, imperial processions and elite or imperial hunts. Thus we have to consider this activity as both trade, as these animals had been made into valuable economic commodities through cultural and political attitudes and necessities, and as status display and political aggrandisement. In their natural environment these animals had a cultural-environmental value as part of a complex ecosystem; once taken away from that environment, transported and traded, the very physicality of these traded creatures made them as much of a commodity as a slave, wine or olive oil.

If traded animals were an important commodity it is also difficult to underestimate the sheer economic importance of animals within the overall Roman economy: guiding ploughs, acting as pack animals, pulling carts and wagons, transporting individual riders, crucial to the operation of some common types of mills, and so on.

Another appropriate comparative text is Keith Thomas's magisterial *Man and the Natural World. Changing Attitudes in England 1500–1800*, first published in 1983 and still a vital and original resource for anyone interested in historical ecology.[6] As a peripatetic archaeologist for much of the 1980s I was always having to jettison some of my accumulated books along the way as I moved house again and again: Thomas's book always went with me and I still have it today.

Medieval Europe had partly derived its economic wealth from a great reliance on animals, both in terms of utilising the ox and horse for labour and transport, and by exploiting animals for food and valuable by-products such as wool and leather. To some extent this had also been true of the Roman world, though slave keeping would have made that society less reliant on animal labour in general. In seventeenth-century England the emerging academic fields of botany and zoology were predicated upon the premise that such scientific studies could ultimately benefit humankind. As Thomas notes, the Royal Society, founded in 1662, encouraged its members to study animals principally in order to determine 'whether they may be of any advantage to mankind, as food or physic; and whether those or any other uses of them can be further improved',[7] rather than for the furtherance of knowledge as a goal in itself.

While a cynic might suggest that Roman attitudes to animals had also been virulently anthropocentric, that is quite specifically skewed towards the interests of humans first and foremost, and above all else, this is to forget that many learned Romans would have been familiar with the writings of Aristotle on Nature and would have been in sympathy with his stance that the natural world was a distinct entity on its own, not necessarily simply geared towards the needs and servicing of the human sphere and therefore somehow subservient to human whims and control.[8] It is perhaps surprising that the philosophical underpinning of the early Royal Society's remit vis-à-vis human-animal relationships was so anti-scientific, as we might understand the goals of much scientific endeavour today.

If one thinks about, for instance, the quite meticulous rendering of details of plants and animals on the Roma frieze on the *Ara Pacis Augustae* in Rome or of the numerous birds in the wall paintings adorning the garden room of the Villa of Livia at Prima Porta we must conclude that such works emerged as a manifestation of the idea that close observation of Nature was an end in itself. These Augustan era artworks suggested that the great peace that Augustan propaganda declared had been brought to the Roman world by the emperor's relentless waging of war extended also to the restitution of peace in Nature – that rupture and schism had not just adversely affected the political and cultural spheres but it had also harmed the natural environment, whose harmonious relationship with humankind equally required remedial healing and restoration to a pre-bellum state. Of course, such propagandistic harnessing of natural imagery for the purposes of political rhetoric marked a manipulative ploy in itself, but underpinning this stratagem would appear to have been a genuine cultural phenomenon and some kind of philosophical watershed. Livia's garden room was, after all, a private space, as opposed to the public nature of the monumental *Ara Pacis*. It is interesting to note that there would appear to have been perhaps little or no difference between the public and private stances on display in both spheres. Yet Roman imperialism and its driving economic imperative was by its very character going to further disrupt the harmony of the natural world in every province that Rome was to rule over.

Of course, rural idylls as portrayed by images on the *Ara Pacis* and in the rich, silver Latin of Virgil's *Georgics* were ridiculous constructs that did little to reflect the true nature of the countryside, either farmed or wild. What went on in the real countryside, in terms of violence affecting animals and wildlife there, was seldom mentioned – predatory animals and birds preyed on other, weaker species; gamekeepers hunted out vermin, as they saw it, and hung their victims up in game-keepers' larders; poachers operated out of necessity, or for profit; human hunters ritually pursued their game; farmers branded their stock, gelded their horses and castrated other livestock, burned dead or diseased stock, slaughtered animals for meat, boiled up carcasses, tanned hides, collected animal excrement to spread as manure, and so on. The countryside was very much muck, blood and guts. It is a wonder anyone ever left the towns.

Roman writers on the natural world, such as Pliny, Virgil, or the agricultural writers such as Varro and Columella, offered no classificatory systems of plants and animals, no organising principles beyond utility and value or lack of it to humankind, which might have created new paradigms or led to changes in public perceptions that impacted on societal behaviour. Of course, we should not really expect that they might have done so.

There was no feeling that interest in the natural world was anything other than an aristocratic pursuit; while pleasure, curiosity and emotional satisfaction might have been among the by-products of such an interest, as reflected in the creation of a personal menagerie or aviary, first and foremost such a move was more cynically connected to the display of status and the exercise of privilege and its numerous connections. There were many recorded instances of exotic animals given as diplomatic gifts, which were at first given due reverence by being paraded or displayed for public edification, and thus also for status enhancement, but which then were surplus to requirements and were dispatched to the arena or simply killed.

Images in Action

As in a number of my previous books I have also found it useful to look at some much, much later artworks to help provide insights of some kind into certain aspects of past behaviours and thoughts in the Roman period, both with regard to the portrayal of exotic or unusual animals and of more common animals given an exaggerated significance in their contemporary societies and times.

In 1515 Albrecht Dürer's woodcut *The Rhinoceros* was published as a print, in celebration of the display of the creature in Lisbon, Portugal, after its receipt as a diplomatic gift and its transportation from Goa in India. While an examination of the artist's other famous animal print, of a hare, reveals the results of a sympathetic study from Nature, the drawing of the rhinoceros is more of a fanciful concoction from which it is evident that Dürer had not ever seen such a beast in the flesh. In preparing his image he apparently had had to rely on a written description and sketch by another artist. Dürer's rhinoceros was a fantastical creature, seemingly wearing plate armour, which acted as *the* image of the animal in Europe until the eighteenth century when further rhinos were brought to Europe for display. Dürer's rhino thus took on a life of its own, being copied and adapted as an illustration in natural history books, appearing as a relief sculpture on the doors of the cathedral in Pisa in central Italy, and as the emblem of the Duke of Florence. The fate of the poor creature needs appreciating. Having been in Lisbon for only a few months King Emmanuel I decided to send the rhino as a gift to Pope Leo X but the ship on which it was being transported sank off the coast of Italy in early 1516. In an echo of Roman imperial hubris, it is worth noting that King Emmanuel had attempted to pit the rhino in a fight against an elephant in his menagerie but the creatures would not co-operate. Dürer's woodcut perhaps represented the first example of a mass media phenomenon linked to the burgeoning public interest in science, and became a symbol of the role that illustration would go on to play in the dissemination of scientific knowledge, despite its inherent inaccuracies.

Later interest in another rhino being brought to Europe also resulted in the production of a significant artwork. The painting of *The Rhinoceros*, in two versions now in *Ca' Rezzonico* in Venice and the National Gallery, London, was painted by Pietro Longhi (1702–1783) in 1751. The subject was the display of Clara the Rhinoceros in Venice as part of her arduous seventeen years touring of Europe in the mid-eighteenth century, after her shipping from Indonesia by the Dutchman Douwemout van der Meer. She was also depicted when in Paris by Jean Baptiste Oudry in 1749, a painting now in the Staatliches Museum, Schwerin, in Germany. Longhi depicted Clara in a stable in the foreground, a black and almost forlorn figure eating hay or grass. Looking on at her from behind a wooden barrier is a very small crowd of Venetians, men and women, most in Carnival costumes. Their studied, jaded boredom and desultory interest throws a pallor of ennui over the scene. The only animated figure in the picture, Clara's keeper, stands to one side, caught perhaps mid lecture. He points at Clara with one hand. In the other, raised hand he holds a whip and, most surprisingly, a rhino's horn. If the viewer had not noticed at first that Clara had no horn, then a second take would be made once the eye has alighted on the figure of the keeper. It is recorded that Clara lost her horn in Rome rubbing it against the sides of her cage or pen, presumably debilitated by stress.

Longhi's painting was perhaps both a record of a historical event and an allegory of sorts, in that the emasculated creature, Nature captured and brought low, was here symbolic of the decline of the Venetian Republic and a searing comment by Longhi on the decadence of his fellow Venetians.

A second relevant painting of an imported exotic creature in Europe is by the Liverpool born artist George Stubbs (1724–1806) and is called *Kongouro from New Holland (The Kangaroo)*, the first depiction of an Australian kangaroo, dating from 1772. The painting is now in the National Maritime Museum in Greenwich, London. Stubbs also painted *A Portrait of a Large Dog (The Dingo)* around about the same time, a depiction of an Australian dingo. These two paintings are viewed as iconic items of Australian national culture, something which was reflected in the failed attempt by the Australian government to buy the pictures when they came on to the open market in 2013. It was equally argued that they were an integral part of England's colonial cultural heritage and their successful 'saving for the nation' by an export ban and a fund-raising campaign became a minor cause célèbre at that time. To muddy the waters somewhat was the fact that Stubbs had not painted the pictures from Nature, that is directly of the animal itself, as was his usual wont, but had painted the stuffed preserved skins of the two specimen animals, which had been brought back in this form from the Cook voyages by Sir Joseph Banks. Thus he was attempting to animate and somehow bring to life two deceased creatures, whose posture and gait he had never seen and whose movements in their natural habitat he had not witnessed. These images are therefore but ghosts of these animals, with no breath inside them and no real sense of presence. Their portrayal was an attempt to produce with a true artist's sensibility a scientific illustration of the creatures, but which sadly failed and simply exoticised these animals in exactly the same way that many Roman artists unfamiliar with creatures such as crocodiles, tigers or giraffes attempted to produce images of them.

The problems encountered by Stubbs in painting the stuffed kangaroo and dingo were not ones encountered by the artists who accompanied Captain Cook on his three Pacific voyages between 1766 and 1779 or those who accompanied what came to be known as the First Fleet that sailed to New South Wales in Australia from Portsmouth in 1787. These artists and illustrators compiled on-the-spot drawings and studies of indigenous peoples and their material culture, and of the indigenous flora and fauna, capturing the strange and, to them, exotic nature of these people, animals and plants. Since Roman artists had encountered and depicted new barbarian peoples, as they saw them, and the exotic mega-fauna of North Africa and India, there cannot have been a time in between these two eras when the contemporary artistic imagination received quite so much stimulation and new information about human, animal and plant life.

To return to Stubbs, he is a particularly interesting artist to consider in this context, given his specialisation in animal subjects, being regarded as a horse painter par excellence. Perhaps some further insights into the nature of animal depiction and its cultural significance at the time can be gained from looking at certain aspects of his broader oeuvre, and this may help inform our understanding of Roman and animal relationships as reflected in Roman art. Such comparative analysis has its own pitfalls, but in this case the value might seem to be outweighed by any degree of obfuscation or conjecture introduced into this study by the application of such a scheme of analysis. A recent exhibition of his work, *Stubbs and the Wild,* at Holburne Museum in Bath in 2016 demonstrated that Stubbs was not as conservative an artistic figure as he might appear when juxtaposed with the art of Modernism and its aftermath, nor was he simply a painter illustrator always ready and willing to take the gentry's shilling to paint their beloved horses, hounds and household pets, as some contemporary and later critics have averred.

Stubbs might even now be considered to have been almost, but not quite, radical in the context of his times, a painter of animals and the natural world in an age of revolution and social and philosophical turmoil against a background of scientific progress and burgeoning rationality. There is a visionary element to some of his work. Certainly he was most comfortable in painting such cosseted animals as racehorses, rather less so with unfamiliar creatures such as the kangaroo and the dingo discussed above or the rather staged encounters depicted in *Horse Frightened by a Lion* of 1763 and in later variant versions, and *Horse Devoured by a Lion*, again of 1763, whose contrived narrative is so very similar to the Pompeian wall painting of a fantasy sexual congress between an ass and a lion discussed in the previous chapter.

Nevertheless, when the study of each individual animal in these rather unsatisfactory compositions is examined Stubbs can be seen to be illustrating the creatures and their poses, movement and anatomy with an astonishing degree of veracity. The petrified horse on suddenly encountering the lion strains every sinew in its body to fight or flee. That we also know that Stubbs took part in the dissection of a horse and produced drawings of the animal's flayed body suggests that his interest in animal anatomy was quite genuinely scientific, even if we may quail at the procedures in which he participated. Another great Stubbs painting is *A Monkey* of 1775 and in later variant versions, with the artist and monkey subject depicted caught in silent, intense contemplation of one another to such an extent that the viewer feels as if they are intruding on some private moment or that they too have their eyes locked together with the small creature as he picks fruit off a tree. Again, in terms of finding a Roman artwork with a similar observational quality we can look at the relief from Ostia depicting a market stall, on which two monkeys sit staring out at the viewer.

While critics are right that the success of many of Stubbs' animal paintings relies not just on the complicity of the viewer but also on their empathy for the subjects, this does not necessarily mean that that empathy was being deliberately manipulated by mawkish or twee subject matter. Rather, the open-minded viewer is invited to be as curious as the artist about these animals and thus to consider their own humanity and place in the natural world by contemplating these images of sentient creatures. The emotion and compassion on display here is not patronising, it is instead somehow liberating in its intensity and authenticity of feeling.

Also of great interest here are a particular genre of English folk art paintings of eighteenth and nineteenth-century farm animals, often rendered in side-on portrait style or being held by a tether by their overtly proud owners, whose wondrous size reflected the results of the improvement of breeding stocks brought about by the wider agricultural revolution of this time.

Earlier in the book I related the details of the notorious episode in the Roman arena when the Roman crowd turned against Pompey during games at which elephants were cruelly treated and slaughtered. This is perhaps the only well attested instance of pity towards animals shown during the arena games. Cicero might have carped, Juvenal cynically talked of bread and circuses, and many Romans doubtless stayed away from the games by choice because of political, moral or philosophical objections. But was any of the contemporary art produced depicting animal killings in the arena produced for didactic purposes, to critique such practices? The pursuit of such a question would entail the writing of another book, but perhaps it is worth briefly dwelling on a much later instance of art criticising cruelty towards animals in order to understand how such a position of resistance could have been established. In 1751 the British artist William Hogarth (1697–1764) produced an extraordinary series of engravings, to be circulated as cheap prints, on the subject of *Four Stages of Cruelty,*[9] charting the depraved behaviour of the fictional Tom Nero who advanced from boyhood cruelty towards animals to their torturing and killing and finally to the murder of a woman, in an escalation that today is a recognised behavioural progression. Caught and hanged, his body ended up on the dissecting table at the Royal College of Physicians. Nero was not alone in his cruel behaviour towards animals at the time and each of the early prints reproduces crowded London street scenes peopled by sadists beating animals, goading them, blinding them, hanging them, and so on, in a veritable pornography of violence. Hogarth's intended aim in producing the prints was to prevent 'in some degree that cruel treatment of poor animals which makes the streets of London more disagreeable to the human mind than anything what ever, the very describing of which gives me pain.'

Scientific Art

In Roman times to some extent looking at anything, be it an animal itself or an image of an animal, represented an act of renewal of some kind. For an artist altering an animal's appearance to distil its essence into a recognisable image was testing the boundaries of what could be recognised and what could be related to. Whether representational or almost abstract, the image had to contain some degree of truth for its potency to have been active.

The exhibiting of Clara the rhinoceros, and other animals such as the Medici giraffe, and the capture and skinning of Joseph Banks' kangaroo and dingo, each marked out a stage in a process of intellectual acquisition of the exotic, whether it masqueraded under the title and rubric of entertainment or of science being perhaps irrelevant. Similar but earlier processes might well have accounted for the prevalence of depictions of *venationes* on mosaic pavements outside of Rome and of Nilotic scenes on mosaics and wall paintings in Rome and Italy in general.

In many of the case studies deployed in this book animals can be viewed as having been treated as veritable cultural artefacts, as much items of Roman material culture as baths, mosaics, silver vessels and pots, and in a deceptively shifting category of 'living artefacts' such as slaves or barbarian people. The mindset that placed sentient creatures in such categories is perhaps difficult for us to engage with. It was, however, not a universal one. Images of contested animal bodies never drew attention to themselves as somehow fake. There was being established here conceptual links between animals and landscapes, and various cross-currents were at work that strained against the leash of contemporary cultural propriety. An appeal to reality and the natural were formidable parts of Roman society's armoury.

But it was not just society at Rome that was changed by its engagement with exotic animals from far provinces or obtained through trading networks and contacts beyond. The trade in such creatures had a profound social impact and consequence in the regions where such animals were native, as well as more significantly a potentially devastating effect on the habitats of these areas. Given the obviously enormous scale of such trade, it would be difficult to argue that this state of affairs was anything other than deleterious to the home region of animals such as hippopotamuses, elephants, lions and tigers. In the case of elephants it is likely that knowledge of how to trap them developed in the service of the provision of creatures for the arena and this also allowed for the trapping and killing of other elephants just for their ivory. The importance and significance of ivory as a luxury commodity, particularly in Late Antiquity, has already been discussed in detail above.

The early environmentalist and essayist Henry David Thoreau's book *Walden* was a nineteenth-century philosophical treatise on the idea of the wilderness, its rocks, plants and animals – 'a living earth' as he termed it, powered by geodynamics that were outside of and therefore beyond culture. Humans could disrupt or destroy the system, but not control it altogether. Birds, in particular, caught his imagination and wing their way through his writings much as they would have done through his retreat at Walden Pond. Emblematic of life and death, and of Nature's endless capacity for renewal, they represented transformation and re-emergence.

In some instances of the discussion of human and animal relationships in academic and popular discourse, animals tend to serve as passive containers, symbols or co-ordinates for political theories, ideologies and histories. In the ancient Roman world there was equally a sense of place, and connection to living plants and wildlife there, but this, perhaps, became skewed by the project of empire. The natural world then became enmeshed in political and other processes that were far more to do with power, control, and economics than with being of or belonging to Nature. That images of fierce arena animal combat (Plate 96) and chariot racers appeared on *opus sectile* mosaics in the Basilica of Junius Bassus, built in AD 331, demonstrated how animals and Roman power were intertwined. As we have seen in Chapter One, the dolphin in Roman art was often a symbol of the place of the sea in the Roman imagination and of the process of colonisation and conquest that underwrote the programme of Roman imperialism. Predator animals and their prey provided metaphors for might, conquest and power.

With respect to this, I would like to return briefly to the subject of the procurement of animals for the arena, by looking at three accounts of different aspects of this phenomenon, the first written in the Republican period and the second and third in Late Antiquity. Writing in 50 BC Cicero, then governor of Cilicia in southern Asia Minor, continued his extended correspondence with his one-time protegé, the politically ambitious Marcus Caelius Rufus over his request for Cicero to help him obtain leopards for the arena in Rome:

> About the panthers, the usual hunters are doing their best on my instructions. But the creatures are in remarkably short supply, and those we have are said to be complaining bitterly because they are the only beings in my province who have to fear designs against their safety. Accordingly they are reported to have decided to leave this province and go to Caria. But the matter is receiving close attention, especially from Patiscus (who had already sent ten animals). Whatever comes to hand will be yours, but what that amounts to I simply do not know.[10]

Although the letter is brief, it raises a whole host of issues. Firstly, it throws some light on the political manoeuvring associated with the animal games and the commodified nature of the creatures involved. Cicero's general air of unhelpfulness in this matter cannot have escaped Rufus, even if his applying of agency to the leopards as reflected in their 'decision' to simply move provinces and avoid capture in so doing might come across to the modern reader as sarcasm. However, it could be the case that leopards really were scarcer at this time than previously and that what we are seeing reflected here in this throwaway piece of information is a genuine ecological impact caused by over-hunting of these creatures.

Quintus Aurelius Symmachus, when urban prefect of the city of Rome in AD 384–385 and consul in AD 391, wrote a number of letters describing preparations for arena games to be given by himself or for his son.[11] In these letters he complains not only about the effort and expense in obtaining animals but also about the poor quality of some of the animals provided. We learn from his self-absorbed carping about the shipping of weak, emaciated bear cubs, of animals that are deemed too old, and of crocodiles that have not eaten in fifty days. No sympathy for these poor creatures was expressed by Symmachus.

The late Roman poet Claudian – Claudius Claudianus – performed his *On Stilicho's Consulship* in or around AD 400. This panegyric to his hero must be read with great caution, but nevertheless the passage quoted here can more or less be taken at face value:

> Some roar enmeshed in snares; some are thrust into wooden cages and carried off. Boats laden with some of the animals traverse seas and rivers; bloodless from terror the rower's hand is stayed, for the sailor fears the merchandise he carries. Others are transported over land in wagons which block the roads with the long procession, bearing the spoils of the mountains. The wild beast is borne a captive by those troubled cattle on whom in times past he sated his hunger, and each time that the oxen turned and looked at their burden they pull away in terror from the pole.[12]

These animals were probably earmarked for participation in consular games given in Milan and Rome. It seems extraordinary that games on this scale were still being arranged at this date and that within the differing political and cultural structures of Late Antiquity many of the trappings of political power and its manifestations were still virtually the same as they had been around 450 years earlier. While what happened to individual animals in the Roman arena was awful in itself, what allowed it to happen and to become normalised was the commodification of such animals that occurred at a very early period as we have seen, and not inherent cruelty per se in the Roman psyche.

What is apparent to us today is the interconnected workings of Nature and human history at all stages of prehistory and history, but the Romans did not intellectualise this concept. Jacob von Uexküll, the influential early twentieth century German biologist, coined the term *Umwelt* to describe the 'surrounding world' of an animal as being more than simply its natural habitat, but rather also its social and sensory environment. It is a field of study that integrates evidence and insights from ecology, archaeology and wildlife biology. In other words the natural behaviour of animals is determined by a complex stew of factors that can be broken or altered by dislocation. In Roman times, as empire led to the annihilation of space and distance, somehow by bringing distant places into mental proximity, a growing interconnectedness came about. This was not a relentlessly homogenising force, but rather a slow, uneven process that may also have served to accentuate differences. Attitudes to animals in Roman society very much reflected this. However, talk about conservation and ecological impact would have had no place in the ancient world.

Today, it is not true to say that Nature no longer exists apart from humanity, even if this is the Anthropocene, the Age of Humans. If the Anthropocene, the newly-coined term for the geological epoch defined by the human race's sometimes detrimental effect on the natural world, is deemed to have begun during the Industrial Revolution, if not some time before, then there certainly were much earlier harbingers in the Roman period. Among these perhaps can be considered the state-sponsored or encouraged methodical exploration for and winning of raw materials through mining and quarrying on an empire-wide basis, the denudation of forests at this time for fuel and building materials, the intensification of farming on marginal lands, particularly in the later Roman period, the late Roman formalisation of hunting as an elite cultural signifier, and the hunting and capture of certain animal species on an extraordinarily large scale for arena games and spectacles, probably leading to severe effects on animal populations and habitats.

The natural world, including its wildlife, was largely seen by the Romans as a resource or a locus for formalised recreation such as hunting. While writers like Virgil might have hymned the countryside almost romantically, and some voices might have been raised in debate about Nature's place in the scheme of things, there was little appreciation of natural life on its own terms. That landscape and Nature were powerful was often recognised – but that it was a sentient world, generally was not.

Ammianus Marcellinus writing in the fourth century AD noted how the hippopotamus, once so common in the Nile delta (Plate 97), now had a much more southern and restricted habitat: 'but now they are nowhere to be found, since, as the inhabitants of those regions conjecture, they became tired of the multitude that hunted them and were forced to take refuge in the land of the Blemmyes.'[13] In lamenting the disappearance of large numbers of hippopotamuses from the Nile, in comparison to the nostalgia of his youth when such creatures were much more common, the historian could be said to have been suffering from some form of what has been termed 'solastalgia', a form of existential dread or distress brought about by localised environmental change. That change, though, was part and parcel of the history of Roman power and violence, such change being encoded in the political presumptions surrounding the imperial programme and its ideology and rhetoric. Personal salvation and self-knowledge could not be found in Nature at the expense of Roman political expediency and cultural imperatives.

Thus the Romans had a profound effect on the animals that found themselves within the Roman empire or within its orbit and spheres of influence. Some of the negative aspects of this had been set in train before the establishment of Roman hegemony in the Mediterranean world, but mostly the blame for instigating damaging change, and certainly for accelerating others, can be laid firmly at their door. The ecological or environmental effects can be classified as being of three types. Firstly, effects caused by the introduction of new species into an area, and as an example one can think of the introduction of goats, rats, and cats. Secondly, effects caused by the depletion of natural habitats principally by deforestation, over-farming and other land-use changes. Thirdly and finally, the wiping out, to the point of extinction of native species in certain areas, or at least an enforced shrinking of their habitat by severe restriction on species numbers and particularly breeding pairs, in both cases by a mixture of deliberate elimination of species seen as pests or threats in primarily agricultural areas, and the gradual wiping out of a species by over hunting, capture, principally for the arena, or killing to exploit animal by-products, such as skins, furs, feathers, and, of course, ivory tusks. So, leopards disappeared from Cilicia after the first century AD; lions were gone from Greece by the first century BC and subsequently from Asia Minor; leopards and hyenas also disappeared from Greece, and other wild creatures such as lynxes and wolves became restricted to the mountains; tigers disappeared from Armenia and northern Iran; elephants, rhinoceroses, and zebras disappeared from North Africa; hippopotamuses and crocodiles disappeared from the lower Nile. The Atlas Bear from North Africa may well have been hunted to extinction during Roman times, or intensive hunting, combined with the destruction of its habitat for natural resources, may have caused its regional extinction.

Less easy to calculate, because we have no contemporary written sources on the matter, are the inevitable animal diseases or epizootics that would undoubtedly have resulted from the substantial trade in exotic animals to Rome and Italy and which would, in all probability, have spread to and affected domestic species. The kind of serious, devastating, widespread outbreaks of animal disease recorded in Ottoman Egypt in the 1850s–1870s as the result of a similar movement of transported animals[14] perhaps provides a comparative model for the Roman period, with equally serious economic consequences.

When viewed alongside the military, political and cultural spheres, such cumulative devastation attested to the cultural sphere's inherent impotence. Relationships, dependencies and symbioses underpinning the natural environment could not keep pace with the hegemonistic transplantation of new political systems, new modes of behaviour, new beliefs, new narratives and new creative forms.

Although principally about animals, this book has reflected upon politics, religion and culture across the Roman world. These are not really sub-divisions of experience, for the cultural identity of Rome was as much linked to its relationship with animals as it was to its relationships with the peoples of its empire and the barbarians beyond it.

One of the main themes of the study has been the consideration of the spread of knowledge about animals, birds and plants from around the Roman world, either through writings on the subject, the representation of unusual or exotic creatures in art, and the gaining of first-hand experience of certain animals by viewing them on display or exhibited and slaughtered in the arena. It is likely that a citizen of Rome itself would have been able to accumulate more such knowledge than a citizen in a smaller Italian town and say a citizen in one of the northern provinces, while an aristocratic Roman was more likely to have gained such knowledge than one of Rome's plebeian class. Such knowledge helped people to comprehend the ideology of empire, to visualise its mass and extent, and to comprehend something of its diverse character. It was part and parcel of being an urban dweller.

A Tale of Two Sites

In order to investigate the idea of variation in knowledge I am going to look at two case studies, knowledge of local species and exotic animals and birds in Pompeii, as far as we can ascertain this from the excavated houses, temples and public buildings there, and knowledge again of local and exotic, non-native creatures at the Roman fort site of Binchester on the northern frontier of the province of Roman Britain. Certain variables will have to be taken into account, such as non-homogeneity in the respective populations and variability in access to such knowledge, and indeed how the respective populations processed and presented that knowledge.

In Pompeii our case study is by necessity finite, temporally ending in AD 79, with the destruction of the town by the eruption of nearby Mount Vesuvius. The natural environment of the town has been the subject of an invaluable monograph *The Natural History of Pompeii* and the following discussion is largely based on data presented in that book.[15] It is possible through analysis of excavated bone assemblages to tell which kinds of animals lived within the town and which were eaten there. Evidence from wall paintings and mosaics can tell us about the kinds of animals that Pompeians, or rather that should be some Pompeians, were familiar with through artistic imagery and thus what knowledge they might have had of less common or exotic creatures. Where such images were located and their context is also information of paramount importance. At Pompeii at least thirty species of mammal are recorded at the site, and thirty-two species are represented in wall paintings, on mosaics or as sculptural representations. Thirteen different types of mammals appeared on *venatio* paintings in Pompeian houses, some creatures such as sheep probably being used as bait to provoke and enrage lions and the like. Bird bones recovered from excavations in the town are few, for various reasons, so evidence in the form of art in the town represents our only form of data, with 113 different species of birds being depicted mainly in wall paintings. Images of six different types of amphibians and reptiles are recorded, and at least twenty-one different families of Mediterranean fish are represented, again mainly as images on mosaics and wall paintings. Of exotic species knowledge is attested of the Algerian mouse,

Barbary ape, brown bear, jackal, mongoose, lion, leopard, tiger, cheetah, lynx, African and Indian elephants, the wild ass or onager, black rhinoceros, hippopotamus, giraffe, gazelle, oryx, three species of ibis, flamingo, Egyptian goose, pheasant, parrot, three species of parakeet, crocodile, and some types of African snakes.

In Roman Britain we know from the writings of the geographer Strabo that the most significant economic exports from pre-Roman Britain to the continent were grain, cattle, gold, silver and iron, along with slaves, hides and hunting dogs,[16] if his account can be accepted as accurate. For many years, in the late 1970s to early 1980s, I led excavations at the Roman fort site of Binchester (*Vinovia*), near Bishop Auckland, in County Durham, northern England, and in 2010 brought out the academic final publication detailing and presenting the results of those excavations.[17] For that reason I intend to look here at the site of Binchester from the point of view of what it can tell us about Roman and animal relationships at this military establishment on the northern frontier of Roman Britain. Of course, excavated data from this site is not strictly comparable in any way with data from Pompeii – the two sites are simply being contrasted here. The evidence at Binchester takes the form of excavated structures, artworks and artefacts from the excavation, and animal bones recovered from all phases of Roman period activity from the late first century AD up to the early to mid-fifth century, that is to beyond the generally accepted date for the end of the formal Roman administration in Britain in AD 410. The analysis of the excavated animal bones from the site has allowed us to flesh out the narrative story of life at Binchester to such an extent that it is sobering to think that prior to the 1950s in Britain it was not necessarily routine to recover and examine such material on archaeological excavations of all periods. Indeed the first general English language manual on the practicalities and methodologies of studying animal bones from archaeological excavations was not published until 1956.

One of the quoin stones on the corner of the mid-fourth century AD commandant's bath house there bears the partially-damaged relief image of an animal, probably a dog or a horse, perhaps the emblem of the military unit stationed there at the time, or who built the bath house. Other finds bearing images of animals include an intaglio decorated with a design of an eagle on an altar; a cockerel-headed carved bone hairpin, a personal possession of someone possibly interested in the god Mercury; a copper alloy key handle in the form of a panther, which may have had Bacchic associations given the links between the god and felines; a lead seal with a bull on it; decorated samian pottery vessels bearing images of numerous scenes involving animals, including dogs chasing hares or stags, lions either on their own or in arena scenes, a panther, birds, eagles, a bear, a hunter holding a dead hare, and, most interesting of all, a vessel on which is a bull leaping scene, perhaps an event in the arena, part of a phenomenon of decorating South Gaulish samian ware with arena scenes involving bulls; and Nene Valley Ware hunt cups decorated with scenes of dogs chasing hares and deer around the bodies of the pot, a very common type of vessel in Roman Britain. A carved jet knife-handle in the form of a dog came from an earlier excavation at the site.

Some time in the later fourth century AD the large stone courtyard commandant's house that our excavations centred on, went out of use as a domestic dwelling house and possibly even ceased to be a military structure. Part of the house was then turned over to use as a slaughterhouse, with a stone slaughtering platform being built and the provision of a stone drain to take away the run-off of blood and urine. Inside this room were deposits of a green cess-like material, obviously representing cattle dung, and articulated cattle bones. Nearby, waste from the slaughterhouse was dumped outside the formerly grand commandant's bath suite, waste that included thousands of animal bones, mainly of cattle. The discovery of a number of dog coprolites in and among the waste from the slaughterhouse showed that untethered dogs were allowed to roam free in this part of the site, possibly scavenging. The fact that a considerable number of articulated bones came from these dumps of slaughterhouse waste demonstrated that bones with meat or muscle or tendon on them were being dumped along with the skulls of poleaxed cattle. One can but imagine the scene, utilising the senses of smell and hearing: the pathetic cries of the animals being slaughtered; the smell or rather stench of the cattle dung and urine inside the slaughterhouse and in the dumps; and rotting flesh in the dumps and stinking dog turds.

In the excavated animal bone assemblage from Binchester were represented: horses; meat animals, as might be expected, principally cattle, sheep, and pig; game animals, including red deer and roe deer, fox, wolf, hare, badger, and otter; dogs; cats; birds such as domestic fowl, domestic duck, mallard, domestic goose, pink footed goose, greylag goose, oystercatcher, raven, rook, crow, white tailed eagle, eagle, lapwing, plover, swan, and song thrush. Despite being a considerable distance away from the coast, fish was represented by the bones of some species of salmon and seafood by more than 700 shells, including oysters, mussels, winkle, cockle, limpet, razor clam, scallop, and clam. This seafood must have been taken there from the coast in tanks or barrels of seawater to keep the creatures alive and fit for subsequent consumption.

It would seem that at one stage of its life the fort operated as a works depot – producing metal items for the military more broadly in northern England and it is possible that the later workshop activity associated with the large scale slaughtering of cattle was also geared towards providing a military market with meat, hides and leather, and possibly also with other animal by-products and artefacts made from bone and horn. The presence of some bone wool combs at the site suggest some small-scale wool processing.

This brief summary analysis of information about human and animal inter-relationships at Binchester Roman fort has demonstrated how significant animals were to the Roman military economy but that knowledge of local species was not articulated here through artistic expression, while representations of exotic animals were few, mainly appearing as images on pottery vessels, though we must remember that the artefacts recovered from the site by excavation would have represented only a small proportion of those that were in use at the site.

Changing Attitudes

In his seminal and highly influential book *Man and the Natural World* historian Keith Thomas examined the way that attitudes to animals and plants changed in the early modern period in England and in Europe more broadly.[18] His study exposed the concurrent schools of thought at the time that either privileged new thinking over old dogma or which allowed for human ascendancy to be both acknowledged and constrained by traditional narratives. This was an age of multiple dilemmas, with differences between town and country becoming more pronounced, as political ideology developed in such a way as to favour conquest and cultivation over conservation and the maintenance of the status quo with regard to human relationships with Nature. Many of the same arguments took place in the Roman period, as has been discussed over the course of this book.

There is no doubt that the Roman period marked a tipping point of some kind in the commodification of the animal world. One of many astonishing things about the provision of animals for the arena in Rome was the fact that this went on for hundreds of years, and the depressing descriptions of trafficked beasts given by Claudian in AD 400 are a manifestation of so many other contemporary cultural currents, and attest to the atrophying of imperial political culture and discourse towards the end of the Roman empire in the west. This continued commodification attested to some degree of moral stagnation and a dearth of progressive ideas for change and renewal.

Although slaves might have been viewed by some in the Roman world as simply being objects, and barbarian peoples might have been thought to have been 'other' by some Romans, alternative narratives about the humanity of slaves and non-Roman people also co-existed. In the same way animals were thought of by some as being part of Nature and by others as being both of Nature and of Roman culture, depending on individual views and, as so often in archaeological and historical studies of the ancient world, on context. Animals in Roman life would appear to us to have been both everywhere, yet at the same time absent. Both barbarians and animals when depicted in Roman art nearly always lacked any essence of their own agency. If it is accepted that to exist is to be observed then at least there was some acknowledgement of their presence.

If I can hijack a well-known academic question, originally relating to Roman women, I would ask: 'Did animals have a Roman empire?'[19] Well, probably hundreds of thousands, if not millions, of animals living during both the Republic and empire died premature and painful deaths as a result of their interactions with Rome. Many others lived out their lives perhaps unaffected. However, if we are to view certain aspects of Roman culture and society as constituting achievements or improvements on a historical scale and ones that we might still recognise as that today, then we must also accept that much was achieved at a cost not only to human lives but also to animal lives. The degraded circumstances of many animals, captured and transported, killed in the arena, sacrificed to the gods, was a heavy price to pay for empire. Of course, attitudes to animals in Roman times were not static or unchanging. But this is difficult to quantify, as over the whole Roman period we can only really chart the history of the relationship between humans and certain farmed food animals and perhaps the relationship between humans and dogs. The key concept underlying discussion of this subject is the concept of commodification. Once it had been accepted that the huge numbers of animals being transported around the Roman empire to take part in the games represented valuable commodities, then such a moment set in place a distancing process that somehow allowed the trade to grow and thrive. These were not only valuable, tradeable commodities, they were also commodities that could be used in the service of status enhancement and political advancement by those sponsoring the games. Favours could be called in, favours could be done, as we have seen through Cicero's letters, all based on provision of these commodified animals.

Animals and Nature as depicted in images in Roman art did not just serve as a symbolic vocabulary divorced from ideas about human and animal inter-relationships. Rather, representation acted to some extent as a mirror refracting cultural moods and emotions, and philosophical approaches to reconciling what we would consider today to be ecological issues with contemporary political, cultural and social realities. However, there is little indication or evidence that the Aristotleian view of an autonomous natural world co-existing with the human world and only to be understood on its own terms informed broader Roman behaviours. Rather, time and time again we have seen examples of the Romans following what they saw as economic or political imperatives over and above any concern for animals or their habitats.

While some modern viewers might take the more anodyne or benign images of animals in Roman art at face value, this would be a mistake or, at worst, a misinterpretation, in that some of these images also encompassed ideas and concepts about greater things, such as death, transgression, love or lust. An animal image sometimes could represent an almost complete cycle of intimacy and alienation.

Once the Romans started to think of animals as commodities it validated and indeed institutionalised the ill treatment that certain kinds of animals experienced in public spectacles. There had never been such a marked instance of this circumstance before – violence towards animals was part of a wider progression towards greater violence of human towards human. The market for exotic animals collapsed after the end of the Roman empire in the west, and this must have allowed damaged ecosystems to start recovering and depleted animal populations to start to grow again.

The anthropomorphising of animals so common today and well attested in Europe from the Medieval period onwards, was often linked to ideas of humour, and we can find numerous examples of this in Roman art, some benign and some satiric or even cruel in intent. It is difficult to agree with those who consider that representations on Roman oil lamps and other items of women committing bestiality with horses, donkeys and bulls necessarily represented amusing vignettes on contemporary rampant or insatiable female sexuality.[20] Surely, rather they might have been to do with male fantasies of domination and transgressive behaviour, or indeed have been satirical comments on the animalistic sexual nature and desires of the Roman alpha male. It was no coincidence that the god Pan was half man half animal, often priapic and voracious.

There is though one example of a *graffito* from the *domus Gelotiana* on the Palatine Hill in Rome and now in the *Museo Palatino* there whose satiric intent is beyond doubt.[21] The *Alexamanos graffito*, or blasphemous *graffito* as it is sometimes also called, used animal imagery in a satiric manner, on this occasion associated with religion. Dating to around AD 200, there is both text and image scratched into the wall plaster in one room in the house. There appears here a large male figure with the head of an ass being crucified. A man or boy looks on. Accompanying text states that 'Alexamanos worships [his] god'.' This would appear to be intended as a pagan's slur on the Christian religion. '*Alaxamanos fidelis*' – 'Alaxamanos is faithful' is a *graffito* riposte to the insult, written on the wall in the room next door.

The importance of animal symbolism in early Christian art and metaphor has been highlighted elsewhere in this book. In early Christian art it should also be of no surprise that three of the most popular representations of Biblical stories and characters were of Daniel in the lion's den, Noah and the flood and, to a lesser extent, Jonah and the whale. All such images, popular on sarcophagi and in paintings in Roman catacombs, centre on man's symbiotic relationship with animals and each made a very specific point about individual aspects of this interaction. The use of a half-man, half-animal figure in the insulting or mocking Palatine *graffito* therefore seems altogether appropriate for the time.

Clarke has also suggested that the threshold mosaics of guard dogs from Pompeii and the attentive dog painted on a pillar at the entrance to the Taverna of Sotericus there represented what he terms 'double takes', that were intended to both surprise or startle their viewers or momentarily take them aback by the realism of the images.[22] In other words, that they had a humorous intent alongside their apotropaic role. More obvious Roman humorous apotropaic images can be found. For instance, a mosaic pavement from a second-century AD house at Antioch bears the single word inscription '*Kaicy*' – 'And you' – a protective or apotropaic formula common in the Greek and Roman worlds. This inscription accompanied a highly-detailed scene of an ithyphallic dwarf, his huge engorged penis swinging back and forth between his legs, playing a musical instrument and facing away from an eye that had both a sword and a trident thrust into it and which was being attacked by a feline of some kind, a dog, a raven or crow, a scorpion, a serpent, and a centipede. All of these items, the eye, the dwarf, the phallus, and each of the creatures, reptiles, and insects depicted represented an apotropaic symbol; together they provided an astonishing protective group for this house and its inhabitants.

In bringing this book to a close I would like to briefly consider the extraordinary image of an owl on a mosaic from a bath house complex at El Djem in Roman Tunisia, and now in the museum at the site (Plate 98). While we have seen few examples of the Roman anthropomorphising of animals in this book this one startling example of the phenomenon tells us a great deal about Roman attitudes to Nature and about the Roman sense of humour. At the centre of the mosaic stands a large owl clad in a toga, looking out at the viewer, as around him other birds fall dead out of the sky and from the branches of the trees that flank the owl on either side. Towards the outer edges of the composition appear two sets of curious standards or insignia. Along the top edge of the pavement is the Latin inscription '*Invidia rumpuntur aves, neque nocta curat*', translated as 'The birds are destroyed by jealousy, but the owl does not care'. Probably sponsored by the hunting sodality the *Telegenii*, this pavement image could have been apotropaic or protective as well as humorous, envious thoughts perhaps being attractive of evil spirits. However, if the toga-clad owl was meant to symbolise Roman knowledge, its indifference to the death of the other birds could be seen as a negative trope, dismissive of Nature. Such was the complexity of the relationship between humans and the natural world that it carried off these contradictions with a certain degree of ambivalence, admitting complexities rather than delivering certainties.

As we have seen throughout this book, when animals were portrayed in Roman art there was often a sense conveyed of some kind of threshold being crossed, almost of hypnagogic vision. Violent human and animal interactions in these images today convey the idea of the Romans as somehow degraded by their culturally-determined behaviour and being lesser species in a polymorphously organic natural world. In terms of their gods they would seem to have gained in stature and by implication in power and wisdom by being closer to the creaturely.

With incredible lucidity and incisiveness the Romans laid bare their difficult relationships with animals and Nature in language, images, literature and metaphor. We can try to interpret the conflict and consensus at that time over this elusive and contested terrain. This Roman discourse was almost a form of metonymy, that mental process that complements metaphor, connecting something familiar with something else that is already familiar. There was a fatal blurring then of the boundaries between true and false, real and artificial in this process, which introduced an elusiveness and ambiguity into everyday life. Cultural agency and the potential of creative, symbolic practices acted as a trigger for change, and when cultural agency and epistemic legitimacy took divergent paths the immediate was converted into the posthumous, while at the same time highlighting its incidents, micro-practices, and inventiveness.

A history of animals in Roman times is not parallel to the history of Roman imperialism or of Roman culture; rather, it is part of the same study, or should be. This book has proposed a way to understand Roman culture through analysing the society's relationship with animals. If negative Roman and animal relationships resulted in some form of psychic damage, at least this account has taken something from the discussion of its once-living subjects, almost their very flesh, skin and breath, and looked at how they were woven into the complex tissue of historical memory that constituted Roman culture, so that these animals may live again conceptually through consideration of their existence.

Academic Notes

Preface
1. Campbell 2015.

Chapter One: Of Mice and Men
1. King 1999 and 2002.
2. On Nilotic scenes see: Barrett 2013; Foucher 1965; Gullini 1956; Hachlili 1998; Meyboom 1995 and 2016; Schrijvers 2007; Spano 1955; Versluys 2000; and Walker 2003.
3. On Egypt and Rome, and Egyptomania see: Bricault *et al.* 2007; Clarke 2007, pp. 87–107; De Vos 1980; Poole 2016; Swetnam-Burland 2015; and Vout 2003.
4. On the Palestrina/Praeneste Nile Mosaic specifically see: Clarke 2007, pp. 89–90; Gullini 1956; Meyboom 1995 and 2016; Schrijvers 2007; Swetnam-Burland 2015, pp. 150–154; and Walker 2003.
5. Swetnam-Burland 2015, p. 150.
6. Clarke 2007, pp. 88–89.
7. On the Cook artists see, for example, Smith 1989. On the First Fleet artists see Anemaat 2014 and Di Tommaso 2012. On Stubbs see this book, Chapter 9, pp. 220–222.
8. Walter Benjamin, 1939 essay *Some Motifs in Baudelaire*.
9. Adams 1987, p. 205.
10. On the philosophical and moral issues relating to animals in Greek and Roman thought see Harden 2013 and Newmyer 2006, 2007, and 2010. On Aristotle specifically see Connell 2016 and Leroi 2014. On Pliny specifically see: Beagon 1992; Bodson 1986; Finkelpearl 2015; French and Greenaway 1986; Moser 2013; and Pollard 2009. On Aelian specifically see: Finkelpearl 2015; Korhonen 2012; and Smith 2014. On Lucretius specifically see: Kyriakidis 2007; Scafoglio 2016; and Shelton 1995 and 1996.
11. On dolphins see: Dodig 2013; Ridgway 1970; Stebbins 1929; and Toynbee 1973, pp. 205–208.

12. On mice see: Jackson 1994 and 2014; Kiernan 2014; and Toynbee 1973, pp. 203–204.
13. On the spread of rats in the Roman world see Armitage 1994 and MacKinnon 2013, pp. 120–121. For rats at Pompeii see King 2002, pp. 442–443.
14. King 2002, pp. 408, 420, and 435.
15. Kiernan 2014.
16. Jackson 1994.

Chapter Two: I Know Why the Caged Bird Sings

1. On Greek and Roman pets principally see: Amat 2002; Ashmead 1978; Bodson 2000; Bradley 1998; Gilhus 2006, pp. 13–14 and 28–31; Kete 1994; Lazenby 1949; MacKinnon 2013 and 2014c; and Podbersek and Paul 2000.
2. MacKinnon 2014 rather ties himself up in knots by both using and questioning the term pet, and indeed refers throughout to 'pet' (sic) in order to distinguish ancient from modern attitudes to what are now often referred to as companion animals. A third alternative name of personal animal, coined in Gilhus 2006, he considers but also rejects.
3. Pliny the Younger Epistles 4.2.
4. Bradley 1998.
5. On birds as pets see: André 1981; Arnott 2007 and 2012; Dyson 2007; Hooper 1985; Hough 1974/75; Johnson 1971; Jones 2013b and 2016; Librán Moreno 2014; Pollard 1977; Tammisto 1997; and Watson 2002.
6. On Lesbia's sparrow see: Dyson 2007; Hooper 1985; Hough 1974/75; Toynbee 1973, pp. 275–279; and Ward Jones 1998.
7. On passer as penis see Ward Jones 1998.
8. Ovid Amores 2.6; Statius Silvae 2.4; and Martial Epigrams 1.7.3.
9. Hough 1974, pp. 2–3.
10. On the garden room of Livia see principally Jones 2013a.
11. Pliny Naturalis Historia 10.43 and 10.59.
12. Martial Epigrams 3.58.14.
13. Suetonius Caligula 57.4.
14. Varro De Re Rustica 3.9.17.
15. On birds at Pompeii see Watson 2002.
16. Van Buren and Kennedy 1919.
17. Varro De Re Rustica 3.8 and Pliny Naturalis Historia 10.141.
18. On Greek and Roman dogs see: Bodson 1980; Bradley 1998; Brewer et al. 2001; Burriss 1935; Clark 2006; Cram 2000; Crockford 2000; Day 1984; De Gross Mazzorin and Minniti 2006; Forster 1940/41; Franco 2014; Giordano and Pelagalli 1957; Gräslund 2004; Harcourt 1974; Horard-Herbin 2000; Jenkins 1957; Johns 2008; Joubert 1958; Karunanithy 2008; King 2002, pp. 410–414; Koch 1984; MacKinnon 2010, 2013, pp. 116–117, and 2014c, pp. 270–274; Merlen 1971; Slater 2010; Smith 2006; Snyder and Moore 2006; Toynbee 1973, pp. 102–124; and Trantalidou 2006.
19. Martial Epigrams 1.109.
20. On the dog casts at Pompeii see King 2002, pp. 411–413.
21. On Helena (CIL VI 19190) see Koch 1984 and Slater 2010.

22. Patricus–CIL X 639; Aminnaranius–CIL VI 29895; Heuresis–CIL VI 39093; and Aeolis–AE 1994.348.
23. On cats in Egypt see Engels 1999 and Malek 1993.
24. On cats at Pompeii see King 2002, pp. 426–427.
25. On cats see: Ashmead 1978; Donaldson 1999; Engels 1999; Huet 2004 and 2008; Johns 2003; Malek 1993; Rogers 1998; and Toynbee 1973, pp. 87–90.
26. Petronius *Satyricon* 46; and Pliny *Naturalis Historia* 29.60, also quoting Cicero.
27. On weasels at Pompeii see King 2002, pp. 435–436.
28. Potter 1985.
29. Deyts 1994 and Vernou 2011.
30. http://curses.csad.ox.ac.uk/sites/uley-curses.shtml.
31. On the fish Juvenal *Satires* 4.
32. On the naming of animals, including pets, in the Roman world see Toynbee 1948.
33. On apes and monkeys see McDermott 1936 and 1938 and Toynbee 1973, pp. 55–60.
34. On monkeys at Pompeii see King 2002, pp. 433–434.
35. Thomas 1983, p. 117.

Chapter Three: Animal Farm

1. On the Roman farming texts see White 1967, 1970, 1975, and 1977.
2. For the best zooarchaeological syntheses for the Roman period see: King 1999 and 2002 and MacKinnon 2004, 2014d, and 2015. Roskams 2015 very much relies on some of these.
3. MacKinnon 2004.
4. Pliny *Naturalis Historia* 10.52.
5. Varro *De Re Rustica* 3.12.
6. Pliny *Naturalis Historia* 8.56.
7. The literature on the *Ara Pacis* is vast. In this context simply see the official guide Rossini 2006.
8. On working animals in general see: MacKinnon 2013 and 2015. On horses specifically see: Anderson 1961; Ascher 2000; Bell and Willekes 2014; Boer 2015; Clutton-Brock 1992; Cooke 2000; Griffith 2006; Hemingway 2004; Hyland 1990, 2003, and 2013; Johns 2006; Kelekna 2009; Langdon 2002; Moreau 2016; Sidnell 2006; Toynbee 1973, pp. 167–185; Walker 2016; and Willekes 2016.
9. Varro *De Lingua Latina* 5.143.
10. On Roman camels see: Albarella *et al.* 1993; Bartosiewicz 1996; Bartosiewicz and Dirjec 2001; Bökönyi 1989; Brogan 1954; Bulliet 1990; Kolendo 1970; Pigière and Henrotay 2012; Potts 2004; Tomczyk 2016; and Voković-Bogdanović and Blažić 2014.
11. Re. London camel bones *pers. comm.* Umberto Albarella. For San Giacomo see Albarella *et al.* 1993.
12. Mikhail 2014.

13. On animals in ancient warfare see: Ambrose 1974; Forster 1940/41; Hyland 2013; Karunanithy 2008; Kistler 2007; Mayor 2014a; Scullard 1974; Sidnell 2006; and Toynbee 1973, pp. 32–38 and 168–171.
14. On Roman veterinary medicine see Goebel and Peters 2014 and Walker 1973.
15. On insects in warfare see Ambrose 1974 and Mayor 2014a, pp. 283–284.
16. Herodian *History of the Empire* 3.9.
17. On animals in later warfare see, for example: Campbell 2015; Cooper 1983; and the film n.d. *The Animals of WW1*.
18. On animals in triumphs see Östenberg 2009 and 2014 and Voisin 1983.
19. Josephus *The Jewish War* 7.136–137.
20. On the Column of Marcus Aurelius see, for example, Ferris 2009.
21. Lippincott and Blühm 2006, pp. 78–80.
22. Livy *History of Rome* 37.59.
23. On ivory working on the Palatine Hill see St Clair 1996 and 2003.
24. On ivory working in Gaul see Béal 2000 and 2007.
25. On ivory see: Béal 2000 and 2007; Carra 1970; Cutler 1993; Krzyshowska 1990; Krzyskowska and Morkot 2000; Lapatin 2001 and 2015, pp. 171–179; MacGregor 1985; St Clair 1996 and 2003; and Stern and Thimme 2007.
26. On ivory as a luxury material see, for instance, Lapatin 2015, pp. 171–179.
27. Pliny *Naturalis Historia* 8.4.
28. Lapatin 2015, p. 191 Note 45.
29. On pearls as a luxury material see, for instance, Lapatin 2015, pp. 182–184.

Chapter Four: Feasting with Panthers

1. On Roman food, eating and drinking in general see: André 1981; Beer 2010; Belayche 2008; Broekaert 2016; Chandezon 2015; Chioffi 1999; Cool 2006; Corbier 1989; Curry 2008; Curtis 1991; Dalby 2000 and 2003; D'Arms 1999; De Ruyt 2008; Detienne and Vernant 1989; Donahue 2014 and 2015; Dunbabin 2003; Ejstrud 2005; Faas 2003; Garnsey 1988 and 1999; Georgoudi *et al.* 2005; Gowers 1993; Grant 2008; King 1999; Lentacker *et al.* 2004; MacKinnon 2004; McInerny 2014; Nadeau 2015; Purcell 1995 and 2003; Roskams 2015; Van Neer *et al.* 2010; and Wilkins and Nadeau 2015.
2. Seneca *Epistulae Morales* 108.22.
3. Curry 2008.
4. http://www.uc.edu/news/NR.aspx?id=19029.
5. On bees and beekeeping see: Carlson 2015; Crane 1999; and Kritsky 2015.
6. For arguments for and against the thesis of Vivien Swan re. African foodways on Hadrian's Wall in Britain see Cool 2006, pp. 39–40.
7. King 1999.
8. King 1999, pp.188–189.
9. On *garum* and other fish sauces see: Bernal-Casasola 2016; Broekaert 2016; Curtis 1984, 1991 and 2014; Ejstrud 2005; and Lowe 2016.
10. On the Scaurus mosaic see Curtis 1984.
11. *Geoponica* 20.46.
12. On Augst see Ejstrud 2005.
13. Pliny *Naturalis Historia* 10.133.
14. Suetonius *Vitellius* 13.2.

15. Varro *De Re Rustica* 3.13.2.
16. Petronius *Satyricon* 31.
17. On edible dormice at Pompeii see King 2002, pp. 428–429.
18. On the sumptuary laws see Dalby 2000 and especially Zanda 2011.
19. Varro *De Re Rustica* 3.12.
20. On fish and fishing see: Beaulieu 2016; Bekker-Nielsen 2002, 2005, and 2016; Bekker-Nielsen and Casasola 2010; Beltrame *et al.* 2011; Curtis 1991; Ejstrud 2005; Kron 2014b; Marzano 2013 and 2015; Marzano and Brizzi 2009; Meyboom 1977; Monteagudo 2010; Palombi 1950; Purcell 1995; Radcliffe 1974; Reese 2002a and 2002b; Van Neer *et al.* 2010; and Wilson 2007.
21. Pliny *Naturalis Historia* 9.82.
22. On the Grado wreck see Beltrame *et al.* 2011.
23. On fish and seafood at Pompeii see: Curtis 1984; Meyboom 1977; and Reese 2002.
24. On murex shells see Giner 2016.
25. Plutarch *Life of Lucullus* 40.1–2.

Chapter Five: The Atrocity Exhibition

1. On animal shows specifically see, for example: Epplett 2001a, 2014, and 2016; Gilhus 2006, 183–187 and 190–191; Rosivach 2006; Shelton 1999, 2004, 2007, and 2014; and Toner 2014. For wider works on the Roman games including discussion of animal shows see: Barton 1989 and 1993; Bird 2012; Brown 1992; Epplett 2016; Fagan 2011; Futrell 1997 and 2006; and Hopkins 1983.
2. Pliny *Naturalis Historia* 8.4.
3. Juvenal *Satires* 4.10.81.
4. King 2002, pp. 404–405, especially p. 405 Table 24.
5. See Toner 2014 and his bibliography.
6. Dio Cassius *Roman History* 73.18–21.
7. Dio Cassius *Roman History* 73.21.1–2.
8. Herodian *History of the Empire* 1.15.3–5.
9. On Romans and elephants see: Daryaee 2016; Finkelpearl 2015; Gowers 1948; Kistler 2007; Krebs 1967; Scullard 1974; Shelton 1999, 2004, and 2006; Toynbee 1973, 32–54. On Pompey's elephant show specifically see Shelton 1999 and her notes and bibliography.The Roman sources on this are: Cicero *Ad Familiares* 7.1; Pliny *Naturalis Historia* 8.20–21; Dio Cassius *Roman History* 39.38; Plutarch *Pompey* 52.4; and Seneca *De Brevitate Vitae* 13.6–7.
10. Cicero *Ad Familiares* 7.1.
11. Pliny *Naturalis Historia* 8.20–21.
12. Seneca *De Brevitate Vitae* 13.6–7.
13. Dio Cassius *Roman History* 39.38.
14. Plutarch *Pompey* 52.4.
15. Shelton 2004, pp. 363–366.
16. Statius *Silvae* 2.5.
17. Cicero *Ad Familiares* 7.1.
18. Josephus *Antiquities of the Jews* 15.8.1.

19. Beste 2006.
20. Dio Cassius *Roman History* 43.23.1–2.
21. See Chapter 4 Note 4.
22. On cocks and cock fighting see: Baird 1981/82; Bradley1998, pp. 545–556; Bruneau 1965; Csapo 1993; Dumont 1988; Hill 1949; and Toynbee 1973, 256–257.
23. Bradley 1998, p. 555.
24. Pliny *Naturalis Historia* 8. 1–15.
25. See Note 11.
26. Pliny *Naturalis Historia* 36.39.
27. Cicero *Ad Familiares* 2.11, 8. 2., 8.4, 8.6, 8.8, and 8.9.
28. On the Magerius mosaic principally see Bomgardner 1992. On the capture of animals and their supply for the arena see: Baratte 1998; Bertrandy 1987; Bomgardner 1992 and 2009; Deniaux 1998; Epplett 2001b and 2003; and MacKinnon 2006.
29. On the *Telegenii* see Bomgardner 1992, pp. 169–170.
30. Bomgardner 1992. p. 170.
31. On such executions see Coleman 1990 and Pasche 2006.
32. Martial *De Spectaculis* 24.21.
33. Martial *De Spectaculis* 10.8.
34. Martial *De Spectaculis* 6.5.
35. On the Zliten mosaic see Aurigemma 1926; Dunbabin 1978, pp. 17–18, 66–67, and 109; and Parrish 1985.
36. On chariot racing see: Bell 2014; Bell and Willekes 2014; Cameron 1976; D'Ambra 2007; Humphrey 1986; and Walker 2016.
37. CIL 6.10002.
38. Gager 1992, pp. 54–55.
39. Gager 1992, pp. 64–67.
40. Toynbee 1948, pp. 26–33.
41. Suetonius *Caligula* 55.
42. On the cosmology of the circus see Bergmann 2002, pp. 386–388.
43. On Roman hunting specifically see: Aymard 1951; Beschaouch 1966; Green 1996; Lavin 1963; MacKinnon 2014b; Tuck 2005; Ward Perkins and Toynbee 1949; and Wootton 2002. On ancient hunting more broadly see: Allsen 2006; Anderson 1985; Barringer 2001; Briant 1991; Camporeale 1984; Carney 2002; Cartmill 1993; Fox 1996; Hughes 2007; Jacobson-Tepfer 2015; Lane Fox 1996; Palagia 2002; Reilly 1993; Scherrer 2014; Trinquier and Vendries 2009; and Vidal-Naquet 1986.
44. RIB 732–733, and 735–738. Vinotonus is named on RIB 732–733 and 737.
45. Tuck 2005.
46. On the hunting *tondi* see Ferris 2013, pp. 55–59 and p. 140 Note 3.
47. On the aesthetics of pain in Antonine art see Ferris 2006.
48. Pliny *Naturalis Historia* 9.5.14–15.

Chapter Six: Venus in Furs

1. Dio Cassius *Roman History* 74.4.3.
2. Herodian *History of the Roman Empire* 4.2.9.

3. Dio Cassius *Roman History* 56.34.1.
4. On owls and Minerva and links with fulling at Pompeii see Flohr 2013a and 2013b.
5. On owls at Pompeii see Watson 2002, pp. 367–369 and 395.
6. On Bacchus and female felines see Jácome 2013, pp. 534–537.
7. Lucian *Alexander* 53–54.
8. Pliny *Naturalis Historia* 36.5.
9. On the statue of Pan and the goat see Fisher and Langlands 2015. On human-animal relationships in Aelian see Korhonen 2012.
10. On Artemis/Diana and bears see Bevan 1986 and 1987.
11. On Epona see Magnen and Thévenot 1953 and Oaks 1986.
12. Pliny *Naturalis Historia* 10.79 and on this curious prescription see McDonough 1999.
13. On the Capitoline wolf see Mazzoni 2010.
14. On animal metaphors, similes and comparative words, many examples can be found in: Adams 1987; Hawtree 2011; and Warren 2010.
15. On the *Hirpi Sorani* see Rissanen 2016.

Chapter Seven: Wise Blood

1. On sacrifice and different aspects of Greek and Roman sacrifice see, for example: Belayche 2005; Bremmer 1983; De Gross Mazzorin and Minniti 2006; Detienne and Vernant 1989; Ekroth 2014; Elsner 2005 and 2012; Faraone and Naiden 2012; Georgoudi *et al.* 2005; Gilhus 2006, pp. 114–161; Gordon 1989; Hitch 2015; Hitch and Rutherford 2015; Jameson 1988; Kadletz 1976; Kosmetatou 1993; Lentacker *et al.* 2004; Méniel 1992; Naiden 2015; Näsström 2004; Petropoulou 2004; Poultney 1956; Scheid 2005 and 2012; Schultz 2016; Sergis 2010; Smith 1996; Van Straten 1995; Stroumsa 2009; Wilkens 2006; and Zaganiaris 1975.
2. See Chapter 3 Note 7.
3. On the sacrificial scenes on the Arch of the Argentarii see Elsner 2005.
4. Posidonius quoted in Athenaeus *Deipnosophistae* 4.153.
5. On the October Horse see: Bennett Pascal 1981 and Vanggaard 1979. On Greek horse sacrifice see Kosmetatou 1993.
6. Polybius *Histories* 12.4; Plutarch *Roman Questions* 97; and Verrius Flaccus quoted in Festus *Breviarium* 190.
7. On the Arval Brethren see, for example, Syme 1980.
8. Ovid *Fasti* 4.681–712.
9. Ovid *Fasti* 5.371.
10. Ovid *Fasti* 4.905–942.
11. On dog sacrifice see: De Gross Mazzorin and Minniti 2006; Sergis 2010; Smith 1996; Wilkens 2006; and Zaganiaris 1975.
12. On Poggio see Soren and Soren 1999.
13. On Mithras and sacrifice see Johnston 2016 and Näsström.
14. On Christian and Jewish views on and opposition to sacrifice see, for example: Elsner 2012, pp. 160–163; and Gilhus 2006, pp. 161–182 and 2014.
15. For circus imagery on children's sarcophagi see D'Ambra 2007.
16. Crummy 2010.

17. On Roman augury see: Bouche-Leclerq 1879–1882; Dubourdieu 2016; Maras 2016; Struck 2014; and Van der Meer 1987.
18. Cicero *De Natura Deorum* 2.7.
19. On *haruspices* see references in Note 17 above and Yébenes 1991.
20. On the liver of Piacenza see Van der Meer 1987.
21. On Roman magic and animals see: Ankarloo and Clark 1999; Blänsdorf 2014; Faraone 1999; Gager 1992; Gordon 2010; Graf 1997; Heintz 2000; Horstmanshoff and Stol 2004; Luck 1985; Ogden 2002 and 2014; and Piranomonte 2009.
22. Pliny *Naturalis Historia* 28.
23. On the fountain of Anna Perenna see Blänsdorf 2014 and Piranomonte 2009.
24. Gager 1992, pp. 143–144.
25. See extracts from Plato, Plutarch, and Porphyry in Newmyer 2011, pp. 87–92.

Chapter Eight: Against Nature

1. On equestrian statues see, for example, Ferris 2009, pp. 79–80 and Ferris 2015, pp. 70, and 77–78.
2. Clarke 2007, pp. 110–120.
3. Clarke 2007, p. 110.
4. Clarke 2007, p. 118.
5. Clarke 2007, p. 166.
6. Barton 1993.
7. On Valcamonica rock art see Bevan 2006.
8. Ferris 2014.
9. On fake monsters see Mayor 2011.
10. Mayor 2011, p. 140.
11. Mayor 2011, p. 143.
12. See Chapter Six, Note 14.
13. Adams 1987, pp. 29–34, 82, 205–208.
14. Adams 1987, pp. 205–208.
15. On Aelian see: Finkelpearl 2015; Korhonen 2012; and Smith 2014.
16. On Lucretius see Scafoglio 2016 and Shelton 1995 and 1996.
17. Thomas 1983, p. 168.
18. Ferris 2000.

Chapter Nine: Lions and Shadows

1. Toynbee 1973.
2. Soranus *Gynaecology* 1.61. On Roman contraception see Hopkins 1965.
3. On Greeks and exotic animals see Bodson 1998.
4. Mikhail 2014.
5. Mikhail 2014, p. 6.
6. Thomas 1983.
7. Thomas 1983, p. 27.
8. For Aristotle see Chapter One, Note 10 above. On wildlife depletion and loss of habitat in the Greek and Roman worlds principally see Hughes 2014, pp. 88–109.

9. On the Hogarth prints see Lippincott and Blühm 2006, pp. 44–45.
10. Cicero *Ad Familiares* 2.11.2.
11. Symmachus Letters 6.35 and 4.63 for example, but his correspondence on these matters was profuse. See Jennison 1937, pp. 95–97 for references to the full corpus.
12. Claudian *De Consulatu Stilichonis* 3.325–332.
13. Ammianus Marcellinus *Roman History* 22.15.19.
14. Mikhail 2014, pp. 151–155.
15. Jashemski and Meyer 2002.
16. Strabo *Geography* 4.5.2.
17. On Binchester see Ferris 2010.
18. Thomas 1983.
19. The original question was 'Did Roman Women Have an Empire?' in an article of the same name by Phyllis Culham in 1977, in M. Golden and P. Toohey (eds) *Inventing Ancient Culture: Historicism, Periodization, and the Ancient World*, London: Routledge, pp. 192–204.
20. Clarke 2007 pp. 226–227.
21. On the crucified donkey-man see, for instance, Gilhus 2006, pp. 231–234 and 242.
22. Clarke 2007, pp. 53–57.

Bibliography

Adams, J.N. (1987) *The Latin Sexual Vocabulary*, London: Duckworth.

Albarella, U., V. Ceglia, and P. Roberts (1993) 'S. Giacomo Degli Schiavoni (Molise): An Early Fifth Century Deposit of Pottery and Animal Bones from Central Adriatic Italy', *Papers of the British School at Rome* LXI, pp. 157–228.

Alison, J. (2014) *Change Me: Stories of Sexual Transformation from Ovid*, Oxford: Oxford University Press.

Allason-Jones, L. and B. McKay (1985) *Coventina's Well. A Shrine on Hadrian's Wall*, Oxford: Oxbow Books.

Allen, M.G. (2015) 'Chasing Sylvia's Stag: Placing Deer in the Countryside of Roman Britain', in K. Baker, R. Carden and R. Madgwick (eds) 2015, pp. 174–186.

Allsen, T. (2006) *The Royal Hunt in Eurasian History*, Philadelphia: University of Pennsylvania Press.

Alroth, B. and C. Scheffer (eds) (2014) *Attitudes Towards the Past in Antiquity: Creating Identities, Proceedings of an International Conference Held at Stockholm University 15–17 May 2009*, Stockholm University Studies in Classical Archaeology 14, Stockholm: Stockholm University.

Álvarez, M.B. (2010) 'Terra Sigillata as a Source for Fishing Gear of the Early Imperial Period', in T. Bekker-Nielsen and D. B. Casasola (eds) 2010, pp. 287–297.

Amat, J. (2002) *Les Animaux Familiers dans la Rome Antique*, Paris: Les Belles Lettres.

Ambrose, J. (1974) 'Insects in Warfare', *Army* December 1974, pp. 33–38.

Ampolo, C. (1988) 'Rome Archaïque: une Société Pastorale?', in C.R. Whittaker (ed) 1988 *Pastoral Economies in Classical Antiquity*, Cambridge: Cambridge University Press, pp. 120–133.

Anderson, J.K. (1961) *Ancient Greek Horsemanship*, Berkeley: University of California Press.

Anderson, J.K. (1985) *Hunting in the Ancient World*, Berkeley: University of California Press.

Andò, V. (2013) *Violenza Bestiale: Modelli dell'Umano nella Poesia Greca Epica e Drammatica*, Caltanissetta, Rome: Salvatore Sciascia Editore.

André, J. (1967) *Les Noms d'Oiseaux en Latin*, Paris: Klincksieck.

André, J. (1981) *L'Alimentation et la Cuisine à Rome*, Paris: Les Belles Lettres.

Andreae, M.T. (1990) 'Tiermegalographien in Pompejanischen Garten. Die Sogennanten Paradeisos Darstellung', *Rivista di Studi Pompeiani* 4, pp. 45–124.

Anemaat, L. (2014) *Natural Curiosity. Unseen Art of the First Fleet*, Sydney: State Library of New South Wales.

Ankarloo, B. and S. Clark (eds) (1999) *Witchcraft and Magic in Europe: Ancient Greece and Rome*, Philadelphia: University of Pennsylvania Press.

Arce, J. (2010) 'Roman Imperial Funerals *in Effigie*', in B.C. Ewald and C.F. Noreña (eds) 2010 *The Emperor and Rome: Space, Representation and Ritual*, Cambridge: Cambridge University Press, pp. 309–324.

Armitage, P. (1994) 'Unwelcome Companions: Ancient Rats Reviewed', *Antiquity* 68, pp. 231–240.

Armitage, P. and H. Chapman (1979) 'Roman Mules', *London Archaeologist* 13.3, pp. 339–346.

Arnott, P.D. (1959) 'Animals in the Greek Theatre', *Greece and Rome* 6, pp. 177–179.

Arnott, W.G. (2007) *Birds in the Ancient World. From A to Z*, London: Routledge.

Arnott, W.G. (2012) 'Lesbia's Pet Bird', in D. Bird (ed) 2012, pp. 11–13.

Arsić, B. (2015) *Bird Relics. Brief and Vitalism in Thoreau*. Cambridge, Massachusetts: Harvard University Press.

Ascher, Y. (2000) 'A Rediscovered Antonine Marble Horseman', *Antike Kunst* 1.43, pp. 102–109.

Ashmead, A. (1978) 'Greek Cats: Exotic Pets Kept By Rich Youths in Fifth Century BC Athens as Portrayed on Greek Vases', *Expedition* 20(3), pp. 38–47.

Aston, E. (2014) 'Part-Animal Gods', in G.L. Campbell (ed) 2014, pp. 366–383.

Atherton, C. (ed) (1998) *Monsters and Monstrosity in Classical Antiquity*, Bari: Levante.

Auguet, R. (1994) *Cruelty and Civilization: the Roman Games*, London: Routledge.

Aurigemma, S. (1926) *I Mosaici di Zliten*, Rome: Società Editrice D'Arte Illustrata.

Avni, G., G. Bowerstock, A. Gorzalczany, J.J. Schwartz, and R. Talgam (2015) *The Lod Mosaic. A Spectacular Roman Mosaic Floor*, New York: Scala.

Awan, H.T. (2003) *Dominus Aquarum: Nilotic Scenes in Roman and Early Byzantine Art*, College Park: University of Maryland Press.

Aymard, J. (1951) *Essai sur les Chasses Romaines des Origines à la Fin du Siècle des Antonins*. Paris: Boccard.

Bacigalupo, MV. (1965) *Il Problema degli Animali nel Pensiero Antico*, Turin: Edizioni di Filosofia.

Baird, L.Y. (1981–1982) 'Priapus Gallinaceus: The Role of the Cock in Fertility and Eroticism in Classical Antiquity and the Middle Ages', *Studies in Iconography* 7, pp. 81–111.

Baker, K., R. Carden and R. Madgwick (eds) (2015) *Deer and People*, Oxford: Windgatherer Press.

Baker, S. (1993) *Picturing the Beast: Animals, Identity and Representation*, Manchester: Manchester University Press.

Baratte, F. (1998) 'Un Témoignage sur les Venatores en Afrique: la Statue de Sidi Ghrib (Tunisie)', *Antiquités Africaines* 34, pp. 215–225.

Barrett, C.E. (2013) 'Nilotic Scenes, Egyptian Religion, and Roman Perceptions', *Journal of Ancient Egyptian Interconnections* 5–4, pp. 3–5.

Barringer, J.M. (2001) *The Hunt in Ancient Greece*, Baltimore: Johns Hopkins University Press.

Barton, C. A. (1989) 'The Scandal of the Arena', *Representations* 27, pp. 1–36.

Barton, C. A. (1993) *The Sorrows of the Ancient Romans. The Gladiator and the Monster*, Princeton: Princeton University Press.

Bartosiewicz, L. (1996) 'Camels in Antiquity: the Hungarian Connection', *Antiquity* 70, pp. 447–453.

Bartosiewicz, L. and J. Dirjec (2001) 'Camels in Antiquity: Roman Period Finds from Slovenia', *Antiquity* 75, pp. 279–285.

Beachem, R. (1999) *Spectacle Entertainments of Early Imperial Rome*, New Haven: Yale University Press.

Beagon, M. (1992) *Roman Nature. The Thought of Pliny the Elder*, Oxford: Clarendon Press.

Beagon, M. (2014) 'Wondrous Animals in Classical Antiquity', in G.L. Campbell (ed) 2014, pp. 414–440.

Béal, J.-C. (2000) 'Objets d'Ivoire, Valeur des Objets, Lieux de Production', in J.-C. Béal and J.-C. Goyon (eds) 2000 *Des Ivoires et des Cornes dans les Mondes Ancien*, Paris: University of Lyon, pp. 101–117.

Béal, J.-C. (2007) 'De la 'Bretagne' à Selongey: Ivoires Romains et Luxe Provincial', in F. Baratte, M. Joly, and J.-C. Béal (eds) 2007 *Autour de Trésor de Mâcon. Luxe et Quotidien en Gaule Romaine*, Mâcon, pp. 207–219.

Beaulieu, M.-C. (2016a) *The Sea in the Greek Imagination*, Philidelphia: University of Pennsylvania Press.

Beaulieu, M.-C. (2016b) 'The Dolphin in Classical Mythology and Religion', in P.A. Johnston, A. Mastrocinque, and S. Papaioannou (eds) 2016, pp. 237–254.

Beer, M. (2010) *Taste or Taboo: Dietary Choices in Antiquity*, Totnes: Prospect Books.

Bekker-Nielsen, T. (2002) 'Fish in the Ancient Economy', in K. Ascani, V. Gabrielsen, K. Kvist, and A.H. Rasmussen (eds) 2002 *Ancient History Matters: Studies Presented to Jens Erik Skydsgaard on His Seventieth Birthday*, Rome: L'Erma di Bretschneider, pp. 29–37.

Bekker-Nielsen, T. (ed) (2005) *Ancient Fishing and Fish Processing in the Black Sea Region*, Aarhus: Aarhus University Press.

Bekker-Nielsen, T. and D. B. Casasola (eds) (2010) *Ancient Nets and Fishing Gear. Proceedings of the International Workshop on Nets and Fishing Gear in Classical Antiquity: a First Approach., Cádiz November 15–17th 2007*, Monographs of the SAGENA Project 2, Aarhus: Aarhus University Press.

Bekker-Nielsen, T. and R. Gertwagen (eds) (2016) *The Inland Seas: Towards an Ecohistory of the Mediterranean and the Black Sea*, Stuttgart: Franz Steiner Verlag.

Belayche, N. (2005) 'Realia Versus Leges? Les Sacrifices de la Religion d'État au IVe Siècle', in S. Georgoudi, R. Koch Piettre and F. Schmidt (eds) 2005 *La Cuisine et l'Autel: les Sacrifices en Questions dans les Sociétés de la Méditerranée Ancienne*, Turnhout: Brepols, pp. 343–370.

Belayche, N. (2008) 'Religion et Consummation de la Viande dans le Monde Romaine: de Réalités Voilées', in W. Van Andringa (ed) 2008 *Sacrifices, Marché de la Viande et Pratiques Alimentaires dans les Cités du Monde Romain*, Turnhout: Brepols, pp. 29–43.

Bell, S. (2014) 'Roman Chariot Racing: Charioteers, Factions, Spectators', in P. Christesen and D.G. Kyle (eds) 2014, pp. 492–504.

Bell, S. and C. Willekes (2014) 'Horse Racing and Chariot Racing', in G.L. Campbell (ed) 2014, pp. 478–490.

Bellelli, V. and M. Mazzi (2013) *Extispicio: Una "Scienza" Divinatoria tra Mesopotamia ed Etruria*, Rome: Scienze e Lettere.

Belozerskaya, M. (2009) *The Medici Giraffe and Other Tales of Exotic Animals and Power*, New York: Little, Brown and Company.

Beltrame, C., D. Gaddi, and S. Parizzi (2011) 'A Presumed Hydraulic Apparatus for the Transport of Live Fish, Found on the Roman Wreck at Grado, Italy', *International Journal of Nautical Archaeology* 40.2, pp. 274–282.

Bennett Pascal, C. (1981) 'October Horse', *Harvard Studies in Classical Philology* 85, pp. 261–291.

Bergmann, B. (1992) 'Exploring the Grove: Pastoral Space on Roman Walls', in J.D. Hunt (ed) 1992 *The Pastoral Landscape*, Studies in the History of Art 36, Washington: University Press of New England, pp. 21–46.

Bergmann, B. (2002) 'Art and Nature in the Villa at Oplontis', in C.Stein and J.H. Humphrey (eds) 2002 *Pompeian Brothels, Pompeii's Ancient History, Mirrors and Mysteries: Art and Nature at Oplontis, and the Herculaneum 'Basilica'*, Journal of Roman Archaeology Supplementary Volume 47, pp. 115–118.

Bibliography

Bergmann, B. (2008a) 'Pictorial Narratives of the Roman Circus', in J. Nelis-Clément and J.-M. Roddaz (eds) 2008 *Le Cirque Romain et Son Image. Actes de Colloque Tenu à l'Institut Ausonius, Bordeaux 2006*, Pessac: Ausonius, pp. 361–392.

Bergmann, B. (2008b) 'Staging the Supernatural: Interior Gardens of Pompeian Houses', in C. Mattusch (ed) 2008 *Pompeii and the Roman Villa: Art and Culture Around the Bay of Naples*, London: Thames and Hudson, pp. 62–64.

Bernal-Casasola, D. (2016) 'Garum in Context: New Times, Same Topics in the Post-Ponsichian Era', in T. Bekker-Nielsen and R. Gertwagen (eds) 2016, pp. 188–215.

Bertrandy, F. (1987) 'Remarques sur le Commerce des Bêtes Sauvage Entre l'Afrique du Nord et l'Italie', *Mélanges d'Archeologie et d'Histoire de l'Ecole Francaise de Rome* 99, pp. 211–241.

Beschaouch, A. (1966) 'La Mosaique de Chasse à l'Amphithéâtre Découverte à Smirat en Tunisie', Paris: *Comptes Rendus des Séances de l'Académie des Inscriptions et Belles-Lettres* 110.1, pp. 134–157.

Beschaouch, A. (1977) 'Nouvelles Recherches sur les Sodalités dans l'Afrique Romaine', *Comptes Rendus des Séances de l'Académie des Inscriptions et Belles-Lettres* 121.3, pp. 486–503.

Beschaouch, A. (1985) 'Nouvelles Observations sur les Sodalités Africaines', *Comptes Rendus des Séances de l'Académie des Inscriptions et Belles-Lettres* 129.3, pp. 453–475.

Beste, H.-J. (2006) 'Documentazione negli Ipogei del Colosseo: Riflettendo su un Metodo Tradizionale', in L. Haselberger and J. Humphrey (eds) 2006 *Imaging Ancient Rome. Documentation-Visualization-Imagination*, Journal of Roman Archaeology Supplementary Series 61, pp. 202–206.

Bettini, M. (2013) *Women and Weasels: Mythologies of Birth in Ancient Greece and Rome*, Chicago: Chicago University Press.

Bevan, E. (1986) *Representations of Animals in Sanctuaries of Artemis and Other Olympian Deities*, British Archaeological Reports International Series 315, Oxford: Archaeopress.

Bevan, E. (1987) 'The Goddess Artemis and the Dedication of Bears in Sanctuaries', *Annual of the British School at Athens* 82, pp. 17–21.

Bevan, L. (2006) *Worshippers and Warriors. Reconstructing Gender and Gender Relations in the Prehistoric Rock Art of Naquane National Park, Valcamonica, Brescia, Northern Italy*, British Archaeological Reports International Series 1485, Oxford: Archaeopress.

Biella, M.C. and E. Giovanelli (eds) (2016) *Nuovi Studi sul Bestiario Fantastico di Età Orientalizzante nella Penisola Italiana*, Trento: Tangram Edizioni Scientifiche.

Biers, J.C. (2004) *A Peaceable Kingdom: Animals in Ancient Art from the Leo Mildenberg Collection*, Mainz: Verlag Philipp von Zabern.

Bird, D. (ed) (2012) *Dating and Interpreting the Past in the Western Roman Empire: Essays in Honour of Brenda Dickinson*, Oxford: Oxbow Books.

Bird, J. (2012) 'Arena Scenes with Bulls on South Gaulish Samian', in D. Bird (ed) 2012, pp. 135–148.

Blanc, N. (1999) 'Des Girafes dans le Thiase. Un Stuc de Tusculum', in N. Blanc and A. Buisson (eds) 1999 *Imago Antiquitatis. Religions et Iconographie du Monde Romain. Mélanges Offerts à Robert Turcan*, Paris: De Bocard, pp. 105–118.

Blänsdorf, J. (2014) 'The Curse Inscriptions and the *Materia Magica* of the Anna-Perenna-Nymphaeum at Rome', in D. Boschung and J.N. Bremner (eds) 2014 *The Materiality of Magic*, Paderborn: Verlag Wilhelm Fink, pp. 293–308.

Blondel, J. and J. Aronson (1999) *Biology and Wildlife of the Mediterranean Region*, Oxford: Oxford University Press.

Bodson, L. (1980) 'Place et Functions du Chien dans le Monde Antique', *Ethnozootechnie* 25, pp. 13–21.

Bodson, L. (1983) 'Attitudes Towards Animals in Greco-Roman Antiquity', *International Journal for the Study of Animal Problems* 4, pp. 312–320.

Bodson, L. (1986) 'Aspects of Pliny's Zoology', in R. French and F. Greenaway (eds) 1986, pp. 98–110.

Bodson, L. (1991) 'Alexander the Great and the Scientific Exploration of the Oriental Countries of His Empire', *Ancient History* 22, pp. 127–138.

Bodson, L. (1998) 'Ancient Greek Views on the Exotic Animal', *Arctos* 32, pp. 61–85.

Bodson, L. (2000) 'Motivations for Pet-Keeping in Ancient Greece and Rome. A Preliminary Survey' in A. Podberscek, E.S. Paul and J.A. Serpell (eds) 2000 *Companion Animals and Us. Exploring the Relationships Between People and Pets*, Cambridge: Cambridge University Press, pp. 27–41.

Bodson, L. (2002) 'Amphibians and Reptiles: Evidence from Wall Paintings, Mosaics, Sculpture, Skeletal Remains, and Ancient Authors', in W.F. Jashemski and E.G. Meyer (eds) 2002, pp. 327–356.

Bodson, L. (2014) 'Zoological Knowledge in Ancient Greece and Rome', in G.L. Campbell (ed) 2014, pp. 556–578.

Boer, R. (2015) 'From Horse Kissing to Beastly Emissions: Paraphilias in the Ancient Near East', in M. Masterson, N.S. Rabinowitz, and J. Robson (eds) 2015 *Sex in Antiquity*, London: Routledge, pp. 67–79.

Bökönyi, S. (1989) 'Camel Sacrifice in Roman Intercisa', *Scientiarum Hungaricae* 61, pp. 399–404.

Bomgardner, D.L. (1992) 'The Trade in Wild Beasts for Roman Spectacles: a Green Perspective', *Anthropozoologica* 16, pp. 161–166.

Bomgardner, D.L. (2000) *The Story of the Roman Amphitheatre*, London: Routledge.

Bomgardner, D.L. (2009) 'The Magerius Mosaic Revisited' in T. Wilmott (ed) 2009 *Roman Amphitheatres and Spectacula: a 21ˢᵗ Century Perspective*, Oxford: Archaeopress, pp. 165–177.

Bouche-Leclerq, A. (1879–1882) *Histoire de la Divination dans l'Antiquité*, Paris: E. Leroux.

Bradley, K. (1998) 'The Sentimental Education of the Roman Child. The Role of Pet-Keeping', *Latomus* 57, pp. 523–557.

Brandt, J.R. (2014) 'Blood, Boundaries and Purification. On the Creation of Identities Between Memory and Oblivion in Ancient Rome', in B. Alroth and C. Scheffer (eds) 2014, pp. 201–216.

Bremmer, J.N. (1983) 'Scapegoat Rituals in Ancient Greece', *Harvard Studies in Classical Philology* 87, pp. 299–320.

Bremmer, J.N., J.H.F. Dijkstra, J.E.A. Kroesen, and Y. Kuiper (eds) 2010 *Myths, Martyrs, and Modernity*, Leiden: Brill.

Brewer, D., T. Clark and A. Phillips (2001) *Dogs in Antiquity: Anubis to Cerberus. The Origins of the Domestic Dog*, Warminster: Aris and Phillips.

Briant, P. (1991) 'Chasses Royales Macédoniennes et Chasses Royales Perses: le Thème de la Chasse au Lion sur la Chasse de Vergina', *Dialogues d'Histoire Ancienne* 17.1, pp. 211–255.

Bricault, L., M.J. Versluys and P.G.P. Meyboom (eds) (2007) *Nile Into Tiber: Egypt in the Roman World: Proceedings of the IIIrd International Conference of Isis Studies, Leiden May 11–14, 2005*, Leiden: Brill.

Brisson, L. (2002) *Sexual Ambivalence. Androgyny and Hermaphroditism in Graeco-Roman Antiquity*, Berkeley: University of California Press.

Broderick, L.G. (ed) (2016) *People With Animals: Perspectives and Studies in Ethnozooarchaeology*, Oxford: Oxbow Books.

Broekaert, W. (2016) 'The Soldiers' Kitchen Along the Limes: Fish Sauce Consumption and Economics', in W. Broekaert, R. Nadeau and J. Wilkins (eds) 2015 *Food,*

Bibliography

Identity and Cross-Cultural Exchange in the Ancient World, Brussels: Éditions Latomus, pp. 64–87.

Brogan, O. (1954) 'The Camel in Roman Tripolitania', *Papers of the British School at Rome*, New Series 9, pp. 126–131.

Brown, S. (1992) 'Death as Decoration: Scenes from the Arena on Roman Domestic Mosaics', in A. Richlin (ed) 1992 *Pornography and Representation in Greece and Rome*, Oxford: Oxford University Press, pp. 180–211.

Bruneau, P. (1965) 'Le Motif des Coqs Affrontés dans l'Imagerie Antique', *Bulletin de Correspondance Hellénique* 89, pp. 90–121.

Bulliet, R.W. (1990) *The Camel and the Wheel*, New York: Columbia University Press.

Burriss, E.E. (1935) 'The Place of the Dog in Superstition as Revealed in Latin Literature', *Classical Philology* 30, pp. 32–42.

Calder, L. (2011) *Cruelty and Sentimentality: Greek Attitudes to Animals 600–300 BC*, British Archaeological Reports International Series 2225, Oxford: Archaeopress.

Calvet, J. and M. Cruppi (1955) *Le Bestiaire de l'Antiquité Classique*, Paris: F. Lanore.

Cambi, N. and G. Koch (eds) (2013) *Funerary Sculpture of the Western Illyricum and Neighbouring Regions of the Roman Empire, Proceedings of the International Scholarly Conference Held in Split from September 27ᵗʰ to the 30ᵗʰ 2009*, Split: Književni Krug.

Cameron, A. (1976) *Circus Factions: Blues and Greens at Rome and Byzantium*, Oxford: Clarendon Press.

Campbell, C. (2015) *Dogs of Courage: When Britain's Pets Went to War*, London: Corsair.

Campbell, G.L. (ed) (2014) *The Oxford Handbook of Animals in Classical Thought and Life*, Oxford: Oxford University Press.

Camporeale, G. (1984) *La Caccia in Etruria*, Rome: G. Bretschneider.

Cannuyer, C. (ed) (2001) *L'Animal dans les Civilizations Orientales*, Brussels: Société Belge d'Études Orientales.

Cannuyer, C. (ed) (2010) *La Girafe dans l'Égypte Ancienne et le Verbe sŕ: Étude de Lexicographie et de Symbolique Animalière*, Brussels: Société Belge d'Études Orientales.

Carandini, A., A. Ricci and M. De Vos (1982) *Filosofiana. La Villa de Piazza Armerina: Imagine di un Aristocrato Romano al Tempo di Costantino*, Palermo: Flaccovio.

Carboni, R. (2016) 'Unusual Sacrificial Victims: Fish and Their Value in the Context of Sacrifices', in P.A. Johnston, A. Mastrocinque, and S. Papaioannou (eds) 2016, pp. 255–280.

Carboni, R., C. Pilo and E. Cruccas (2012) *Res Sacrae: Note su Alcuni Aspetti Culturali della Sardegna Romana*, Cagliari: Edizioni AV.

Carlson, R.D. (2015) *The Honey Bee and Apian Imagery in Classical Literature*, Unpublished PhD Thesis, University of Washington, Seattle, Ann Arbor: University Microfilms International..

Carney, E. (2002) 'Hunting and the Macedonian Elite: Sharing the Rivalry of the Chase', in D. Ogden (ed) 2002 *The Hellenistic World: New Perspectives*, London: Duckworth, pp. 59–80.

Carra, M. (1970) *Ivories of the West*, London: Hamlyn.

Cartmill, M. (1993) *A View to a Death in the Morning: Hunting and Nature Through History*, Cambridge, Massachusetts: Harvard University Press.

Cassin, B. and J.-L. Labarrière (eds) (1997) *L'Animal dans l'Antiquité*, Paris: J. Vrin.

Castignone, S. and G. Lanata (eds) (1994) *Filosofi e Animali nel Mondo Antico*, Pisa: Edizioni ETS.

Centre de Recherches A. Piganiol (ed) (1995) *Homme et Animal dans l'Antiquité Romaine: Actes do Colloque de Nantes 1991*, Tours: Centre de Recherches A. Piganiol.

Chadwick, W. (1985) *Women Artists and the Surrealist Movement*, London: Thames and Hudson.

Chandezon, C. (2015) 'Animals, Meat, and Alimentary By-Products: Patterns of Production and Consumption', in J. Wilkins and R. Nadeau (eds) 2015, pp. 135–146.

Chioffi, L. (1999) *Caro: il Mercato della Carne nell'Occidente Romano: Riflessi Epigrafici ed Iconografici*, Rome: L'Erma di Bretschneider.

Chomel, C. (1900) *Histoire du Cheval dans l'Antiquité et Son Rôle dans la Civilisation*, Paris: Lecaplain and Vidal.

Christesen, P. and D.G. Kyle (eds) (2014) *A Companion to Sport and Spectacle in Greek and Roman Antiquity*, Oxford: Wiley-Blackwell.

Cima, M. and E. La Rocca (1998) *Horti Romani: Atti del Convegno, Roma 1995*, Bullettino della Commissione Archeologica Communale di Roma, Rome: L'Erma di Bretschneider.

Cima, M. and E. Talamo (2008) *Gli Horti di Roma Antica*, Rome: Quaderni Capitolini. Electa.

Clark, K. (1977) *Animals and Men: Their Relationship as Reflected in Western Art from Prehistory to the Present Day*, London: Thames and Hudson.

Clark, K. (2006) *Guides, Guards and Gifts to the Gods: Domesticated Dogs in the Art and Archaeology of Iron Age and Roman Britain*, British Archaeological Reports British Series 422, Oxford: Archaeopress.

Clarke, J.R. (1996) 'Landscape Paintings in the Villa of Oplontis', *Journal of Roman Archaeology* 9, pp. 81–107.

Clarke, J.R. (2003) *Art in the Lives of Ordinary Romans. Visual Representation and Non-Elite Viewers in Italy, 100 BC–AD 315,* Berkeley: University of California Press.

Clarke, J.R. (2007) *Looking at Laughter. Humor, Power, and Transgression in Roman Visual Culture, 100 BC–AD 250,* Los Angeles: University of California Press.

Clarke, M. (1995) 'Between Lions and Man: Images of the Hero in the Iliad', *Greek, Roman and Byzantine Studies* 36, pp. 137–160.

Clavel-Lévêque, M. (1984) *L'Empire en Jeux. Espace Symbolique et Pratique Sociale dans le Monde Romain*, Paris: Éditions du Centre National de la Recherche Scientifique.

Clutton-Brock, J. (1992) *Horse Power. A History of the Horse and the Donkey in Human Societies*, Cambridge, Massachusetts: Harvard University Press.

Clutton-Brock, J. (1999) *A Natural History of Domesticated Mammals*, Second Edition, Cambridge: Cambridge University Press.

Cohen, A. (1997) *The Alexander Mosaic: Stories of Victory and Defeat*, Cambridge: Cambridge University Press.

Cohen, A. and J.B. Rutter (eds) (2007) *Constructions of Childhood in Ancient Greece and Italy*. Hesperia Supplement 41, Athens: The American School of Classics at Athens.

Coleman, K. (1990) 'Fatal Charades: Roman Executions Staged as Mythological Enactments', *Journal of Roman Studies* 80, pp. 44–73.

Coleman, K. (1993) 'Launching Into History: Aquatic Displays in the Early Empire', *Journal of Roman Studies* 83, pp. 48–74.

Coleman, K. (2011) 'Public Entertainments', in M. Peachin (ed) 2011 *The Oxford Handbook of Social Relations in the Roman World*, Oxford: Oxford University Press, pp. 335–357.

Coleman, K. and P. Derron (2014) *Le Jardin dans l'Antiquité: Introduction et Huit Exposés Suivis de Discussions*, Entretiens sur l'Antiquité Classique 60, Vandoeuvres: Fondation Hardt.

Collins, B.J. (ed) (2002) *A History of the Animal World in the Ancient Near East*, Leiden: Brill.

Conan, M. (1986) 'Nature Into Art: Gardens and Landscape in the Everyday Life of Ancient Rome', *Journal of Garden History* 6, pp. 348–356.

Connell, S.M. (2016) *Aristotle on Feminine Animals: a Study of the Generation of Animals*, Cambridge: Cambridge University Press.

Cooke, B. (2000) *Imperial China: the Art of the Horse in Chinese History. An Exhibition Catalogue*, Lexington: Kentucky Horse Park.

Cool, H.E.M. (2006) *Eating and Drinking in Roman Britain*, Cambridge: Cambridge University Press.

Cooper, J. (1983) *Animals in War*, London: Heinemann.

Corbier, M. (1989) 'The Ambiguous Status of Meat in Ancient Rome', *Food and Foodways* 3, pp. 223–264.

Cornwall, I.W. (1956) *Bones for the Archaeologist*, London: Phoenix House.

Cosentino, A. (2016) 'Persephone's Cockerel', in P.A. Johnston, A. Mastrocinque, and S. Papaioannou (eds) 2016, pp. 189–212.

Cram, L. (2000) 'Varieties of Dog in Roman Britain', in S.J. Crockford (ed) 2000, pp. 171–180.

Crane, E. (1999) *The World History of Beekeeping and Honey Hunting*, New York: Routledge.

Crane, S. (2013) *Animal Encounters: Contacts and Concepts in Medieval Britain*, Philadelphia: University of Pennsylvania Press.

Crockford, S.J. (ed) (2000) *Dogs Through Time: An Archaeological Perspective*, British Archaeological Reports International Series 889, Oxford: Archaeopress.

Crofton-Sleigh, L. (2016) 'The Mythical Landscapers of Augustan Rome', in J. McInerny and I. Sluiter (eds) 2016, pp. 383–407.

Croisille, J.M. (1965) *Les Natures Mortes Campaniennes*, Brussels: Collection Latomus 76.

Croisille, J.M. (2015) *Natures Mortes dans la Rome Antique. Naissance d'un Genre Artistique*, Paris: Picard.

Crummy, N. (2010) 'Bears and Coins: the Iconography of Protection in Late Roman Infant Burials', *Britannia* 41, pp. 37–93.

Csapo, E. (1993) 'Deep Ambivalence: Notes on a Greek Cockfight', Part I *Phoenix* 47, 1–28, Parts II–IV *Phoenix* 47, pp. 115–124.

Curry, A. (2008) 'The Gladiator Diet', *Archaeology* 61 No. 6, pp. 28–30.

Curtis, R.I. (1984) 'A Personalized Floor Mosaic from Pompeii', *American Journal of Archaeology* 88.4, pp. 557–566.

Curtis, R.I. (1991) *Garum and Salsamenta: Production and Commerce in Materia Medica*, Leiden: Brill.

Curtis, R.I. (2014) 'From Fish to Fish Sauce: Seafood in the Ancient Roman World', in S.D. Pevnick (ed) 2014, pp. 95–110.

Curtis, R.I. (2016) 'Ancient Processed Fish Products', in T. Bekker-Nielsen and R. Gertwagen (eds) 2016, pp. 160–187.

Cutler, A. (1993) 'Five Lessons in Late Roman Ivory', *Journal of Roman Archaeology* 6, pp. 167–192.

Dalby, A. (2000) *Empire of Pleasures: Luxury and Indulgence in the Roman World*, London: Routledge.

Dalby, A. (2003) *Food in the Ancient World From A to Z*, London: Routledge.

D'Ambra, E. (2007) 'Racing With Death: Circus Sarcophagi and the Commemoration of Children in Roman Art', in A. Cohen and J.B. Rutter (eds) 2007, pp. 339–351.

D'Arms, J.H. (1999) 'Performing Culture: Roman Spectacle and the Banquets of the Powerful', in B. Bergmann and C. Kondoleon (eds) 1999 *The Art of Ancient Spectacle*, New Haven: Yale University Press, pp. 301–320.

Daryaee, T. (2016) 'From Terror to Tactical Usage: Elephants in the Partho-Sasanian Period', in V.S. Curtis, E.J. Pendleton, M. Alram, and T. Daryaee (eds) 2016 *The Parthian and Early Sasanian Empires: Adaption and Expansion*, Oxford: Oxbow Books, pp. 36–41.

Davies, M.I.J. and F.N. M'Mbogori (eds) (2013) *Humans and the Environment: New Archaeological Perspectives for the Twenty-First Century*, Oxford: Oxford University Press.

Day, L. P. (1984) 'Dog Burials in the Greek World', *American Journal of Archaeology* 88, pp. 21–32.

De Caro, S. (2001) *La Natura Morta nelle Pitture e nei Mosaici delle Città Vesuviane*, Naples: Museo Archeologico Nazionale di Napoli and Electa.

De Grossi Mazzorin, J. (2006) 'Cammelli nell'Antichita: le Presenze in Italia', in B. Sala and U. Tecchiati (eds) 2006 Archaeozoological Studies in Honour of Alfredo Riedel, Bolzano: Ripartizione Beni Culturali, pp. 231–242.

De Grossi Mazzorin, J. and C. Minniti (2006) 'Dog Sacrifice in the Ancient World: a Ritual Passage?', in L.M. Snyder and E.A. Moore (eds) 2006, pp. 62–66.

Deniaux, E. (1998) 'L'Importation d'Animaux d'Afrique à l'Époque Républicaine et les Relations de Clientele', in M. Khanoussi, P. Ruggeri and C. Vismara (eds) 1998 *L'Africa Romana* Atti del XIII Convegno di Studio Djerba, Rome: Carocci, pp. 1299–1307.

De Ruyt, C. (2008) 'Les Produits Vendus au Macellum', in W. Van Andringa (ed) 2008, pp. 135–150.

Detienne, M. and J.-P. Vernant (eds) (1989) *The Cuisine of Sacrifice Among the Greeks*, Chicago: University of Chicago Press.

De Vos, M. (1980) *L'Egittomania in Pitture e Mosaici Romano-Campani della Prima Età Imperiale*, Leiden: Brill.

Deyts, S. (1994) *Un Peuple de Pelerins. Offrandes de Pierre et de Bronze des Sources de la Seine*, Dijon: Revue Archéologique de l'Est et du Centre-Est, Trezieme Supplement.

Di Tommaso, L. (2012) *Images of Nature: the Art of the First Fleet*, London: Natural History Museum.

Dixon, K.R. and P. Southern (1992) *The Roman Cavalry*, London: Batsford.

Dodge, H. (2011) *Spectacle in the Roman World*, London: Bristol Classical Press.

Dodig, R. (2013) 'Dolphin Representations on Funerary Monuments in the Interior of Dalmatia', in N. Cambi and G. Koch (eds) 2013, pp. 481–504.

Donahue, J.F. (2014) *Food and Drink in Antiquity: a Sourcebook*, London: Bloomsbury.

Donahue, J. F. (2015) 'Roman Dining', in J. Wilkins and R. Nadeau (eds) 2015, pp. 253–264.

Donaldson, M.D. (1999) *The Domestic Cat in Roman Civilization*, Lampeter: the Edwin Mellen Press.

Dorcey, P.F. (1992) *The Cult of Silvanus: a Study in Roman Folk Religion*, Leiden: Brill.

Dubois, P. (1982) *Centaurs and Amazons. Women and the Pre-History of the Great Chain of Being*, Ann Arbor: University of Michigan Press.

Dubourdieu, A. (2016) 'Le Savoir des Augures Comme *Interpretes Iovis* Chez Cicéron (*De Legibus, De Natura Deorum, De Divinatione*)', in V. Gasparini (ed) 2016 *Vestigia: Miscellanea di Studi Storico-Religiosi in Onore di Filippo Coarelli nel 80 Anniversario*, Stuttgart: Franz Steiner Verlag, pp. 327–336.

Dulière, C. (1979) *Lupa Romana. Recherches d'Iconographie et Essai d'Interprétation*, Brussels: Institut Historique Belge de Rome.

Dumont, J. (1988) 'Les Combats de Coq Furent-Ils Un Sport?', *Pallas* 34, pp. 33–47.

Dumont, J. (2001) *Les Animaux dans l'Antiquité*, Paris: L'Harmattan.

Dunbabin, K.M.D. (1978) *The Mosaics of Roman North Africa: Studies in Iconography and Patronage*, Oxford: Clarendon Press.

Dunbabin, K.M.D. (2003) *The Roman Banquet: Images of Conviviality*, Cambridge: Cambridge University Press.

Durand, J.-A. and F. Lissarrague (1979) 'Les Entrailles de la Cité', *Hephaistos* 1, pp. 92–108.

Dwyer, E.J. (1978) 'The Fowler and the Asp: Literary Versus Generic Illustration in Roman Art', *American Journal of Archaeology* 82, pp. 400–404.

Dyson, J.T. (2007) 'The Lesbia Poems', in M. Skinner (ed) 2007 *A Companion to Catullus*, Oxford: Wiley-Blackwell, pp. 254–275.

Eason, C. (2008) *Fabulous Creatures, Mythological Monsters, and Animal Power Symbols: a Handbook*, Westport: Greenwood Publishing Group.

Egerton, F. (2012) *Roots of Ecology. Antiquity to Haeckel*, Berkeley: University of California Press.

Ejstrud, B. (2005) 'Size Matters: Estimating Trade in Wine, Oil and Fishsauce from Amphorae in the First Century AD', in T. Bekker-Neilsen (ed) 2005, pp. 171–181.

Ekroth, G. (2014) 'Animal Sacrifice in Antiquity', in G.L. Campbell (ed) 2014, pp. 324–354.

Elsner, J. (2005) 'Sacrifice and Narrative on the Arch of the Argentarii at Rome', *Journal of Roman Archaeology* 18.1, pp. 83–99.

Elsner, J. (2012) 'Sacrifice in Late Roman art', in C.A. Faraone and F.S. Naiden (eds) 2012, pp. 120–166.

Engels, D. (1999) *Classical Cats: the Rise and Fall of the Sacred Cat*, London: Routledge.

Epplett, C. (2001a) *Animal Spectacula of the Roman Empire*, Unpublished PhD Thesis, University of British Columbia.

Epplett, C. (2001b) 'The Capture of Animals by the Roman Military', *Greece and Rome* 48.2, pp. 210–222.

Epplett, C. (2003) 'The Preparation of Animals for Roman Spectacula: Vivaria and Their Administration', *Ludica* 9, pp. 76–92.

Epplett, C. (2014) 'Roman Beast Hunts', in P. Christesen and D.G. Kyle (eds) 2014, pp. 505–519.

Epplett, C. (2016) *Gladiators and Beast Hunts: Arena Sports of Ancient Rome*, Barnsley: Pen and Sword Military.

Erdkamp, P., K. Verboven, and A. Zuiderhoek (eds) (2015) *Ownership and Exploitation of Land and Natural Resources in the Roman World*, Oxford: Oxford University Press.

Evans, J.D. (1963) 'Cretan Cattle-Cults and Sports', in A.E. Mourant and F.E. Zeuner (eds) 1963 *Man and Cattle*, London: Royal Anthropological Institute, pp. 138–143.

Faas, P. (2003) *Around the Roman Table: Food and Feasting in Ancient Rome*, Chicago: University of Chicago Press.

Fagan, B. (2015) *The Intimate Bond: How Animals Shaped Human History*, New York: Bloomsbury Press.

Fagan, G.G. (2011) *The Lure of the Arena: Social Psychology and the Crowd at the Roman Games*, Cambridge: Cambridge University Press.

Faraone, C.A. (1999) *Ancient Greek Love Magic*, Cambridge, Massachusetts: Harvard University Press.

Faraone, C.A. and F.S. Naiden (eds) (2012) *Greek and Roman Animal Sacrifice: Ancient Victims, Modern Observers*, Cambridge: Cambridge University Press.

Fer, B. (1999) 'The Work of Art, the Work of Psychoanalysis', in G. Perry (ed) 1999 *Gender and Art*, New Haven: Yale University Press, pp. 240–251.

Ferris, I.M. (2000) *Enemies of Rome. Barbarians Through Roman Eyes*, Stroud: Sutton.

Ferris, I.M. (2006) 'Suffering in Silence: the Aesthetics of Pain in Antonine Art', in T. Pollard and I. Banks (eds) 2006 *Past Tense: Studies in the Archaeology of Conflict*, Leiden: Brill, 67–92.

Ferris, I.M. (2009) *Hate and War. The Column of Marcus Aurelius*, Stroud: History Press.

Ferris, I.M. (2010) *The Beautiful Rooms Are Empty. Excavations at Binchester Roman Fort, County Durham 1976–1981 and 1986–1991*, Durham: Durham County Council Excavation Monograph.

Ferris, I.M. (2013) *The Arch of Constantine. Inspired by the Divine*, Stroud: Amberley Publishing.

Ferris, I.M. (2014) 'A Roman Carved Jet Dog from Binchester Roman Fort, County Durham', *Durham Archaeological Journal* 19, pp. 23–32.

Ferris (2015) *The Mirror of Venus. Women in Roman Art*, Stroud: Amberley Publishing.

Finkelpearl, E. (2015) 'Elephant Tears: Animal Emotion in Pliny and Aelian', in C.A. Clark, E. Foster and J.P. Hallett (eds) 2015 *Kinesis: the Ancient Depiction of Gesture, Motion, and Emotion. Essays for Donald Lateiner*, Ann Arbor: University of Michigan Press, pp. 173–187.

Fisher, K. and R. Langlands (2015) 'Bestiality in the Bay of Naples: the Herculaneum Pan and Goat Statue', in K. Fisher and R. Langlands (eds) 2015 *Sex, Knowledge, and Receptions of the Past*, Oxford: Oxford University Press, pp. 86–110.

Flohr, M. (2013a) *The World of the Fullo: Work, Economy, and Society in Roman Italy*, Oxford: Oxford University Press.

Flohr, M. (2013b) 'Ulula, Quinquatrus and the Occupational Identity of Fullones in Early Imperial Italy', in M. Gleba and J. Pásztókai-Szeőke (eds) 2013 *Making Textiles in Pre-Roman and Roman Times. Peoples, Places, Identities. Ancient Textiles Series Vol. 13*, Oxford: Oxbow Books, pp. 192–207.

Forster, E.S. (1940/1941) 'Dogs in Ancient Warfare', *Greece and Rome* 10, pp. 114–117.

Foucher, L. (1965) 'Les Mosaiques Nilotiques Africaines', in *La Mosaique Greco-Romaine*, Paris: Éditions du Centre National de la Recherche Scientifique.

Fox, R.L. (1996) 'Ancient Hunting: from Homer to Polybius', in G. Shipley and J. Salmon (eds) 1996, pp. 119–154.

Franco, C. (2014) *Shameless: The Canine and the Feminine in Ancient Greece*, Berkeley: University of California Press.

Frayn, J.N. (1984) *Sheep-Rearing and the Wool Trade in Italy During the Roman Period*, Liverpool: Francis Cairns Publications Limited.

French, R. (1994) *Ancient Natural History: Histories of Nature*, London: Routledge.

French, R. and F. Greenaway (eds) (1986) *Science in the Early Roman Empire: Pliny the Elder, His Sources and Influence*, London: Croom Helm.

Freyburger, G. (2016) 'Lament on the Sacrificial Bull in Ovid, Metamorphoses 15: 120–42', in P.A. Johnston, A. Mastrocinque, and S. Papaioannou (eds) 2016, pp. 299–308.

Furley, W. and V. Gysembergh (2015) *Reading the Liver. Papyrological Texts on Ancient Greek Extispicy*, Studien und Texte zu Antike und Christentum 94, Tübingen: Mohr Siebeck.

Futrell, A. (1997) *Blood in the Arena: the Spectacle of Roman Power*, Austin: University of Texas Press.

Futrell, A. (2006) *The Roman Games: Historical Sources in Translation*, Oxford: Blackwell.

Gager, J.G. (1992) *Curse Tablets and Binding Spells from the Ancient World*, Oxford: Oxford University Press.

Gardeisen, A. (ed) (2005) Les Équidés dans le Monde Méditerranéen Antique, Lattes: Édition de l'Association pour le Développement d'Archéologie en Languedoc-Roussillon.

Garnsey, P. (1988) *Famine and Food Supply in the Graeco-Roman World*, Cambridge: Cambridge University Press.

Bibliography

Garnsey, P. (1999) *Food and Society in Classical Antiquity*, Cambridge: Cambridge University Press.

Gatier, P.-L. (1996) 'Des Girafes pour l'Empereur', *Topoi* 6, pp. 903–941.

Gentili, G.V. (1964) *Mosaics of Piazza Armerina: the Hunting Scenes*, Milan: Arti Grafiche Ricordi.

Georgoudi, S., R. Koch Piettre and F. Schmidt (eds) (2005) *La Cuisine et l'Autel: les Sacrifices en Questions dans les Societés de la Méditerranée Ancienne,* Turnhout: Brepols.

Georgoudi, S., R. Koch Piettre and F. Schmidt (eds) (2012) *La Raison des Signes. Présages, Rites, Destin dans les Societés de la Méditerranée Ancienne*, Leiden: Brill.

Ghigi, A. (1939) *Poultry Farming as Described by the Writers of Ancient Rome*, Milan: Raffaello Bertieri.

Gilhus, I.S. (2006) *Animals, Gods and Humans. Changing Attitudes to Animals in Greek, Roman and Early Christian Ideas*, London: Routledge.

Gilhus, I.S. (2014) 'Animals in Late Antiquity and Early Christianity', in G.L. Campbell (ed) 2014, pp. 355–365.

Giner, C.A. (2016) 'Purple in the Ancient Mediterranean World: Social Demand and the Exploitation of Marine Resources', in T. Bekker-Nielsen and R. Gertwagen (eds) 2016, pp. 138–159.

Giordano, C. and G. Pelagalli (1957) 'Cani e Canili nella Antica Pompei', *Atti della Accademia Pontaniana* New Series 7, pp. 165–201.

Glassner, J.-J. (2012) 'La Fabrique des Présages en Mésopotamie: la Sémiologie des Devins', in S. Georgoudi, R. Koch Piettre and F. Schmidt (eds) 2012, pp. 29–53.

Goebel, V. and J. Peters (2014) 'Veterinary Medicine', in G.L. Campbell (ed) 2014, pp. 589–606.

Goguey, D. (2003) *Les Animaux dans la Mentalité Romaine*, Brussels: Éditions Latomus.

Golden, M. (1997) 'Equestrian Competition in Ancient Greece: Difference, Dissent, Democracy', *Phoenix* 51, pp. 327–344.

Gontier, T. (1999) *L'Homme et l'Animal. La Philosophie Antique*, Paris: Presses Universitaires de France.

Gordon, R. (1989) 'The Moment of Death: Art and the Ritual of Greek Sacrifice', in I. Lavin (ed) 1989 *World Art: Themes of Unity in Diversity*, Pennsylvania: Pennsylvania State University Press, pp. 567–573.

Gordon, R. (2010) 'Magian Lessons in Natural History: Unique Animals in Graeco-Roman Natural Magic', in J.N. Bremmer, J.H.F. Dijkstra, J.E.A. Kroesen, and Y. Kuiper (eds) 2010, pp. 249–270.

Gowers, E. (1993) *The Loaded Table: Representations of Food in Roman Literature*, Oxford: Clarendon Press.

Gowers, W. (1948) 'African Elephants and Ancient Authors', *African Affairs* 47, pp. 173–180.

Graf, F. (1997) *Magic in the Ancient World*, Cambridge, Massachusetts: Harvard University Press.

Grant, A. (1989) 'Animals in Roman Britain' in M. Todd (ed.) 1989 *Research on Roman Britain 1960–1989*, London: Society for the Promotion of Roman Studies, pp. 135–146.

Grant, A. (1991) 'Economic or Symbolic? Animals and Ritual Behaviour' in P. Garwood, D. Jennings, R. Skeates and J. Toms (eds.) 1991 *Sacred and Profane*, Oxford: Oxbow Books, pp. 109–114.

Grant, M. (2008) *Roman Cookery: Ancient Recipes for Modern Kitchens*, Second Edition, London: Serif.

Grant, R.M. (1999) *Early Christians and Animals*, London: Routledge.

Gräslund, A-S. (2004) 'Dogs in Graves-a Question of Symbolism?, in B. Santillo-Frizell (ed) 2004, pp. 167–176.

Green, C.M.C. (1996) 'Did the Romans Hunt?', *Classical Antiquity* 15, pp. 222–260.

Green, M.J. (1992) *Animals in Celtic Life and Myth,* London: Routledge.

Green, M.J. (2001) 'Animal Iconographies: Metaphor, Meaning and Identity', in G. Davis, A. Gardner and K. Lockyear (eds) *TRAC 2000 Proceedings of the Tenth Annual Theoretical Roman Archaeology Conference,* Oxford: Oxbow Books, pp. 80–93.

Greenewalt, C.H. (1976) *Ritual Dinners in Early Historic Sardis,* Berkeley: University of California Press.

Griffith, M. (2006) 'Horsepower and Donkeywork: Equids and the Ancient Greek Imagination', *Classical Philology* 101, pp. 185–246.

Grigson, C. (2016) *Menagerie: the History of Exotic Animals in England,* Oxford: Oxford University Press.

Grimm, J.M. (2010) 'A Bird for All Occasions: the Use of Birds at the Romano-British Sanctuary of Springhead, Kent (UK)', in W. Prummel, J.T. Zeiler and D.C. Brinkhuizen (eds) 2010, pp. 187–195.

Groot, M. (2016) *Livestock for Sale: Animal Husbandry in a Roman Frontier Zone. The Case Study of the Civitas Batavorum,* Amsterdam: Amsterdam University Press.

Guarisco, D. (2016) 'Acting the She-Bear: Animal Symbolism and Ritual in Ancient Athens', in P.A. Johnston, A. Mastrocinque, and S. Papaioannou (eds) 2016, pp. 419–430.

Gullini, G. (1956) *I Mosaici di Palestrina,* Rome: Archeologia Classica Supplementary Volume 1.

Hachlili, R. (1998) 'Iconographic Elements of Nilotic Scenes on Byzantine Mosaic Pavements in Israel', *Palestine Exploration Quarterly* 130.2, pp. 106–120.

Hales, S. (2003) *The Roman House and Social Identity,* Cambridge: Cambridge University Press.

Harcourt, R.A. (1974) 'The Dog in Prehistoric and Early Historic Britain', *Journal of Archaeological Science* 1, pp. 151–175.

Harden, A. (2013) *Animals in the Classical World: Ethical Perspectives from Greek and Roman Texts,* New York: Palgrave MacMillan.

Harden, A. (2014) 'Animals in Classical Art', in G.L. Campbell (ed) 2014, pp. 24–60.

Hawtree, L.J. (2011) *Wild Animals in Roman Epic,* Unpublished PhD Thesis, University of Exeter.

Heintz, F. (2000) 'Magic Tablets and the Games at Antioch', in C. Kondoleon (ed) 2000 *Antioch: the Lost Ancient City,* Princeton: Princeton University Press, pp. 163–167.

Hekster, O. (2002) *Commodus: an Emperor at the Crossroads,* Amsterdam: J.C. Gieben.

Hemingway, S. (2004) *The Horse and Jockey from Artemision: a Bronze Equestrian Monument of the Hellenistic Period,* Berkeley: University of California Press.

Henig, M. (1984) *Religion in Roman Britain,* London: Batsford.

Henig, M. (1995) *The Art of Roman Britain,* London: Batsford.

Heyob, S.K. (1975) *The Cult of Isis Among Women in the Greco-Roman World,* Leiden: Brill.

Higginbotham, J. (1997) *Piscinae: Artificial Fishponds in Roman Italy,* Chapel Hill: University of North Carolina Press.

Hill, D.K. (1949) 'Greek Cock Fighting', *Bulletin of the Walters Art Gallery* 2, No. 3.

Hitch, S. (2015) 'Sacrifice', in J. Wilkins and R. Nadeau (eds) 2015, pp. 337–347.

Hitch, S. and I. Rutherford (eds) (2015) *Animal Sacrifice in the Ancient Greek World,* Cambridge: Cambridge University Press.

Holleman, A.W.J. (1985) 'Lupus, Lupercalia, Lupa', *Latomus* 44.3, pp. 609–614.

Holliday, P.J. (1993) 'The Sarcophagus of Titus Aelius Evangelus and Gaudenia Nicene', *J. Paul Getty Museum Journal* 21, pp. 85–100.

Hooper, R.W. (1985) 'In Defence of Catullus' Dirty Sparrow', *Greece and Rome* 32:2, pp. 162–178.

Bibliography

Hopkins, K. (1965) 'Contraception in the Roman Empire', *Comparative Studies in Society and History* 8 No.1, pp. 124–151.

Hopkins, K. (1983) *Death and Renewal*, Cambridge: Cambridge University Press.

Horard-Herbin, M-P. (2000) 'Dog Management and Use in the Late Iron Age: the Evidence from the Gallic Site of Levroux (France)' in S.J. Crockford (ed.) 2000 *Dogs Through Time: An Archaeological Perspective, Proceedings of the 1ˢᵗ ICAZ Symposium on the History of the Domestic Dog, Eighth Congress of the International Council for Archaeozoology (ICAZ98), 1998, Victoria, Canada*, British Archaeological Reports International Series 889. Oxford: Archaeopress, pp. 115–121.

Horstmanshoff, H.F.J. and M. Stol (eds) (2004) *Magic and Rationality in Ancient Near Eastern and Graeco-Roman Medicine*, Leiden: Brill.

Hough, J.N. (1974/1975) 'Bird Imagery in Roman Poetry', *Classical Journal* 70, pp. 1–13.

Houlihan, P.F. (1996) *The Animal World of the Pharaohs*, London: Thames and Hudson.

Houlihan, P.F. (2002) 'Animals in Egyptian Art and Hieroglyphs', in B.J. Collins (ed) 2002, pp. 97–144.

Hubbell, H.M. (1935) 'Ptolemy's Zoo', *Classical Journal* 31, pp. 68–76.

Huet, V. (2008) 'Le Sacrifice Disparu: les Relifs de Boucherie', in W. Van Andringa (ed) 2008, pp. 197–223.

Huet, V. (2004) 'Les Sacrifices dans le Monde Romain', *Thesaurus Cultus et Rituum Antiquorum* 1, pp. 183–235.

Huet, V. (2015) 'Watching Rituals', in R. Raja and J. Rüpke (eds) 2015, pp. 144–154.

Hughes, J.D. (2003) 'Europe as Consumer of Exotic Biodiversity: Greek and Roman Times', *Landscape Research* 28.1, pp. 21–31.

Hughes, J.D. (2007) 'Hunting in the Ancient Mediterranean World', in L. Kalof (ed) 2007 *A Cultural History of Animals in Antiquity*, Oxford: Berg, pp. 47–70.

Hughes, J.D. (2014) *Environmental Problems of the Greeks and Romans: Ecology in the Ancient Mediterranean*, Baltimore: Johns Hopkins University Press.

Hull, D.B. (1964) *Hounds and Hunting in Ancient Greece*, Chicago: University of Chicago Press.

Humphrey, J.H. (1986) *Roman Circuses: Arenas for Chariot-Racing*, Berkeley: University of California Press.

Hurwit, J. (2006) 'Lions, Lizards and the Uncanny in Early Greek Art', *Hesperia* 75, pp. 121–136.

Hyland, A. (1990) *Equus. The Horse in the Roman World*, London: Batsford.

Hyland, A. (2003) *The Horse in the Ancient World*, Stroud: Sutton.

Hyland, A. (2013) 'War and the Horse', in B. Campbell and L.A. Tritle (eds) 2013 *The Oxford Handbook of Warfare in the Classical World*, Oxford: Oxford University Press, pp. 493–526.

Ingold, T. (2000) 'From Trust to Domination: an Alternative History of Human-Animal Relations', in T. Ingold (ed) 2000 *The Perception of the Environment: Essays in Livelihood, Dwelling and Skill*, London: Routledge, pp. 61–76.

Isler, P. (1984) 'The Meaning of the Animal Frieze', in E.C. Polomé (ed) 1984 Essays in Memory of Karl Kerényi, Washington: Institute for the Study of Man, pp. 123–144.

Jackson, R. (1994) 'The Mouse, the Lion and 'the Crooked One': Two Enigmatic Roman Handle Types', *Antiquaries Journal* 74, pp. 325–332.

Jackson, R. (2014) 'Tailpiece: Roman Mice in Art, Allegory and Actuality'. In R. Collins and F. McIntosh (eds) 2014 *Life in the Limes. Studies of the People and Objects of the Roman Frontiers*, Oxford: Oxbow Books, pp. 217–231.

Jacobson-Tepfer, E. (2015) *The Hunter, the Stag, and the Mother of Animals: Image, Monument, and Landscape in Ancient North Asia*, Oxford: Oxford University Press.

Jácome, P.M. (2013) 'Bacchus and Felines in Roman Iconography: Issues of Gender and Species', in A. Bernabé, M.H. de Jáuregui, A.I.J. San Cristóbal, and R.M. Hernández (eds) 2013 *Redefining Dionysos*, Berlin: Walter de Gruyter, pp. 526–540.

Jameson, M.H. (1988) 'Sacrifice and Animal Husbandry in Classical Greece', in C.R. Whitaker (ed) 1988 *Pastoral Economies in Classical Antiquity*, Cambridge: Cambridge University Press, pp. 87–119.

Jameson, M.H. (2014) *Cults and Rites in Ancient Greece: Essays on Religion and Society* (edited by A.B. Stallsmith), Cambridge: Cambridge University Press.

Jashemski, W.F. and E.G. Meyer (eds) (2002) *The Natural History of Pompeii*, Cambridge: Cambridge University Press.

Jenkins, F. (1957) 'The Role of the Dog in Romano-Gaulish Religion', *Collection Latomus* XVI, pp. 60–78.

Jennison, G. (1937) *Animals for Show and Pleasure in Ancient Rome*, Manchester: Manchester University Press.

Jeskins, P. (1998) *Environment and the Classical World*, London: Bristol Classical Press.

Jesnick, I.J. (1997) *The Image of Orpheus in Roman Mosaic: an Exploration of the Figure of Orpheus in Graeco-Roman Art and Culture with Special Reference to its Expression in the Medium of Mosaic in Late Antiquity*, British Archaeological Reports International Series 671, Oxford: Archaeopress.

Johns, C. (1995) 'Mounted Men and Sitting Ducks: the Iconography of Romano-British Plate-Brooches' in B. Raftery, V. Megaw and V. Rigby (eds.) 1995 *Sites and Sights of the Iron Age: Essays on Fieldwork and Museum Research Presented to Ian Mathieson Stead*, Oxbow Monograph 56, Oxford: Oxbow Books, pp. 103–109.

Johns, C. (2003) 'The Tombstone of Laetus' Daughter: Cats in Gallo-Roman Sculpture', *Britannia* 34, pp. 53–63.

Johns, C. (2006) *Horses: History, Myth, Art*, London: British Museum Press.

Johns, C. (2008) *Dogs: History, Myth, Art*, London: British Museum Press.

Johns, C. (2011) *Cattle: History, Myth, Art*, London: British Museum Press.

Johnson, L.R. (1971) 'Birds for Pleasure and Entertainment in Ancient Rome', *Maryland Historian* 2, pp. 76–92.

Johnston, P.A. (2016) 'The Importance of Cattle in the Myths of Hercules and Mithras', in P.A. Johnston, A. Mastrocinque, and S. Papaioannou (eds) 2016, pp. 281–298.

Johnston, P.A., A. Mastrocinque, and S. Papaioannou (eds) (2016) *Animals in Greek and Roman Religion and Myth*, Newcastle Upon Tyne: Cambridge Scholars Publishing.

Jones, F.M.A. (2011) *Virgil's Garden: the Nature of Bucolic Space*, London: Bristol Classical Press.

Jones, F.M.A. (2013a) 'Drama, Boundaries, Imagination, and Columns in the Garden Room at Prima Porta', *Latomus* 72, pp. 997–1021.

Jones, F.M.A. (2013b) 'The Caged Bird in Roman Life and Poetry: Metaphor, Cognition, and Value', *Syllecta Classica* 24, pp. 105–123.

Jones, F.M.A. (2016) *The Boundaries of Art and Social Space in Rome: the Caged Bird and Other Art Forms*, London: Bloomsbury Academic.

Joubert, C.J. (1958) *Le Chien dans le Monde Antique*, Toulouse: Soubiron.

Kadletz, E. (1976) *Animal Sacrifice in Greek and Roman Religion*, PhD Thesis University of Washington, Seattle, Ann Arbor: University Microfilms International.

Kalof, L. (ed) (2007) *A Cultural History of Animals in Antiquity Volume One*, Oxford: Berg.

Karunanithy, D. (2008) *Dogs of War: Canine Use in Warfare from Ancient Egypt to the 19th Century*, London: Yarak.

Keesling, C.M. (2009) 'Exemplary Animals: Greek Animal Statues and Human Portraiture', in T. Fögen and M.M. Lee (eds) 2009 *Bodies and Boundaries in Graeco-Roman Antiquity*, Berlin: Walter de Gruyter, pp. 283–310.

Bibliography

Kelekna, P. (2009) *The Horse in Human History*, Cambridge: Cambridge University Press.

Kenner, H. (1970) *Das Phänomen der Verkehrten Welt in der Griechisch-Römischen Antike*, Klagenfurt: Ernst Ploetz.

Kete, K. (1994) *The Beast in the Boudoir: Petkeeping in Nineteenth-Century Paris*, Berkeley: University of California Press.

Kiernan, P. (2014) 'The Bronze Mice of Apollo Smintheus', *American Journal of Archaeology* 118 No. 4, pp. 601–626.

King, A. (1999) 'Diet in the Roman World: a Regional Inter-Site Comparison of the Mammal Bones', *Journal of Roman Archaeology* 12, pp. 168–202.

King, A. (2002) 'Mammals. Evidence from Wall Paintings, Sculpture, Mosaics, Faunal Remains, and Ancient Literary Sources', in W.F. Jashemski and F.G. Meyer (eds) 2002, pp. 401–450.

Kisling, V.N. (2001) 'Ancient Collections and Menageries', in V.N. Kisling (ed) 2001 *Zoo and Aquarium History: Ancient Animal Collections to Zoological Gardens*, Boca Raton, Florida: CRC Press, pp. 1–47.

Kistler, J.M. (2007) *War Elephants*, Lincoln: University of Nebraska Press.

Kitchell, K.F. (2013) *Animals in the Ancient World From A to Z*, London: Routledge.

Klingender, F.D. (1971) *Animals in Art and Thought: to the End of the Middle Ages*, London: Routledge and Kegan Paul.

Koch, G. (1984) 'Zum Grabrelief der Helena', *J. Paul Getty Museum Journal* 12, pp. 59–72.

Kolendo, J. (1970) 'Epigraphie et Archéologie: le *Praepositus Camellorum*' dans une Inscription d'Ostie', *Klio* 51, pp. 287–298.

Korhonen, T. (2012) 'On Human-Animal Sexual Relationships in Aelian's Natura Animalium', *Arctos, Acta Philologica Fennica* XLVI, pp. 65–78.

Korhonen, T. and E. Ruonakoski (2017) *Human and Animal in Ancient Greece: Empathy and Encounter in Classical Literature*, London: I.B. Tauris.

Kosmetatou, E. (1993) 'Horse Sacrifices in Greece and Cyprus', *Journal of Prehistoric Religion* 7, pp. 31–41.

Kosmin, P.J. (2014) *The Land of the Elephant Kings. Space, Territory, and Ideology in the Seleucid Empire*, Cambridge: Cambridge University Press.

Kozloff, A.P. (1981) *Animals in Ancient Art from the Leo Mildenberg Collection*, Cleveland: Cleveland Museum of Art.

Kozloff, A.P. (1986) *More Animals in Ancient Art from the Leo Mildenberg Collection*, Mainz: Verlag Philipp von Zabern.

Krebs, W. (1967) 'Zur Rolle der Elephanten in der Antike', *Forschungen und Fortschritte* 41, pp. 85–87.

Krekoukias, D. (1970) *Gli Animali nella Meteorologia Popolare: degli Antichi Greci, Romani e Bizantini*, Florence: L.S. Olschki.

Kritsky, G. (2015) *The Tears of Re: Beekeeping in Ancient Egypt*, Oxford: Oxford University Press.

Kron, G. (2014a) 'Animal Husbandry', in G.L. Campbell (ed) 2014, pp. 109–135.

Kron, G. (2014b) 'Ancient Fishing and Fish Farming', in G.L. Campbell (ed) 2014, pp. 192–202.

Krzyskowska, O. (1990) *Ivory and Related Materials. An Illustrated Guide*, London: Institute of Classical Studies Bulletin Supplement 59.

Krzyskowska, O. and R. Morkot (2000) 'Ivory and Related Materials', in P.T. Nicholson and I. Shaw (eds) 2000 *Ancient Egypt: Material and Technology*, Cambridge: Cambridge University Press, pp. 320–331.

Kuttner, A.L. (1999) 'Looking Outside Inside: Ancient Roman Garden Rooms', in J.D. Hunt (ed) 1999 *The Immediate Garden and the Larger Landscape*, Special Issue of Studies in the History of Gardens and Designed Landscapes 1, pp. 7–35.

Kyle, D.G. (1995) 'Animal Spectacles in Ancient Rome: Meat and Meaning', *Nikephoros* 7, pp. 181–205.

Kyle, D.G. (2015) *Sport and Spectacle in the Ancient World*, Second Edition, Oxford: Wiley-Blackwell.

Kyriakidis, S. (2007) *Catalogues of Proper Names in Latin Epic Poetry: Lucretius-Virgil-Ovid*, Newcastle: Cambridge Scholars Publishing.

Lane Fox, R.L. (1996) 'Ancient Hunting: from Homer to Polybios', in J. Salmon and G. Shipley (eds) 1996 *Human Landscapes in Classical Antiquity: Environment and Culture*, London: Routledge, pp. 119–153.

Langdon, J. (2002) *Horses, Oxen and Technological Innovation: the Use of Draught Animals in English Farming 1066–1500*, Cambridge: Cambridge University Press.

Lapatin, K.D.S. (2001) *Chryselephantine Statuary in the Ancient Mediterranean World*, Oxford: Oxford University Press.

Lapatin, K.D.S. (2015) *Luxus. The Sumptuous Arts of Greece and Rome*, Los Angeles: J. Paul Getty Museum.

Larew, H.G. (2002) 'Insects: Evidence from Wall Paintings, Sculpture, Mosaics, Carbonized Remains, and Roman Authors', in W.F. Jashemski and E.G. Meyer (eds) 2002, pp. 315–326.

Lauwerier, R.C.G.M. (2004) 'The Economic and Non-Economic Animal: Roman Depositions and Offerings', in S. Jones O'Day, W. Van Neer and A. Ervynck (eds) 2004 *Behaviour Behind Bones: the Zooarchaeology of Ritual, Religion, Status and Identity*, Oxford: Oxbow Books, pp. 66–72.

Lavin, I. (1963) 'The Hunting Mosaics of Antioch and Their Sources', *Dumbarton Oaks Papers* 17, pp. 179–286.

Lazenby, F.D. (1949) 'Greek and Roman Household Pets', *Classical Journal* 44 No. 4, pp. 245–252 and pp. 299–307.

Leach, E.A. (1988) *The Rhetoric of Space: Literary and Artistic Representations of Landscape in Republican and Augustan Rome*, Princeton: Princeton University Press.

Lecocq, F. (2016) 'Inventing the Phoenix: a Myth in the Making Through Words and Images', in P.A. Johnston, A. Mastrocinque, and S. Papaioannou (eds) 2016, pp. 449–478.

Lentacker, A, A. Ervynck, and W. Van Neer (2004) 'Gastronomy or Religion? The Animal Remains from the Mithraeum at Tienen (Belgium)', in S. Jones O'Day, W. Van Neer, and A. Ervynck (eds) 2004 *Behaviour Behind Bones: the Zooarchaeology of Ritual, Religion, Status and Identity*, Oxford: Oxbow Books, pp. 66–72.

Lepetz, S. (1996) 'L'Animal dans la Société Gallo-Romaine de la France du Nord', Amiens: *Révue Archéologique de Picardie*.

Leroi, A.M. (2014) *The Lagoon. How Aristotle Invented Science*, London: Bloomsbury.

Lhermitte, J.-F. (2015) *L'Animal Verteux dans la Philosophie Antique a l'Époque Impériale*, Paris: Classiques Garnier.

Librán Moreno, M. (2014) 'La Avifauna en le Poesia Latina de Amor', in R.M. Soldevila and J. Martos (eds) 2014 Amor y Sexo en la Literatura Latina, Supplementos de Exemplaria Classica 4, Huelva: University of Huelva, pp. 57–93.

Li Causi, P. (2003) *Sulle Tracce del Manticora. La Zoologia dei Confini del Mondo in Grecia e a Roma*, Palermo: Palumbo.

Lippincott, L. and Blühm, A. (2005) *Fierce Friends. Artists and Animals, 1750–1900*, Merrell, London.

Lloyd-Jones, H. (1980) *Mythical Beasts,* London: Duckworth.

Loisel, G. (1912) *Histoire des Ménageries de l'Antiquité à Nos Jours*, Paris: Octave Doin et Fils.

Loughlin, E. (2004) 'Grasping the Bull By the Horns: Minoan Bull Sports', in S. Bell and G. Davies (eds) 2004 *Games and Festivals in Classical Antiquity*, British Archaeological Reports International Series 1220, Oxford: Archaeopress, pp. 1–8.

Lovejoy, A.O. and G. Boas (1935) *Primitivism and Related Ideas in Antiquity*, Baltimore: Johns Hopkins University Press.

Lowe, B.J. (2016) 'The Trade in Fish Sauce and Related Products in the Western Mediterranean', in T. Bekker-Nielsen and R. Gertwagen (eds) 2016, pp. 216–237.

Lowe, D. (2015) *Monsters and Monstrosity in Augustan Poetry*, Ann Arbor: University of Michigan Press.

Lucas, A.T. (1989) *Cattle in Ancient Ireland*, Kilkenny: Boethius Press.

Luck, G. (1985) *Arcana Mundi: Magic and the Occult in the Greek and Roman Worlds*, Baltimore: Johns Hopkins University Press.

Ludwig, A. (2015) *Kameldarstellungen aus Metall im Vorislamischen Südarabien. Eine Archäologische Fallstudie zu den Kulturkontakten Zwischen Arabia Felix und der Mittelmeerwelt*, Wiesbaden: Jenaer Archäologische Schriften.

Luff, R.-M. (1982) *Zooarchaeological Study of the Roman North-Western Provinces*, British Archaeological Reports International Series 137, Oxford: Archaeopress.

MacGregor, A. (1985) *Bone, Antler, Ivory and Horn: the Technology of Skeletal Materials Since the Roman Period*, London: Croom Helm.

MacKinnon, M. (2004) *Production and Consumption of Animals in Roman Italy: Integrating the Zooarchaeological and Textual Evidence*, Journal of Roman Archaeology Supplementary Series 54.

MacKinnon, M. (2006) 'Supplying Exotic Animals for the Roman Amphitheatre Games: New Reconstructions Combining Archaeological, Ancient Textual, Historical and Ethnographic Data', *Mouseion* Series III Volume 6, pp. 1–25.

MacKinnon, M. (2010) 'Sick as a Dog: Zooarchaeological Evidence for Pet Dog Health and Welfare in the Roman World', *World Archaeology* 42(2), pp. 290–309.

MacKinnon, M. (2013) 'Pack Animals, Pets, Pests, and Other Non-Human Beings', in P. Erdkamp (ed) 2013 *The Cambridge Companion to Ancient Rome*, Cambridge: Cambridge University Press, pp. 110–130.

MacKinnon, M. (2014a) 'Fauna of the Ancient Mediterranean World', in G.L. Campbell (ed) 2014, pp. 156–179.

MacKinnon, M. (2014b) 'Hunting', in G.L. Campbell (ed) 2014, pp. 203–215.

MacKinnon, M. (2014c) 'Pets', in G.L. Campbell (ed) 2014, pp. 269–281.

MacKinnon, M. (2014d) 'Animals in the Urban Fabric of Ostia: Initiating a Comparative Zooarchaeological Synthesis', *Journal of Roman Archaeology* 27, pp. 175–201.

MacKinnon, M. (2015) ' Changes in Animal Husbandry as a Consequence of Developing Social and Economic Patterns from the Roman Mediterranean Context', in P. Erdkamp, K. Verboven, and A. Zuiderhoek (eds) (2015), pp. 249–276.

Magnen, R. and E. Thévenot (1953) *Epona*, Bordeaux: Delmas.

Mahoney, A. (2001) *Roman Sport and Spectacles: a Sourcebook*, Newburyport: Focus Publishing.

Malek, J. (1993) *The Cat in Ancient Egypt*, London: British Museum Press.

Mander, J. (2012) *Portraits of Children on Roman Funerary Monuments*, Cambridge: Cambridge University Press.

Manning, A. and J. Serpell (eds) (1994) *Animals and Human Society: Changing Perspectives*, London: Routledge.

Mantzilas, D. (2016) 'Sacrificial Animals in Roman Religion: Rules and Exceptions', in P.A. Johnston, A. Mastrocinque, and S. Papaioannou (eds) 2016, pp. 19–38.

Maras, D.F. (2016) '*Numero Avium Regnum Trahebant*: Birds, Divination, and Power Amongst Romans and Etruscans', in P.A. Johnston, A. Mastrocinque, and S. Papaioannou (eds) 2016, pp. 85–114.

Marinatos, N. (1989) 'The Bull as Adversary: Some Observations on Bull-Hunting and Bull-Leaping', *Ariadne* 5, pp. 23–32.

Mariantos, N. (1994) 'The "Export" Significance of Minoan Bull Hunting and Bull-Leaping Scenes', *Egypt and the Levant* 40, pp. 89–93.

Markoe, G. and N.J. Serwint (1985) 'The "Lion Attack" in Archaic Greek Art: Heroic Triumph', *Classical Antiquity* 8, pp. 86–115.

Martens, M. (2015) 'Communal Dining: Making Things Happen', in R. Raja and J. Rüpke (eds) 2015, pp. 167–180.

Marzano, A. (2013) *Harvesting the Sea: the Exploitation of Maritime Resources in the Roman Mediterranean*, Oxford: Oxford University Press.

Marzano, A. (2015) 'The Variety of Villa Production: from Agriculture to Aquaculture', in P. Erdkamp, K. Verboven, and A. Zuiderhoek (eds) (2015), pp. 187–206.

Marzano, A. and G. Brizzi (2009) 'Costly Display Or Economic Investment? A Quantitative Approach to the Study of Marine Aquaculture', *Journal of Roman Archaeology* 22, pp. 215–230.

Mason, J. (2007) 'Animals: From Souls and the Sacred in Prehistoric Times to Symbols and Slaves in Antiquity', in L. Kalof (ed) 2007, pp. 17–46.

Massa, F. (2014) *Tra la Vigna et la Croce: Dionisio nei Discorsi Letterari e Figurativi Cristiani (II–IV Secolo)*, Potsdamer Altertumswissenschaftliche Beiträge Bd.47, Stuttgart: Franz Steiner Verlag.

Mastrocinque, A. (2016) 'Birds and Love in Greek and Roman Religion', in P.A. Johnston, A. Mastrocinque, and S. Papaioannou (eds) 2016, pp. 213–226.

Matteucig, G. (1974) 'Aspetti Naturalistici Desumibili da una Prima Elencazione delle Forme Animali Rappresentate nell'Antica Pompei', *Bolletino della Società di Naturalisti in Napoli* 83, pp. 177–211.

Mayor, A. (2011) *The First Fossil Hunters. Dinosaurs, Mammoths, and Myth in Greek and Roman Times*, Princeton: Princeton University Press.

Mayor, A. (2014a) 'Animals in Warfare', in G.L. Campbell (ed) 2014, pp. 282–293.

Mayor, A. (2014b) 'Ancient Fossil Discoveries and Interpretations', in G.L. Campbell (ed) 2014, pp. 579–588.

Mazzoni, C. (2010) *She-Wolf. The Story of a Roman Icon*, Cambridge: Cambridge University Press.

McDermott, W.C. (1936) 'The Ape in Roman Literature', *Transactions of the American Philological Association* 67, pp. 148–167.

McDermott, W.C. (1938) *The Ape in Antiquity*, Baltimore: Johns Hopkins University Press.

McDonald, A. (2004) *The British Museum Pocket Dictionary of Ancient Egyptian Animals*, London: British Museum Press.

McDonald, A. (2014) 'Animals in Egypt', in G.L. Campbell (ed) 2014, pp. 441–460.

McDonough, C.M. (1999) 'Forbidden to Enter the Ara Maxima: Dogs and Flies, or Dogflies', *Mnemosyne* LII.4, pp. 464–477.

McGregor, J.H.S. (2015) *Back to the Garden: Nature and the Mediterranean World from Prehistory to the Present*, New Haven: Yale University Press.

McInerny, J. (2010) *The Cattle of the Sun: Cows and Culture in the World of the Ancient Greeks*, Princeton: Princeton University Press.

McInerny, J. (2014) 'Civilization, Gastronomy, and Meat-Eating', in G.L. Campbell (ed) 2014, pp. 248–268.

McInerny, J. and I. Sluiter (eds) (2016) *Valuing Landscape in Classical Antiquity: Natural Environment and Cultural Imagination*, Leiden: Brill.

McKnight, L.M. And S. Atherton-Woolham (2015) *Gifts for the Gods: Ancient Egyptian Animal Mummies and the British*, Liverpool: Liverpool University Press.

Méniel, P. (1992) *Les Sacrifices d'Animaux chez les Gaulois*, Paris: Éditions Errance.

Méniel, P. (2015) 'Killing and Preparing Animals', in R. Raja and J. Rüpke (eds) 2015, pp. 155–166.

Merlen, R.H.A. (1971) *De Canibus: Dog and Hound in Antiquity*, London: J.H. Allen.

Merrills, A. (2017) *Roman Geographies of the Nile: from the Late Republic to the Early Empire*, Cambridge: Cambridge University Press.

Merten, E. (1991) 'Venationes in der Historia Augusta', in K. Rosen (ed) 1991 Bonner Historia-Augusta Colloquium 1986/1989, Bonn, pp. 139–178.

Meyboom, P.G.P. (1977) 'I Mosaici Pompeiani Configure di Pesci', *Mededelingen van het Nederlands Instituut te Rome* 39 New Series 4, pp. 49–93.

Meyboom, P.G.P. (1995) *The Nile Mosaic of Palestrina: Early Evidence of Egyptian Religion in Italy,* Leiden: Brill.

Mikhail, A. (2011) *Nature and Empire in Ottoman Egypt: an Environmental History,* Cambridge: Cambridge University Press.

Mikhail, A. (2014) *The Animal in Ottoman Egypt,* Oxford: Oxford University Press.

Miles, M.M. (2016) 'Birds Around the Temple: Constructing a Sacred Environment', in J. McInerny and I. Sluiter (eds) 2016, pp. 151–195.

Miziur, M. (2016) 'Fierce Felines in the Cult of Dionysus: Bacchic Mania and What Else?', in P.A. Johnston, A. Mastrocinque, and S. Papaioannou (eds) 2016, pp. 361–392.

Monteagudo, G.L. (2010) 'Nets and Fishing Gear in Roman Mosaics from Spain', in T. Bekker-Nielsen and D. B. Casasola (eds) 2010, pp. 161–185.

Morales Muniz, A., J.A. Riquelme and C. Liseau von Lettow-Vorbeck (1995) 'Dromedaries in Antiquity: Iberia and Beyond', *Antiquity* 69, pp. 368–375.

Moreau, T. (2016) 'The Horse, the Theology of Victory, and the Roman Emperors of the 4th Century CE', in P.A. Johnston, A. Mastrocinque, and S. Papaioannou (eds) 2016, pp. 335–360.

Morgan, L. (1995) 'Of Animals and Men: the Symbolic Parallels', in C. Morris (ed) 1995 Klados: Essays in Honour of J.N. Coldstream, *Bulletin of the Institute of Classical Studies* Supplement 63, pp. 171–184.

Morgan, M.G. (1975) 'Three Non-Roman Blood Sports', *Classical Quarterly* 25, pp. 117–122.

Moritz, L.A. (1958) *Grain-Mills and Flour in Classical Antiquity,* Oxford: Clarendon Press.

Morphy, H. (ed) (1989) *Animals Into Art,* London: Unwin Hyman.

Morris, C. (2007) 'Animals into Art in the Ancient World', in L. Kalof (ed) 2007, pp. 175–198.

Moser, B, (2013) *The Roman Ethnozoological Tradition: Identifying Exotic Animals in Pliny's Natural History,* Unpublished MA Thesis University of Western Ontario.

Myers, W. (2015) *Bio Art. Altered Realities,* London: Thames and Hudson.

Nadeau, R. (2015) 'Cookery Books', in J. Wilkins and R. Nadeau (eds) 2015, pp. 53–58.

Naiden, F.S. (2015) *Smoke Signals for the Gods. Ancient Greek Sacrifice from the Archaic Through Roman Periods,* Oxford: Oxford University Press.

Näsström, B-M. (2004) 'The Sacrifices of Mithras', in B. Santillo-Frizell (ed) 2004, pp. 108–111.

Newby, Z. (2015) 'Roman Art and Spectacle', in B.E. Borg (ed) 2015 *A Companion to Roman Art,* Oxford: Wiley Blackwell, pp. 552–568.

Newmyer, S.T. (2006) *Animals, Rights, and Reason in Plutarch and Modern Ethics,* London: Routledge.

Newmyer, S.T. (2007) 'Animals in Ancient Philosophy: Conceptions and Misconceptions', in L. Kalof (ed) 2007, pp. 151–174.

Newmyer, S.T. (2010) *Animals in Greek and Roman Thought: a Sourcebook,* London: Routledge.

Newmyer, S.T. (2016) *The Animal and the Human in Ancient Thought: the 'Man Alone of Animals' Concept,* London: Routledge.

Normand, H. (2015) *Les Rapaces dans les Mondes Grec et Romain: Catégorisation, Répresentations Culturelles et Pratiques,* Bordeaux, Scripta Antiqua 80.

Oaks, S. (1986) 'The Goddess Epona: Concepts of Sovereignity in a Changing Landscape', in M. Henig and A. King (eds) (1986) *Pagan Gods and Shrines of the Roman Empire,* Oxford: Oxford University Committee for Archaeology, pp. 77–83.

O'Day, S.J., W. Van Neer and A. Ervynck (eds) (2004) *Behaviour Behind Bones: the Zooarchaeology of Ritual, Religion, Status and Identity*. Proceedings of the 9th Conference of the International Council of Archaeozoology (Durham August 2002), Oxford: Oxbow.

Ogden, D. (2002) *Magic, Witchcraft, and Ghosts in the Greek and Roman Worlds: a Sourcebook*, Oxford: Oxford University Press.

Ogden, D. (2010) 'Binding Spells: Curse Tablets and Voodoo Dolls in the Greek and Roman Worlds', in J.N. Bremmer, J.H.F. Dijkstra, J.E.A. Kroesen, and Y. Kuiper (eds) 2010, 38–86.

Ogden, D. (2014) 'Animal Magic', in G.L. Campbell (ed) 2014, pp. 294–309.

Olsen, S.L. (2000) 'The Secular and Sacred Roles of Dogs at Botai, North Kazakhstan', in S.J. Crockford (ed) 2000, pp. 71–92.

Osborn, C. (2007) *Dumb Beasts and Dead Philosophers. Humanity and the Humane in Ancient Philosophy and Literature*, Oxford: Clarendon Press.

Östenberg, I. (2009) *Staging the World: Spoils, Captives, and Representations in the Roman Triumphal Procession*, Oxford: Oxford University Press.

Östenberg, I. (2014) 'Animals and Triumphs', in G.L. Campbell (ed) 2014, pp. 491–506.

Padgett, J.M. (2003) *The Centaur's Smile: the Human Animal in Early Greek Art*, Princeton: Princeton University Press.

Palagia, O. (2002) 'Hephaestion's Pyre and the Royal Hunt of Alexander', in A.B. Bosworth and E.J. Baynham (eds) 2002 *Alexander the Great in Fact and Fiction*, Oxford: Oxford University Press, pp. 167–206.

Palombi, A. (1950) 'La Fauna Marina nei Mosaici e nei Dipinti Pompeiani', in A. Maiuri (ed) 1950 *Pompeiana: Raccolta di Studi per il Secondo Centenario degli Scavi di Pompei*, Naples: Biblioteca della Parola del Passato Vol. 4, pp. 425–455.

Parker, H.N. (2015) 'Vaseworld: Depiction and Description of Sex at Athens', in R. Blondell and K. Ormand (eds) 2015 *Ancient Sex: New Essays. Classical Memories/ Modern Identities*, Columbus: Ohio State University Press, pp. 23–142.

Parker, R. and G. Pollock (1981) *Old Mistresses. Women, Art and Ideology*, London: Pandora.

Parrish, D. (1985) 'The Date of the Mosaics from Zliten', *Antiquités Africaines* 21, pp. 137–158.

Paschke, B.A. (2006) 'The Roman *Ad Bestias* Execution as a Possible Historical Background for I Peter 5.8', *Journal for the Study of the New Testament* 28(4), pp. 489–500.

Peters, W. (1963) *Landscape in Romano-Campanian Mural Painting*, Assen: Van Gorcum and Prakke.

Petrakis, V. (2014) 'The Religious Significance of Insects in the Aegean Bronze Age: Three Notes', in G. Touchais, R. Laffineur, and F. Rougemont (eds) 2014 *Physis. L'Environment Naturel et la Relation Home-Milieu dans le Monde Égéen Protohistorique*, Aegeum 37, Liège-Austin, pp. 525–529.

Petropoulou, M.-Z. (2004) *Animal Sacrifice in Ancient Greek Religion, Judaism, and Christianity, 100 BC to AD 200*, Oxford: Oxford University Press.

Pevnick, S.D. (ed) (2014) *Poseidon and the Sea: Myth, Cult, and Daily Life*, Tampa: Tampa Museum of Art.

Pigière, F. and D. Henrotay (2012) 'Camels in the Northern Provinces of the Roman Empire', *Journal of Archaeological Science* 39.5, pp. 1531–1539.

Pimentel, J. (2017) *The Rhinoceros and the Megatherium: an Essay in Natural History*, Cambridge, Massachusetts: Harvard University Press.

Piranomonte, M. (2009) 'Religion and Magic at Rome: the Fountain of Anna Perenna', in M. Simón and R.L. Gordon (eds) 2009 *Magical Practice in the Latin West, Papers of the International Conference Held at the University of Zaragoza 30 Sept–1 Oct 2005*, Leiden: Brill, pp. 191–214.

Piranomonte, M. (2014) *Via Flaminia: Villa di Livia*. Milan: Electa.

Plumb, C. (2015) *Georgian Menagerie: Exotic Animals in Eighteenth-Century London*, London: I.B. Tauris.

Podberscek, A.L. and E.S. Paul (2000) *Companion Animals and Us: Exploring the Relationships Between People and Pets*, Cambridge: Cambridge University Press.

Polara, G. (1983) *Le Venationes: Fenomeno Economico e Construzione Giuridica*, Milan: A. Giuffrè.

Pollard, E.A. (2009) 'Pliny's Natural History and the Flavian Templum Pacis: Botanical Imperialism in First Century CE Rome', *Journal of World History* 20, pp. 320–324.

Pollard, J. (1977) *Birds in Greek Life and Myth*, London: Thames and Hudson.

Poole, F. (ed) (2016) *Il Nilo a Pompei. Visioni d'Egitto nel Mondo Romano*. Catologo della Mostra, Museo Egizio Torino, Modena: Franco Cosimo Panini Editore.

Potter, D.S. and D.J. Mattingly (eds) (1999) *Life, Death, and Entertainment in the Roman Empire*, Ann Arbor: University of Michigan Press.

Potter, T. (1985) 'A Republican Healing Sanctuary at Ponte di Nona Near Rome and the Classical Tradition of Votive Medicine', *Journal of the British Archaeological Association* 138, pp. 23–47.

Potts, D.T. (2004) 'Camel Hybridization and the Role of Camelus Bactrianus in the Ancient Near East', *Journal of the Economic and Social History of the Orient* 47.2, pp. 143–165.

Poultney, J.W. (1956) 'The Two Boar-Sacrifices in the Iguvine Tablets', *American Journal of Philology* 78, pp. 177–180.

Prieur, J. (1988) *Les Animaux Sacrés dans l'Antiquité. Art et Religion du Monde Méditerranéen*, Rennes: Ouest-France.

Prummel, W., J.T. Zeiler and D.C. Brinkhuizen (eds) (2010) *Birds in Archaeology. Proceedings of the 6th Meeting of the ICAZ Bird Working Group in Groningen 2008*, Eelde Groningen: Barkhuis.

Purcell, N. (1995) 'Eating Fish: the Paradoxes of Seafood', in J. Wilkins, D. Harvey, and M. Dobson (eds) 1995 *Food in Antiquity*, Exeter: Exeter University Press, pp. 132–149.

Purcell, N. (2003) 'The Way We Used to Eat: Diet, Community, and History at Rome', *American Journal of Philology* 124, pp. 329–358.

Purdy, J. (2015) *After Nature: A Politics for the Anthropocene*, Cambridge, Massachusetts: Harvard University Press.

Radcliffe, W. (1974) *Fishing from the Earliest Times*, Chicago: Ares Publishers.

Rafanelli, S. and L. Donati (2004) 'Il Sacrificio nel Mondo Etrusco', *Thesaurus Cultus et Rituum Antiquorum* I, pp. 135–182.

Raja, R. and J. Rüpke (eds) (2015) *A Companion to the Archaeology of Religion in the Ancient World*, Oxford: Wiley Blackwell.

Reese, D.S. (2002a) 'Fish: Evidence from Specimens, Mosaics, Wall Paintings, and Roman Authors', in W.F. Jashemski and E.G. Meyer (eds) 2002, pp. 274–291.

Reese, D.S. (2002b) 'Marine Invertebrates, Freshwater Shells, and Land Snails: Evidence from Specimens, Mosaics, Wall Paintings, Sculpture, Jewelry, and Roman Authors', in W.F. Jashemski and E.G. Meyer (eds) 2002, pp. 292–314.

Reilly, L.C. (1993) 'The Hunting Frieze from Vergina', *Journal of the Hellenic Society* 113, pp. 160–162.

Retford, K. (2006) *The Art of Domestic Life: Family Portraiture in Eighteenth-Century England*, New Haven: Yale University Press.

Richter, G.M.A. (1930) *Animals in Greek Sculpture*, London: Oxford University Press.

Riddehough, G.B. (1959) 'Man-Into-Beast Changes in Ovid', *Phoenix* 13, pp. 201–209.

Ridgway, B.S. (1970) 'Dolphins and Dolphin-Riders', *Archaeology* 23, pp. 86–95.

Ridley, G. (2004) *Clara's Grand Tour: Travels with a Rhinoceros in Eighteenth-Century Europe*, New York: Grove Press.

Riess, W. and G.G. Fagan (eds) (2016) *The Topography of Violence in the Greco-Roman World*, Ann Arbor: University of Michigan Press.

Rissanen, M. (2012) 'The Hirpi Sorani and the Wolf Cults of Central Italy', *Arctos, Acta Philologica Fennica* XLVI, pp. 115–136.

Robbins, L.E. (2002) *Elegant Slaves and Pampered Parrots: Exotic Animals in Eighteenth-Century Paris*, Baltimore: Johns Hopkins University Press.

Rogers, K.M. (1998) *The Cat and the Human Imagination: Feline Images from Bast to Garfield*, Ann Arbor: University of Michigan Press.

Rosivach, V. (2006) 'The First Venatio', *New England Classical Journal* 33, pp. 271–278.

Roskams, S. (2015) 'Food for Thought: the Potential and Problems of Faunal Evidence for Interpreting Late Antique Society', in L. Lavan and M. Mulryan (eds) 2015 *Field Methods and Post-Excavation Techniques in Late Antique Archaeology*, Leiden: Brill, pp. 513–552.

Rossini, O. (2006) *Ara Pacis*, Milan: Electa.

Russell, N. (2011) *Social Zooarchaeology: Humans and Animals in Prehistory*, Cambridge: Cambridge University Press.

Salisbury, J.E. (2011) *The Beast Within: Animals in the Middle Ages*, Second Edition, London: Routledge.

Santillo-Frizell, B. (ed) (2004) *Pecus: Man and Animal in Antiquity, Proceedings of the Conference at the Swedish Institute in Rome September 9th–12th 2002*, Rome: Swedish Institute in Rome.

Santillo-Frizell, B. (2010) *Lana, Carne, Latte: Paesaggi Pastorali Tra Mito e Realta*, Florence: M. Pagliai Edizioni Polistampa.

Scafoglio, G. (2016) 'Men and Animals in Lucretius' *De Rerum Natura*', in P.A. Johnston, A. Mastrocinque, and S. Papaioannou (eds) 2016, pp. 39–50.

Scheid, J. (2003) 'Hierarchy and Structure in Roman Polytheism: Roman Methods of Conceiving Action', in C. Ando (ed) 2003 *Roman Religion*, Edinburgh: Edinburgh University Press, pp. 164–189.

Scheid, J. (2005) *Quand Faire, C'Est Croire: les Rites Sacrificiels des Romains*, Paris: Aubier.

Scheid, J. (2012) 'Roman Animal Sacrifice and the System of Being', in C.A. Faraone and F.S. Naiden (eds) 2012 *Greek and Roman Animal Sacrifice: Ancient Victims, Modern Observers*, Cambridge: Cambridge University Press, pp. 84–95.

Scherrer, P. (2014) 'Hunting the Boar-the Fiction of a Local Past', in B. Alroth and C. Scheffer (eds) 2014, pp. 113–119.

Schrijvers, P.H. (2007) 'A Literary View on the Nile Mosaic at Praeneste', in L. Bricault, M.J. Versluys and P.G.P. Meyboom (eds) 2007, pp. 223–244.

Schönfelder, M. (1994) 'Bear-Claws in Germanic Graves', *Oxford Journal of Archaeology* 13.2, pp. 217–227.

Schultz, C. E. (2016) 'Roman Sacrifice, Inside and Out', *Journal of Roman Studies* 106, pp. 58–76.

Schwabe, C.W. (1994) 'Animals in the Ancient World', in A. Manning and J. Serpell (eds) 1994, pp. 36–58.

Scullard, H.H. (1974) *The Elephant in the Greek and Roman World*, London: Thames and Hudson.

Scullard, H.H. (1981) *Festivals and Ceremonies of the Roman People*, Ithaca, New York: Cornell University Press.

Scurlock, J. (2002) 'Animals in Ancient Mesopotamian Religion', in B.J. Collins (ed) 2002, pp. 361–387.

Sergis, M.G. (2010) 'Dog Sacrifice in Ancient and Modern Greece: from the Sacrifice Ritual to Dog Torture (*Kynomartirion*)', *Folklore: Electronic Journal of Folklore* 45, pp. 61–88.

Sestili, A. (2011) *Venator Equus. Il Cavallo da Caccia nel Mondo Antiquo*, Rome: Aracne Editrice.

Shaw, B.D. (2011) *Sacred Violence: African Christians and Sectarian Hatred in the Age of Augustine*, Cambridge: Cambridge University Press.

Shelton, J.-A. (1995) 'Contracts with Animals: Lucretius, *De Rerum Natura*', *Between the Species* 11, pp. 115–121.

Shelton, J.-A. (1996) 'Lucretius and the Use and Abuse of Animals', *Eranos* 94, pp. 48–64.

Shelton, J.-A. (1999) 'Elephants, Pompey, and Reports of Popular Displeasure in 55 BC', in S.N. Byrne and E. Cueva (eds) 1999 *Veritatis Amicitiaeque Causa: Essays in Honor of Anna Lydia Motto and John R. Clark*, Wauconda: Bolchazy-Carducci Publishers, pp. 231–271.

Shelton, J.-A. (2004), 'Dancing and Dying: the Display of Elephants in Ancient Roman Arenas', in M. Joyal and R. Egan (eds) 2004 *Daimonopylai: Essays in Classics and the Classical Tradition Presented to Edmund G. Berry*, Winnipeg: University of Manitoba Centre for Hellenic Civilization, pp. 363–382.

Shelton, J.-A. (2006) 'Elephants as Enemies in Ancient Rome', *Literary and Cultural Studies* 32, pp. 3–25.

Shelton, J.-A. (2007) 'Beastly Spectacles in the Ancient Mediterranean World', in L. Kalof (ed) 2007, pp. 97–126.

Shelton, J.-A. (2014) 'Spectacles of Animal Abuse', in G.L. Campbell (ed) 2014, pp. 461–477.

Shipley, G. and J. Salmon (eds) (1996) *Human Landscapes in Classical Antiquity: Environment and Culture*, London: Routledge.

Sidnell, P. (2006) *Warhorse: Cavalry in Ancient Warfare*, London: Continuum.

Simpson, G. and Blance, B. (1998) 'Do Brooches Have Ritual Associations?' in J. Bird (ed.) 1998 *Form and Fabric: Studies in Rome's Material Past in Honour of B.R. Hartley*, Oxford: Oxbow Books, pp. 267–279.

Slater, N.W. (2010) 'Mourning Helena: Emotion and Identification in a Roman Grave Stela (71.AA.271)', *Getty Research Journal* 2, pp. 139–146.

Smith, B. (1989) *European Vision and the South Pacific*, Third Edition, New Haven: Yale University Press.

Smith, C. (1996) 'Dead Dogs and Rattles: Time, Space and Ritual Sacrifice in Iron Age Latium' in J.B. Wilkins (ed.) 1996 *Approaches to the Study of Ritual: Italy and the Ancient Mediterranean*, Accordia Specialist Studies on the Mediterranean Vol. 2. Accordia Research Centre, University of London, pp. 73–89.

Smith, K. (2006) *Guides, Guards and Gifts to the Gods. Domesticated Dogs in the Art and Archaeology of Iron Age and Roman Britain*, British Archaeological Reports British Series 422, Oxford: Archaeopress.

Smith, S.D. (2014) *Man and Animal in Severan Rome: the Literary Image of Claudius Aelianus. Greek Culture in the Roman World*, Cambridge: Cambridge University Press.

Snyder, L.M. and E.A. Moore (eds) (2006) *Dogs and People in Social, Working, Economic or Symbolic Interaction*, Oxford: Oxbow Books.

Sorabella, J. (2007) 'Eros and the Lizard: Children, Animals, and Roman Funerary Sculpture', in A. Cohen and J.B. Rutter (eds) 2007, pp. 353–370.

Sorabji, R. (1993) *Animal Minds and Human Morals: the Origins of the Western Debate*, Ithaca: Cornell University Press.

Soren, D. and N. Soren (1999) *A Roman Villa and a Late Roman Infant Cemetery: Excavation at Poggio Gramignano, Lugnano in Teverina*, Rome: Bibliotheca Archaeologica 23. L'Erma di Bretschneider.

Spano, G. (1955) 'Paesaggio Nilotico con Pigmei Difendentisi Magicamente dai Coccodrilli', *Atti delle Accademia Nazionale dei Lincei. Memorie* Series 8.6, 335–368.

Spencer, D. (2002) *The Roman Alexander: Reading a Cultural Myth*, Exeter: University of Exeter Press.

Spencer, D. (2011) *Roman Landscape: Culture and Identity*, Cambridge: Cambridge University Press.

Starac, A. (2013) 'Funerary Sculptures in Istria: Animal and Mythological Figures', in N. Cambi and G. Koch (eds) 2013, pp. 193–221.

St Clair, A. (1996) 'Evidence for Late Antique Bone and Ivory Carving on the Northeast Slope of the Palatine: the Palatine East Excavations', *Dumbarton Oaks Papers* 50, pp. 369–374.

St Clair, A. (2003) *Carving as Craft. Palatine East and the Greco-Roman Bone and Ivory Carving Tradition*, Baltimore: Johns Hopkins University Press.

Stebbins, E.R. (1927) *The Dolphin in the Literature and Art of Greece and Rome*, Baltimore: Johns Hopkins University Press.

Steiner, G. (2005) *Anthropocentrism and its Discontents: the Moral Status of Animals in the History of Western Philosophy*, Pittsburgh: University of Pittsburgh Press.

Stern, W. and D.H. Thimme (2007) *Kenchreia. Port of Corinth. VI Ivory, Bone and Related Finds*, Leiden: Brill.

Stevenson, M. and L. Twentyman-Jones (2000) *Far Away and Long Ago*, London: Michael Graham-Stewart Gallery.

Van Straten, F. (1995) *Hiera Kala: Images of Animal Sacrifice in Archaic and Classical Greece*, Leiden: Brill.

Strong, D.E. (1973) 'Roman Museums', in D.E. Strong 1973 (ed) *Archaeological Theory and Practice. Essays Presented to Professor W.F. Grimes*, London: Seminar Press, pp. 247–264.

Stroumsa, G.G. (2009) *The End of Sacrifice: Religious Transformations in Late Antiquity*, Chicago: Chicago University Press.

Struck, P. (2014) 'Animals and Divination', in G.L. Campbell (ed) 2014, pp. 310–323.

Swetnam-Burland, M. (2015) *Egypt in Italy. Visions of Egypt in Roman Imperial Culture*, Cambridge: Cambridge University Press.

Sykes, N. (2014) *Beastly Questions. Animal Answers to Archaeological Issues*, London: Bloomsbury.

Syme, R. (1980) *Some Arval Brethren*, Oxford: Oxford University Press.

Tammisto, A. (1985) 'Representations of the Kingfisher (*Alcedo atthis*) in Graeco-Roman Art', *Arctos* 19, pp. 217–242.

Tammisto, A. (1986) 'Phoenix *Felix et Tu*: Remarks on the Representation of the Phoenix in Roman Art', *Arctos* 20, pp. 171–225.

Tammisto, A. (1989) 'The Representations of the Capercaille (*tetrao urogallus*) and the Pheasant (*Phasianus colchicus*) in Romano-Campanian Wall Paintings and Mosaics', *Arctos* 23, pp. 223–249.

Tammisto, A. (1997) *Birds in Mosaics. A Study on the Representation of Birds in Hellenistic and Romano-Campanian Tesselated Mosaics to the Early Augustan Age*, Rome: Institutum Romanum Finlandiae.

Thomas, K. (1983) *Man and the Natural World. Changing Attitudes in England 1500–1800*, Harmondsworth: Allen Lane.

Thommen, H. (2009) *An Environmental History of Ancient Greece and Rome*, Translation of 2012, Cambridge, Cambridge University Press.

Thorson, R.M. (201) *Walden's Shore: Henry David Thoreau and Nineteenth-Century Science*, Cambridge, Massachusetts: Harvard University Press.

Thumiger, C. (2014) 'Metamorphosis: Human into Animals', in G.L. Campbell (ed) 2014, pp. 384–413.

Tomczyk, W. (2016) 'Camels on the Northeastern Frontier of the Roman Empire', *Papers from the Institute of Archaeology* 26 (1), p.Art.2. DOI: http://doi.org/10.5334/pia-485.

Bibliography

Toner, J. (2014) *The Day Commodus Killed a Rhino: Understanding the Roman Games*, Baltimore: Johns Hopkins University Press.

Toynbee, J.M.C. (1948) 'Beasts and Their Names in the Roman Empire', *Papers of the British School at Rome* Vol. XVI, New Series Vol. III, pp. 24–37.

Toynbee, J.M.C. (1973) *Animals in Roman Life and Art*, London: Thames and Hudson.

Trantalidou, K. (2006) 'Companions from the Oldest Times: Dogs in Ancient Greek Literature, Iconography and Osteological Testimony', in L.M. Snyder and E.A. Moore (eds) 2006 *Dogs and People in Social, Working, Economic or Symbolic Interaction*, Oxford: Oxbow Books, pp. 96–120.

Trautman, T.R. (2015) *Elephants and Kings. An Environmental History*, Chicago: University of Chicago Press.

Trinquier, J. and C. Vendries (eds) (2009) *Chasses Antiques. Pratiques et Représentations dans le Monde Gréco-Romain*, Rennes: Rennes University Press.

Tuck, S. L. (2005) 'The Origins of Roman Imperial Hunting Imagery: Domitian and the Redefinition of *Virtus* Under the Principate', *Greece and Rome* 52, pp. 221–245.

Tuck, S.L. (2014) 'Representations of Spectacle and Sport in Roman Art', in P. Christesen and D.G. Kyle (eds) 2014, pp. 422–437.

Tutrone, F. (2010) 'Confini in Discesa. Rappresentazioni della Violenza e della Bestialità nella Cultura Romana', in V. Andò and N. Cusumano (eds) 2010 *Come Bestie?: Forme e Paradossi della Violenza tra Mondo Antico e Disagio Contemporaneo*, Caltanissetta, Rome: Salvatore Sciascia Editore, pp. 209–234.

Uhlenbrock, J.P. (1986) *Herakles. Passage of the Hero Through 1000 Years of Classical Art*, Annandale-on-Hudson, New York: Aristide D. Caratzas Publisher, New York and The Edith C. Blum Art Institute, Bard College.

Van Buren, A.W. and R.M. Kennedy (1919) 'Varro's Aviary at Casinum', *Journal of Roman Studies* 9, 59–66.

Van der Meer, L.B. (1987) *The Bronze Liver of Piacenza*, Amsterdam: J.C. Gieben.

Vanggaard, J.H. (1979) 'The October Horse', *Temenos*, pp. 81–95.

Vendries, C. (2009) 'L'Auceps, les Gluax et l'Appeau. À Propos de la Ruse et de L'Habileté du Chasseur d'Oiseaux, in J. Trinquier and C. Vendries (eds) 2009, pp. 119–140.

Van Neer, W., A. Ervynck and P. Monsieur (2010) 'Fish Bones and Amphorae: Evidence for the Production and Consumption of Salted Fish Products Outside the Mediterranean Region', *Journal of Roman Archaeology* 23, pp. 161–195.

Vernou, C. (2011) *Ex-Voto Retour aux Sources. Les Bois des Sources de la Seine*, Dijon: Musée Archéologique de Dijon.

Versluys, M.J. (2000) *Aegyptiaca Romana: Nilotic Scenes and the Roman Views of Egypt*, RGRW 144, Leiden: Brill.

Vidal-Naquet, P. (1986) 'The Black Hunter and the Origin of the Athenian Ephebia', in P. Vidal-Naquet (ed) 1986 *The Black Hunter: Forms of Thought and Forms of Society in the Greek World*, Baltimore: Johns Hopkins University Press.

Vigne, J.-D., J. Guilaine, K. Debue, L. Haye and P. Gérard (2004) 'Early Taming of the Cat in Cyprus', *Science* 304, p. 259.

Vigneron, P. (1968) *Le Cheval dans L'Antiquité Gréco-Romaine*, Nancy: Berger-Levrault.

Voisin, J.-L. (1983) 'Le Triumphe Africain de 46 et l'Idéologie Césarienne', *Antiquités Africaines* 19, pp. 7–33.

Von Hofsten, S. (2007) *The Feline-Prey Theme in Archaic Greek Art: Classification, Distribution, Origin, Iconographical Context*, Stockholm: Almquist and Wiksell.

Vout, C. (2003) 'Embracing Egypt', in C. Edwards and G. Woolf (eds) 2003 *Rome the Cosmopolis*, Cambridge: Cambridge University Press, pp. 177–202.

Voković-Bogdanović, S. and S. Blažić (2014) 'Camels from Roman Imperial Sites in Serbia', *Anthropozoologica* 49.2, pp. 281–295.

Walker, H.J. (2015) *The Twin Horse Gods: the Dioscuri in Mythologies of the Ancient World*, London: I.B. Tauris.

Walker, H.J. (2016) 'Horse Riders and Chariot Drivers', in P.A. Johnston, A. Mastrocinque, and S. Papaioannou (eds) 2016, pp. 309–334.

Walker, R.E. (1973) 'Roman Veterinary Medicine', in J.M.C. Toynbee 1973, pp. 301–343.

Walker, S. (2003) 'Carry-On at Canopus: the Nilotic Mosaic from Palestrina and Roman Attitudes to Egypt', in R. Matthews and C. Roemer (eds) 2003 *Ancient Perspectives on Egypt*, London: Routledge, pp. 191–202.

Ward, A. (1968) 'The Cretan Bull Sports', *Antiquity* 42, pp. 117–122.

Ward Jones, J. (1998) 'Catullus' *Passer* as *Passer*', *Greece and Rome* 45:2, pp. 188–194.

Ward Perkins, J.B. and J.M.C. Toynbee (1949) 'The Hunting Mosaics of Lepcis Magna', *Archaeologia* 93, pp. 165–195.

Warren, R. (2010) *Animal Comparisons and Analogies in the Portrayal of Northern Europeans in Roman Late Republican and Imperial Literature*, Unpublished M.A. Thesis, Lund University.

Watson, G.E. (2002) 'Birds: Evidence from Wall Paintings, Mosaics, Sculpture, Skeletal Remains, and Ancient Authors', in W.F. Jashemski and E.G. Meyer (eds) 2002, pp. 357–400.

Wengrow, D. (2013) *The Origins of Monsters. Image and Cognition in the First Age of Mechanical Reproduction*, Princeton: Princeton University Press.

Wheeler, R.E.M. and T.V. Wheeler (1932) *Report on the Excavation of the Prehistoric, Roman, and Post-Roman Site in Lydney Park, Gloucestershire*, Reports of the Research Committee of the Society of Antiquaries of London No. IX.

White, K.D. (1967) *Agricultural Implements of the Roman World*, Cambridge: Cambridge University Press.

White, K.D. (1970) *Roman Farming*, London: Thames and Hudson.

White, K.D. (1975) *Farm Equipment of the Roman World*, Cambridge: Cambridge University Press.

White, K.D. (1977) *Country Life in Classical Times*, London: Paul Elek.

Wiedemann, T. (1992) *Emperors and Gladiators*, London: Routledge.

Wilkens, B. (2006) 'The Sacrifice of Dogs in Ancient Italy', in L.M. Snyder and E.A. Moore (eds) 2006, pp. 131–136.

Wilkins, J. (1993) 'Social Status and Fish in Greece and Rome', in G. Mars and V. Mars (eds) 1993 *Food, Culture and History*, London: London Food Seminar, pp. 191–203.

Wilkins, J. and R. Nadeau (eds) (2015) *A Companion to Food in the Ancient World*, Oxford: Blackwell.

Willekes, C. (2016) *The Horse in the Ancient World: from Bucephalus to the Hippodrome*, London: I.B. Tauris.

Wilson, I.A. (2007) 'Fishy Business: Roman Exploitation of Marine Resources', *Journal of Roman Archaeology* 19, pp. 525–537.

Wiseman, T.P. (1987) *Catullus and His World: a Reappraisal*, Cambridge: Cambridge University Press.

Witt, R.E. (1971) *Isis in the Greco-Roman World*, London: Thames and Hudson.

Witts, P. (2016) *A Mosaic Menagerie: Creatures of Land, Sea and Sky in Romano-British Mosaics*, Oxford: Archaeopress.

Woodford, S. (2003) *Images of Myths in Classical Antiquity*, Cambridge: Cambridge University Press.

Wootton, W. (2002) 'Another Alexander Mosaic: Reconstructing the Hunt Mosaic from Palermo', *Journal of Roman Archaeology* 15, pp. 265–274.

Bibliography

Wylie, D. (2013) *Crocodile*, London: Reaktion Books.

Yale, E. (2016) *Sociable Knowledge: Natural History and the Nation in Early Modern Britain*. Philadelphia: University of Pennsylvania Press.

Yébenes, S.P. (1991) 'Haruspex Legionis', *Gérion 9*, pp. 175–193.

Zaganiaris, N.J. (1975) 'Sacrifices de Chiens dans l'Antiquité Classique', *Platon 27*, pp. 322–329.

Zaleski, J. (2014) 'Religion and Roman Sport', in P. Christesen and D.G. Kyle (eds) 2014, pp. 590–602.

Zanda, E. (2011) *Fighting Hydra-Like Luxury: Sumptuary Regulation in the Roman Republic*, London: Bristol Classical Press.

Zanker, P. (1988) *The Power of Images in the Age of Augustus*, Ann Arbor: University of Michigan Press.

Zanker, P. and B.C. Ewald (2012) *Living With Myths: the Imagery of Roman Sarcophagi*, Oxford: Oxford University Press.

Filmography

n.d. *The Animals of WWI*. Imperial War Museum, London. Commentary by Matthew Lee.

Image Credits

Index

Index